Holy Ground

Holy Ground

The Importance of the Body, Posture, and Liturgy in Worship

L. Charles Jackson

WIPF & STOCK · Eugene, Oregon

HOLY GROUND
The Importance of the Body, Posture, and Liturgy in Worship

Copyright © 2024 L. Charles Jackson. All rights reserved. Except for brief quotations in critical publications or reviews, no part of this book may be reproduced in any manner without prior written permission from the publisher. Write: Permissions, Wipf and Stock Publishers, 199 W. 8th Ave., Suite 3, Eugene, OR 97401.

Wipf & Stock
An Imprint of Wipf and Stock Publishers
199 W. 8th Ave., Suite 3
Eugene, OR 97401

www.wipfandstock.com

PAPERBACK ISBN: 978-1-5326-9401-1
HARDCOVER ISBN: 978-1-5326-9402-8
EBOOK ISBN: 978-1-5326-9403-5

VERSION NUMBER 02/19/24

Contents

Acknowledgements | vii

Introduction | 1

1 What is Worship? | 22
2 What Does God Want in Worship? | 52
3 Praise in Worship | 70
4 Prayer in Worship | 98
5 Preaching in Worship | 112
6 The Sacraments in Worship | 129
7 Holy Communion | 144
8 Grape Juice Christianity | 167

Conclusion | 192

Bibliography | 199

Acknowledgements

Most anything worthwhile is never done alone. I thank my faithful congregation at Covenant Presbyterian Church in Dayton, Ohio. For years when I was their pastor they faithfully, lovingly, and patiently worshipped with me as their minister. Their eager longing for God-centered, deep, and Spirit-filled worship was a constant encouragement to me and it always drove me to try to do better especially in worship. It was in Dayton that my interest in worship developed in the context of faithful elders and a wonderful congregation who loved the Lord. A pastor could not have wished for more!

I acknowledge my brothers and sisters here in Africa for teaching me so much about worship. Their enthusiastic, fully embodied worship has been a rich blessing to me and rekindled in me a desire that all worship should be recognized as embodied worship.

I thank Elisabeth Bloechl for her willingness to edit, and her careful editing in spite of my sometimes careless work. This helped me so much as a busy missionary juggling too many other tasks at the same time and helped bring this little project to the finish line.

As always, I give thanks to my wife, Connie. Her encouragement to write this little book was steady and helpful. I could not have done it without her. All that I do, I do with her at my side and I'm thankful. Thank you dear.

Introduction

> When the LORD saw that he turned aside to see, God called to him out of the bush, "Moses, Moses!" And he said, "Here I am." Then he said, "Do not come near; take your sandals off your feet, for the place on which you are standing is holy ground." (Exod. 3: 4–5, English Standard Version)

IN THE SCRIPTURES, WHENEVER someone is on holy ground their posture always changes. What makes the ground holy? It's not the dirt or the rocks that are somehow sacred—it's God's presence that makes a place holy. This means that wherever God comes down to meet with his people they are standing on holy ground. When this happens, just like Moses at the burning bush our posture should always change when we are on holy ground, and it's because we are in the presence of God.

Holy ground is where heaven and earth meet—a powerful cosmic interaction that is unlike anything else we experience. Holy ground is a mysterious, supernatural place where God meets with his people. This is why in many Bible stories we see the saints dramatically changing their postures in the presence of God—they fall down on their knees, they take off their sandals, they lower their heads, or they raise their hands. These are the natural responses to holy ground—our posture always adjusts appropriately when we meet with God, which is the fitting and proper response of any human being in the presence of Almighty God. This is exactly what should happen in worship.

This little book is directed to the most important topic of our lives—worship. More pointedly I hope to challenge readers to think seriously not only about the centrality of worship, but also about the role of the body, posture, and liturgy in worship. I admit that tackling this subject I feel a bit like the ancient church father, Sulpitius who pleaded with his readers not to be distracted by what he called his "somewhat unpolished style." He continued saying, "I should be deemed highly worthy of general reprehension for having too boldly laid hold of a subject which ought to have been reserved for truly eloquent writers."[1] Even if the style of this little book is not that of an eloquent author, please receive it as an introductory study that is worthy of attention. In daring to contribute to the subject of worship I am reminded of an odd but accurate phrase—some things are so important they are worth doing poorly.

So why write another book on worship? There are already all kinds of books that are trying to make scriptural arguments for worship. However, none of them aim at the issue of embodied worship or the role of the body and liturgy in worship. I am a Presbyterian, and my own tradition has a long history of arguing for biblical standards for worship. Still, I have not discovered a single book on worship that combines scriptural principles for God-centered worship (sometimes called the regulative principle) while also giving sustained attention to the role of the body in worship. Some of them, while trying to argue against either ritualistic repetition and/or charismatic extremes neglect the role of the body or ignore it altogether—as if the body doesn't really matter. Still others cite the "regulative principle" as if citing it eliminates a serious discussion of raising hands, kneeling, or other questions about posture and liturgy.

It may seem ironic, but Protestants who once argued strenuously against the use of thoughtless and/or superstitious traditions in worship are captive to new traditions that do not have strong biblical foundations. In fact, because of deeply entrenched and inflexible traditions in worship, I'm convinced that now is the time for another Reformation—a reformation of worship. This is particularly true for what is called Evangelical and Reformed Theology. Just as the church of the late Middle Ages had become rotten with deeply rooted corruption Evangelicalism and some Reformed traditions have become similarly corrupted and saturated with the man-centered principles of pop culture and/or dead traditions.

---

1. Severus, "On St. Martin," 4.

Although much of its theology is stellar, Reformed Protestants have serious problems regarding worship. Worship has become stale in some of Reformed circles, which in many cases has transformed worship into a kind of boring theological lecture series, punctuated with long and oftentimes inaccessible prayers and esoteric hymns (which always seem musically and linguistically awkward and for some reason written prior to 1878). All of these things tend to sap worship of its deep joy and threaten to dry up the bottomless wells of enthusiasm we might otherwise experience in worship.

In fact, to speak of worship as an experience will cause many Reformed leaders to wince with agony like a vampire sprinkled with holy water. Ahh, they say, worship is not about our experience—it's about God! But why couldn't it be both? Why couldn't we structure our worship and liturgy upon theological excellence that is intimately and simultaneously linked with thoughtful and scriptural postures and liturgies? This is a substantial challenge and Protestants whose tradition includes a serious interest in always reforming their lives according to the Holy Scriptures do not seem presently willing to take a serious look at their own worship practices particularly as they relate to posture and liturgy.

If worship conforms to the Scriptures, then it involves bodily activity, and we should think carefully about this activity in light of the Scriptures especially if we take the Bible seriously. Many traditions that sincerely believe the Bible—do not take it seriously in regard to embodied worship. For instance, God tells us that worship is an activity, yet many churches require their people to sit passively for most of the worship service. We sit passively as the preacher preaches (often lifeless, long, and complex theological tomes). We sit passively as the offering plate is handed to us (sometimes the box is in the back, and one never gets the opportunity to praise God with an offering). We sit passively (and sleepily) as the pastor prays over us (super long theological prayers!). We sit passively as the sacraments are distributed to us (even though it hardly ever actually happens). The posture of sitting passively should be reconsidered, in light of the scriptures exhortation everywhere that we should worship the Lord actively. There is a reason that many of us in such traditions speak of ourselves as the frozen chosen.

Unfortunately, there seem to be many churches who take some aspects of worship theology very earnestly, but this does not include the role of the body in their considerations. Instead, pastors everywhere ought to think about every aspect of worship and include our bodies in their thinking. This, however, can open us to some serious challenges. For example, one serious problem may be that many Bible-believing Christians simply don't care about the body in their theology of worship: revealing a dreadful theological problem.

This should strike us as unsettling since the Scriptures command us in very strong language that our bodies are central to worship. Like a guiding principle Rom. 12:1-2 says,

> I appeal to you therefore, brothers, by the mercies of God, to present your bodies as a living sacrifice, holy and acceptable to God, which is your spiritual worship.

God tells us that presenting our bodies is our spiritual worship. For me this verse has become something of a controlling feature when thinking about worship. God demands embodied worship. Since there is no such thing as disembodied worship, it stands to reason that all worship is by definition an embodied experience. Rom. 12:1 it is God himself who commands embodied worship.

In worship God doesn't call us to purely theological meditation or rational theological reflection. He doesn't tell us to approach him with religious contemplation or reflection alone. No, God calls us to present our bodies as liturgy, as worship, which means that God specifically calls us to embodied worship.

In worship God connects the body and soul together in perfect harmony. In fact, in Rom. 12:1 the body is so central to worship that our bodies stand in place of the whole person. Because on this earth there is no such thing as a living human being without a body, Paul speaks of the body as the same as the person.

Paul says present your bodies. For those who may think that because the body is physical it is less important than the soul, which is spiritual, the scriptures teach something very different. Paul tells us that physically offering our bodies is a spiritual act of worship —there is no separation. Worship is an embodied activity!

Evidently the Bible does not have a problem linking spiritual worship with bodily liturgy—they are one and the same. In fact, the Greek word Paul uses in Rom. 12:1 as spiritual "worship" is a word connected to our English word, liturgy. The noun λειτουργία (*leitourgia*) means service, role in serving, or ministry. In classical culture the word liturgy was derived from the public civil service offered by a political or religious authority and in scriptural use the word liturgy is also related to the service a minister (and a worshipper) offers in public worship.

Liturgy has roots in classical culture as pointing to the public acts of worship among pagan priests who would sacrifice to their gods as a public service to their community. Such worship might take place as part of the beginning of a civic religious feast or celebration. It might have included the dedication of a building or perhaps in preparing the armies for a war. In the Scriptures the word liturgy is used in the same way regarding the acts of priests, but here in Rom. 12:1, it is used to refer to everyone's service offered in worship to God, which is always embodied.

In Rom. 12:1, Paul uses it to refer to an act of worship offered by individual Christians. According to one theological dictionary,

> Luke 1:23 says that Zechariah went home when his days of service (*leitourgia*) in the temple ended. All the vessels within the temple are described in Heb. 9:21 as being used for service (*leitourgia*). Although in New Testament the word is mostly used for temple worship, Paul refers to giving a monetary offering as a service (*leitourgia*) that provides for physical needs and results in thanksgiving to God.[2]

Liturgy is the physical, embodied activity of worship. In short, liturgy is what we do in worship–liturgy is worship. There is no such thing as worship without liturgy. Everyone has a liturgy because everyone does something in worship. The question is not whether you believe in liturgy, the question is what kind of liturgy do you practice?

I have so many friends who say that they don't like liturgical worship, but what they mean is they don't like Roman Catholic or high church Anglican styles of worship. They don't realize that everyone who worships God has a liturgy, because liturgy is another way of describing what we do in worship. The real question is whether you have a good liturgy or a bad one. Therefore, we need to rediscover what the scriptures teach us about liturgy and the use of our bodies in worship.

To worship God is to use our bodies in order to bring physical, offerings of love and obedience to him—the most important of which is one's whole self, or as Paul puts it, present your bodies. In worship we offer to God the whole of who we are as embodied beings. This includes literal offerings such as money, but it also includes thanksgiving, prayers, praise, requests for forgiveness and even eating and drinking

---

2. Clark and McLaurin III, *Lexham Theological Wordbook*, see entry on worship.

together with God and one another. These are literal acts of worship. Thus, worship is always embodied, which requires us to include gestures, rites, kneeling, raising hands, etc.

The following dictionary helps:

> Bodily gestures are the principal means by which one expresses the highest forms of one's spiritual, intellectual, and artistic experiences, and the principal ways in which humans communicate with each other. Rite and ceremony have been used by all religions both to intensify and to communicate the interior dispositions of the soul. Gestures, no less than words, are a part of human language, the one appealing to sight, the other to hearing—the two senses closest to the intellect and therefore closest to the spiritual life. Each is a language unto itself, yet normally they depend upon each other for the full expression of one's inner self—words calling upon gestures to give them greater force, intensity, and eloquence, and gestures calling upon words to make their meaning more articulate. Any act or movement of the human body becomes a gesture when it gives expression to meaning within an interpersonal relationship. Liturgical gestures in their turn express specific meanings within the relationship between God and human persons in community celebrations.[3]

This reality has been ignored or forgotten among many Protestants. It may be as simple as a reflexive kind of anti-Catholicism. In fact, a common charge against anyone arguing for more liturgical worship is that they are "proto-Catholic." One of many such overreactions may have led some people to a general understanding that worship should exclusively or primarily emphasize one of the following: the rational or the emotional. The beauty of embodied worship is that it includes both—providing us with the most robust and powerful experience of worship.

The reaction of some Protestants may be connected to traditions that have tended to reduce worship to repetitive rituals with very little theological instruction. We might think of a traditional Roman Catholic or Greek Orthodox worship service where many of the worshippers could easily recite the forms of service and they could definitely tell you when to bow, when to do the sign of the cross and when to stand. They would not, however, have as much clarity as to the theological and/or scriptural underpinnings of their rituals. They repeat rituals without much thought.

3. "Liturgical Gestures," para. 1.

This has caused many Protestants to overreact to the whole idea of rituals. For them rituals are inherently thoughtless and therefore worthless.

In my own Protestant tradition, and perhaps in response to overly ritualistic traditions many Christians have a very limited view of worship as rational, cerebral, or theological. Things such as teaching theology or listening to a good sermon are for them the primary purpose of a worship service, period. Whatever else happens before or after the sermon is tangential and not really pertinent to the central feature of worship, which is the sermon.

Finally, there are vast swaths of Evangelical/charismatic/Protestant Christians all over the world who have reduced worship to an emotional experience. Perhaps you have heard someone say that a good worship experience really charges their spiritual batteries. They go to worship essentially for an emotional experience that reinforces their existing religious convictions, which are very generic. They want to feel great from their worship experience, but they would probably not be able to recite the Ten Commandments or repeat the Lord's Prayer or even the simplest of doctrinal truths. After all, they say, it's a relationship—not a religion (whatever this is supposed to mean).

Theologically informed, embodied worship is fuller than either of these kinds of worship practices because it combines all the best elements of each tradition. Following the scriptural teachings on worship, as we contemplate the glory of the Lord in theologically powerful prayers and praise—we lift up our hands. As a result, theologically powerful prayers become even more powerful.

When considering our need for the forgiveness of our sins we can use well-crafted prayers of confession, kneeling as we confess our sins to God in prayer—again providing us with an even more powerful experience in our prayers (good theology and good posture). We don't do either one or the other—we do both in embodied worship. If this is true, then it means that many Christians and especially pastors should seriously rethink their worship practices in light of our embodied reality.

It also means that thinking seriously about embodied worship can provide Christians with the most robust and powerful worship experience that God wants us to practice. Since we are by faith obeying God's command to offer our bodies in worship, God will be given glory and he promises to bless us in Christ. Embodied worship provokes the blessings of God.

We would also restore to worship the beautiful, powerful, and ancient practices of frequent Holy Communion with God and with each other. This is a challenge because many Christians, especially Protestants do not care about embodied worship as commanded in the scriptures. This may account at least in part for the almost derisive neglect of the sacraments, especially the Lord's Supper sometimes called the Eucharist.

While historically shocking, some Protestants do not practice the Eucharist as a central or normative part of worship. This historically peculiar practice of infrequent Holy Communion is in many ways parallel to the odd and contorted practices of the late Middle Ages when the clergy withheld the bread from the laymen and essentially worshipped it. They improperly transformed the supper into something the average Christian had little chance to experience. Though doing so for different reasons, many Protestants today have withheld the Lord's Supper from their people strangely depriving them of something God says they should do in remembrance of him. This seems extremely different from our savior's warm invitation to his disciples at the last supper—take, eat!

Whenever I hear the reasons for infrequent Eucharist it also seems like a peculiar combination of anti-Catholic/anti-ritualistic fear and an overly rationalistic view of worship: an odd kind of fearful, theological rationalism. For these types of people communion has become an empty memorial that is merely another way of "remembering" Christ. When you combine this with a common belief that the body doesn't really matter, then it makes sense why they neglect Eucharist. Why eat and drink in worship if it doesn't really matter? Quite simply they don't care about the body and thus they don't care about Holy Communion.

If Jesus had said take and think, then Protestants in my own Reformed tradition would already be three steps ahead. However, Jesus did not say take and think, he said take and eat. Since many Christians don't acknowledge the spiritual benefit of doing something with one's body they disregard the Eucharist, even though this physical ritual has been considered scripturally and traditionally a central feature of worship for almost two thousand years.

Eating is about as physical of an activity that one can do so if your tradition doesn't care about the body in worship, it won't take the sacraments seriously. Sadly, this is a pervasive practice among many Protestants in worship today, especially in America.

While it reveals a low view of the sacraments, this is most likely linked to a prevalent notion that the "real you" is your soul, which is somehow trapped or shackled to a body. Thus, the "real" you is not your body, but your soul, which basically means that the body is not centrally important as it relates to religion. This view argues that it's the soul that matters more than anything else. Christians should beware of such ideas because they are essentially pagan ideas—not from God.

These bad ideas are not new; they are quite ancient and come to us from Greek philosophy and an old heresy: Gnosticism. In the first few centuries of church history orthodox Christians fought against a false teaching sometimes called Gnosticism. Gnosticism though more of a loosely associated group of teachers became a dangerous influence in the early church and was rejected as a heresy.

Gnostics taught some strange things. For instance, they taught that "god" was a monad who somehow produced a physical world with the demiurge and the physical world was basically bad. This was a core belief of Gnostics—the material world was something negative and our physical existence was like a trap for the spark of divine creation which we might identify the soul. They tended to divide all things into a dualism or two categories of the spiritual and material. Very simply, the spiritual is good, and the physical is bad.

Gnostics taught that salvation comes from spiritual enlightenment of the soul. For Gnostics the soul was the most central element of humanity, and the soul was the spiritual center for humans. They believed that the soul which is spiritual is trapped in a body, which is physical, and the ultimate goal of spiritual blessing is to be somehow free of the physical body. Many Christians have gnostic propensities in their worship practices.

Creation

These ideas stand in stark contrast to orthodox Christian teachings. For orthodox Christians, when God created the first man, he breathed into Adam the breath of life. As such Adam became a living being. The breath of God animated his body and Adam did not become a living soul, but a living body. The soul is not the "real" person, but the animating breath of the body without which there is no life. The soul and body live in harmony together because a soul without a body is a dead person. The soul and body live together in harmony as one because human beings are embodied beings.

The exception to this occurs at death. It is traditional Christian theology to teach that upon death the soul is separated from the body and soul of a believer immediately passes into glory, but this is not a permanent solution to death. Because humans are embodied beings, this condition is temporary and when the body is reunited with the soul at the final resurrection, we will be fully alive again in our permanent transformed, but physical, embodied estate.

Incarnation

The coming of Jesus Christ into world also affirms the reality of embodied human life because Jesus himself become flesh. John 1:14 says that the word became flesh and dwelt among us. The term, John uses for flesh is a powerful word that could almost be translated as meat. Jesus become flesh, which was necessary for him to become a true human because humans are embodied beings.

This is one of the most central Christian doctrines—the incarnation. When the scriptures tell us that the Word became flesh and dwelt among us, we see the physical human body affirmed as central to Christianity. The incarnate, enfleshed, and embodied Son of God redeems people as whole human beings—body and soul. Christianity asserts the incarnation as central to salvation and it's unique in this doctrine. Our God became a human being—100%. Though paradoxical, Jesus was God and man. He was as the great creeds affirm fully God and fully man without confusion.

Many religions have taught that that their gods have come to earth in the form of human beings, but none of these pagan religions teach that their gods actually became a human being. The incarnation is uniquely Christian. The Greek and Roman stories tell of the gods coming as messengers in the form of boys, maidens, etc., but no Greek myth ever speaks of the gods becoming enfleshed true human beings—never.

For the Greeks, the mortality of human flesh was a weakness that the immortal gods could never countenance. The Greek words for their gods described them as "the ones without death," or the "undying ones." In contrast to the gods, humans were said to be the dying ones. Human beings have physical, mortal bodies which by definition would be a weakness for the gods. For Christians the incarnation allowed Jesus Christ to take on flesh so that as he experienced death for his people he would also be raised from the dead, on behalf of his people. Christ's goal in redemption was to save us as whole human beings—body and soul.

For more on the importance of the incarnation you can read one of the early church's greatest warriors, Athanasius. He wrote his famous book, *On the Incarnation* in part as a response to the false teachings of Gnosticism. Athanasius' views represent the orthodox position on the centrality of the incarnation for salvation.

Jesus did not come as the God/Man to save only our souls, but to save us as whole, embodied beings. Thus, we see in his bodily resurrection from the dead a clamoring for us to understand the role of the body in Christian theology as a whole, but particular to this study, the resurrection requires an undeniable centrality to bodily liturgy in worship. At the final resurrection God in Christ will affirm us as embodied beings forever and we will worship him forever as embodied humans.

Jesus also requires us to acknowledge embodied humanity when he meets with his disciples after the resurrection. In Luke 24 Jesus appears to his disciples and eats with them. It's when they were eating that their eyes were opened. When he wants to encourage them, he physically urges them to touch him.

> See my hands and my feet, that it is I myself. Touch me and see. For a spirit does not have flesh and bones as you see that I have." And when he had said this, he showed them his hands and his feet. And while they still disbelieved for joy and were marveling, he said to them, "Have you anything here to eat?" They gave him a piece of broiled fish, and he took it and ate before them. (Luke 24:39)

To provide spiritual encouragement Jesus physically touches them. Our savior's physical, tactile—literal touching of others—is a central characteristic of Jesus' ministry. Everywhere he moved in his public ministry he either touched or was touched by people. This is most poignant in Jesus' work because he touched the untouchable and in touching them— they were transformed! In many ways physical touching embodies the ministry and work of Jesus among needy sinners. Think of the woman with the issue of blood in Luke 8 who merely touched the edge of Jesus' robes and immediately was healed because righteousness and healing went out to her as she touched him.

This little book on worship is not an attempt to explain or delineate various positions on theological psychology as it relates to the relationship between the body and emotions. However, this book assumes a complex, but clear connection between the body, the mind, and the emotions, particularly in worship. My work assumes the reality of embodied existence for human beings that cannot be separated from "spiritual" things—it's what we might call a given. As such I'm working on the orthodox assumption that as embodied beings we need to think carefully about the body in worship. Though a mystery, embodied existence is a given. Almost all the basic Bible encyclopedias and reference books say something like the following:

> Man is viewed as a psychophysical unity in which, contrary to Greek philosophy and to some modern psychology, the body is not separated from the spiritual aspect of man.[4]

I am challenging pastors and elders everywhere to rethink every single aspect of worship first from the scriptures and as such with reference to engaging human beings as embodied beings. When we greet our people in worship, we might consider raising our hands with palms facing to them. They could respond with raised hands and palms facing upward as recipients of God's gracious greeting. The same posture might conclude our worship as minister's hands are raised speaking the benediction, the people of God's hands are lifted upwards helping them by faith to receive the blessings of God.

It's curious that even the "nonphysical" aspects of worship such as reading words, singing songs or listening to sermons all involve the physical senses and thus the body and should include some consideration of posture. When we read, we use our eyes and the sense of sight, but we're reading the word of God so perhaps standing in reverence helps us to hear it well. When we sing, we use our larynx or voice box, our lungs and our mouths connected to the sense of hearing and don't miss the fact that in singing praises we feel the music through our ears and thus the music touches our souls! Music may be the most instructive as to how a physical noise enters our bodies through the ears and moves our souls deeply.

This approach to worships provokes some people to great fear. Nonetheless, when thinking about liturgy we cannot allow our fear to guide us; we must be guided by faith. Fear may be the most powerful obstacle for many people to think scripturally and freely about worship. For instance, if God says raise your hands, then find the appropriate time and raise your hands. If God commends kneeling, then kneel. Raising

---

4. Bass, "Body," 528.

hands will not make you Pentecostal any more than kneeling will make you a crypto Roman Catholic—this is a fear-based approach.

If God has recommended a posture, we should not fear it, but find the best or most appropriate place for it in our worship services and worship God in faith. If we have no place in our worship for God's recommended postures, then perhaps we should rethink our liturgy. Let faith in God's own recommendations guide you more than fear of some perceived or real abuse from another tradition. This is very liberating!

In my opinion, there is a kind of Reformation rationalism and/or charismatic chaos that tends to dominate Protestant thinking on worship today. Thinking scripturally about embodied worship will give us liberty from these unnecessary dilemmas. It will also liberate us from the fear that casts shadows so many of our discussions about worship. I have seen otherwise sturdy elders turn ashen gray when asked if it's OK to raise hands in worship. Why the fear? Why not replace this fear with faith especially in worship.

The subject of worship is so important that it may be the most central matter in our lives and most certainly one of the most crucial issues of our times. For instance, it's typical for people to account for today's lamentable political and cultural decline by looking to presidential politics, economic conditions, supreme court decisions, consumerism, social injustice, and of course the reprehensible condition of secondary and university education. These are the usual suspects. While I agree that all these things are important and many are deplorable, I, however, am convinced that they are not ultimate. Worship is ultimate because of the ancient idea—*lex orandi lex credenda*—the rule of prayer (worship) is the rule of belief. We could modify and slightly update saying, as goes worship, so goes the culture.

The appalling and disgraceful condition of contemporary worship is far more critical, pivotal, and ultimate to the decline of American and western civilization in general than many of the items we tend to deem as foundational. For instance, we live in a culture once characterized by at least an outward nod to the claims of God, but which is now characterized by lauding mentally ill perverts and self-mutilating people as "courageous" heroes. You would expect that lauding perverts as heroes would come from deeply pagan sources, unfortunately the homage and the praise which is so prominent in our culture is also coming from those who claim to be Christians.

The problem is pervasive. Sometimes after the rock concert, light shows and loud music, that poses as Christian worship, we will hear a "courageous" testimony of someone who simultaneously scolds the church for its historic gender intolerance and bigoted treatment of gays while providing an effusive story about their personal lustful perversions that the audience is expected to affirm. This happens in what passes for "worship."

In many ways this book is a series of queries asking the question—what if? What if worship were understood as a God-centered and embodied experience that acts as a means of discipleship which shapes God's people into a pious community as it simultaneously calls down the mighty presence of God? Add to this the often-overlooked reality that when God's people worship him humbly in spirit and in truth, he is inclined to hear them, he is inclined to answer their prayers and their praise with history-changing providential intervention. If you, the reader, will bear with me, I hope to convince you that historic Christian worship as a first principle of life might create a very different effect then we can ever imagine. Our experience of faithful, embodied and God-centered worship transforms us and calls upon God to change history on our behalf.

We will need to change our minds a bit. For example, we need to recognize that significant, historic change does not come solely from electing a good president or appointing conservative justices to the Supreme Court per se, but rather from God's response to worship. (I would love to have a good president and judges who respect our constitution). We are living in radical times of revolution and slowing down the revolution is not enough. Too often I hear people say, "we need revival." I have a bad feeling that simple revival as they might mean it is not even close to the answer. We must respond to this radicalism with a radical or "to the root" response of our own—we must respond with worship. If we do, then we find that God responds to us and when he does respond, amazing things happen.

In the scriptures God offers us a glimpse of what happens when he responds to our worship. We see this in Ps. 18:6–15:

> In my distress I called upon the LORD; to my God I cried for help. From his temple he heard my voice, and my cry to him reached his ears. Then the earth reeled and rocked; the foundations also of the mountains trembled and quaked, because he was angry. Smoke went up from his nostrils, and devouring fire from his mouth; glowing coals flamed forth from him. He

bowed the heavens and came down; thick darkness was under his feet. He rode on a cherub and flew; he came swiftly on the wings of the wind. He made darkness his covering, his canopy around him, thick clouds dark with water. Out of the brightness before him hailstones and coals of fire broke through his clouds. The LORD also thundered in the heavens, and the Most High uttered his voice, hailstones and coals of fire. And he sent out his arrows and scattered them; he flashed forth lightnings and routed them. Then the channels of the sea were seen, and the foundations of the world were laid bare at your rebuke, O LORD, at the blast of the breath of your nostrils.

When God's people sincerely and humbly kneel before him in worship, he looks down upon them with his favor and kindness. This is why Christians who are concerned about cultural decline should put first things first—focusing almost entirely on worship because worship makes the ultimate difference.

If we look solely to the events of history in our own times, we may be fooled into thinking that the events around us are ultimate. For example, when the Roman Empire fell, many Christians lamented what they thought to be the end of the world. Yet, the supposed "end of the world" motivated monks to copy and maintain treasures of literary and theological wisdom. It motivated many to become missionaries who trekked to the uncivilized lands of the "barbarians" where God transformed these pagan cannibals into what today we call Europe. When God's people appeal directly to the supreme court of heaven with whom they have original jurisdiction through Jesus Christ the results are the stuff of historians.

In fact, if the great St. Augustine is correct, whether it's the fall of the city of Rome or the decline of the sanity in the whole western world, the city that matters the most is the city of God—the church of Jesus Christ. Earthly kingdoms rise and fall, but the church of Christ will one day prevail against the gates of hell. Only the church has this promise.

Egypt, Assyria, Babylon, Persia, the Greeks, and the Romans have all fallen into the dust bin of history. However, God used each of these kingdoms to shape, to sanctify and to perfect his bride, the church, which is the ultimate purpose of history. When these kingdoms served his purpose for the church, they fell into the forgotten sands of time. Like the great Ozymandias whose inscription hailed his subjects to look on his breathtaking works and despair; the poem concludes reminding us that his broken and shattered visage was sinking into the desert as "the lone and level sands stretch far away." Today we may be at a very low point in the history of the world and even the life of the church, yet "the lone and level sands" will never ultimately cover the church of Jesus Christ.

Some historians consider the rising and falling of these kingdoms as the stuff of history. To the contrary, they are the backdrop of history that God uses to sanctify his church—the church is at the center of God's providential work: a lesson the powerful ancient king, Nebuchadnezzar learned in Dan. 4:30–32:

> and the king answered and said, "Is not this great Babylon, which I have built by my mighty power as a royal residence and for the glory of my majesty?" While the words were still in the king's mouth, there fell a voice from heaven, "O King Nebuchadnezzar, to you it is spoken: The kingdom has departed from you, and you shall be driven from among men, and your dwelling shall be with the beasts of the field. And you shall be made to eat grass like an ox, and seven periods of time shall pass over you, until you know that the Most High rules the kingdom of men and gives it to whom he will."

God is sovereign and he displays his almighty rule in raising up and smashing down earthly kingdoms though not arbitrarily—he does it all for the purpose of loving and caring for his church. The church is the center of history as outlined in Eph. 1:20–23:

> that he worked in Christ when he raised him from the dead and seated him at his right hand in the heavenly places, far above all rule and authority and power and dominion, and above every name that is named, not only in this age but also in the one to come. And he put all things under his feet and gave him as head over all things to the church, which is his body, the fullness of him who fills all in all.

As kingdoms rise and fall just like in the days of Daniel, the church is humbled into a renewed submission and ultimate allegiance to her true king, Jesus Christ. To the many people experiencing the collapse of a culture, it appears to be the end of the world as they know it. And to a certain extent it is. However, God uses such forlorn times to renew a simple trust and obedience in the hearts of his people and their proper response is worship.

In fact, such humility is often seen most poignantly and beautifully in the reformation of godly worship. It appears in many, many ways that America and the western world in general is experiencing just such a fall. This book is a call to respond to the providences of God with radical reformation and renewal in worship—not merely for cultural renewal per se, but primarily to put first things first in faithful obedience and then let God take care of everything else. The good news is that he does—God always has and always will take care of everything for his own glory and for the loving sanctification of his bride, the church.

Since God loves his church so much that he gave his one and only son for her, then we also must join with our God as we seek the glory of his church. Unfortunately for our days, this requires us to be rather critical and even harsh in pointing to the undignified and perhaps even rebellious practices of the church in worship. The intent of this little book is not to be harsh for the sake of cruelty, rather the intent is to expose the pervasive array of worship malpractice with the hope that it will provoke change in the church and ultimately a reformation of which historians might one day record as a blessed moment in history.

We live in times where rebellious people demand complete affirmation of their rebellion. When no such affirmation is given, the one demanding it believes that his or her essential rights as a sovereign individual are under assault. The irony is that worship is a genuine assault on the rebellious idea that human beings and their wills are sovereign. God-centered worship is a direct strike against all kinds of similar man-centered ideas. Consequently, even a basic criticism of popular, man-centered worship practices will provoke a battle. Yet, I am convinced that it is a battle worth fighting because in many ways, the very heart of Christianity is at stake when it comes to matters of worship.

One contribution that I hope this work will offer is my attempt to expose one of the most unstudied yet potent issues in worship—the body, posture, and liturgy. Neglect of the body has led to effectively eliminating one of the most ancient and central practices of worship, Holy Communion or the eucharist. This has pushed the Lord's Supper out of any meaningful place in Christian worship, sometimes replacing it and the gospel with a kind of Christian rationalism or an Evangelical moralism, which is driven unfortunately at the behest of an obsession with pop culture. Using pop culture as a guide for worship, massive numbers of Christians have essentially eradicated worship as something once riveting our attention and praise to God and they have repositioned human beings at the center of worship.

Contemporary worship has replaced historic practices such as the Eucharist, a reverent, ordered liturgy and scriptural preaching with boring theological diatribes or with rock bands and "worship leaders." I hope to address all these subjects in this work, but on a very basic level this book is a clarion call for a return to embodied worship and even more particularly to the Eucharist as a regular part of worship.

The first few chapters are an attempt to define the nature and purpose of Cristian worship. I try to define worship using the scriptures as our ultimate standard. Woven into the definition of worship is a basic assumption that human beings are made in the image of God and are by nature embodied, worshipping beings. Worship is our highest and most noble activity. Alexander Schmemann describes a human, as "a worshipping being, *homo adorans*: the one for whom worship is the essential act which both posits his being and fulfills it."[5] We are created with an essential hunger for God and because of the centrality of worship in feeding this hunger, we are what James K.A. Smith describes as "liturgical animals," creatures who can't *not* worship and who are fundamentally formed by worship practices."[6] This is why Daniel I. Block states simply and frankly, "to be human is to worship."[7]

My study of worship not only investigates the nature of worship as individuals, but more importantly worship as a corporate activity. This means the doctrine of the church is at the center of worship. Worship and ecclesiology go hand in hand. A proper understanding of worship will reverse the silly but popular phrase—it's a relationship not a religion. Actually, it's about a relationship that produces true religion.

The church is not merely a collection of individuals who desire a "religious" experience. The church is a gathered, worshipping community—most importantly the church gathers in formal worship to meet with her God through Jesus Christ. I use a courtroom illustration as the most appropriate image of formal, gathered worship. This is a helpful illustration of at least part of the scriptural idea of formal worship, and it's also something that we desperately need to rediscover—the idea of an official, formal gathering of God's people to meet with the judge of all the earth is an idea that comes from the scriptures. It seems to be an idea that is lost to modern worship practices, especially when it includes reverence and awe.

As I define worship, I also include a forgotten aspect of worship as warfare. In many ways worship involves aggressive, military imagery of

5. Schmemann, *Life of the World*, 118.
6. Smith, *Imagining the Kingdom*, 3.
7. Block, *Glory of God*, 1.

God's engagement with the forces of darkness. In worship we declare that God is the ultimate judge and that one day he will judge all people everywhere who refuse to bow their knees to his majestic authority. We should sing about this when we sing the Psalms in worship, which have fallen into disuse.

Once worship is defined, the book moves into the elements of worship again attempting to use the Bible as the sole standard for what God wants us to do in worship and with particular interest in role of the body and liturgy in worship. In some ways, this work is simple, yet in other ways it is an attempt to reveal the stunning beauty of worship as an embodied experience where God's ordinances are not rules per se, but they are deeply enriching and liberating practices designed to bless us as those made in the image of God.

Praise in worship, for instance, is an incredible gift from God that shapes and directs not only our songs in worship but praise also possesses an astonishing way of shaping our lives as well. Praise is an embodied experience that has mysterious strength to bless us and to give glory to God. God is kind in using embodied experiences such as singing, eating, and drinking in worship to disciple us and to enrich our lives at the same time.

In this little outline of worship, I tackle the issue of preaching, praise, prayer, and the sacraments in worship—all with a particular focus on the importance of worship as an embodied experience. I attempt to do all of this with an interest in embodied worship motivated by faith and not by fear.

For each item I have a simple approach to worship that is also applicable to life: say what God says and do what God says to do. In worship as with so many issues of theology and life people who claim allegiance to the scriptures are apt to wiggle and maneuver around what the Bible actually says when it comes to issues with which they disagree with God's word. I marvel when the opening chapter of Ephesians teaches in multiple and undeniable ways the doctrine of predestination. To the person who disagrees with it, this chapter suddenly becomes a "problem" passage. For them, the passage can't really say what it obviously says. From here the person begins to dismantle this "problem" passage and explain it away.

In worship practices we find the same approach. If the scriptures encourage us to raise our hands, then some unemotional Presbyterians feel the need to say something differently than what God says about it–it's appropriate to raise hands in worship. If emotional charismatics think that kneeling is too liturgical and smells of Roman Catholicism, they still need to say what God says—kneeling is an appropriate posture of worshipping God.

I laughed recently when a Reformed minister read a Psalm to open worship where God says to clap your hands all ye nations. I laughed to myself because I know full well that this church has effectively forbidden clapping in any part of the worship service. They might clap before worship starts at the announcement that Uncle Bob and Aunt Betty had a 50th wedding anniversary, but they will never allow for clapping hands in worship itself. So much for the call to worship telling us to clap our hands? When this kind of thing happens—a direct clash between clear scriptural statements and contemporary worship practices—we should ask why. Why is it that God encourages something that we discourage? This should give us serious pause.

I am challenging us to remember that we are not allowed to pick and to choose what we want to say because we prefer something other than what God says about it. While the place, manner, and practice of raising hands, clapping hands and kneeling may be appropriately discussed and debated, we may not dismiss these postures as if they were not appropriate for worship at all. Rather, we need to say what God says about them—with faith and not fear.

Even the most frigid Presbyterian must at least acknowledge that they are OK with raising hands in worship. Beyond a begrudging acknowledgment that God says to raise hands in prayer, I'm arguing that we need to start listening to God's recommendations and thus engaging the full person in worship without apology or fear. This engages people without gimmicks or techniques (for which everyone is clamoring)—it engages them in ways that God has already recommended, which means they are appropriate and will bless us.

Too often people define their worship practices in opposition to other traditions that they perceive to be bad. If charismatics raise their hands, then Presbyterians who fear the dangers of chaotic worship refuse to raise their hands. If Anglicans kneel for confessions of sin, then charismatics, Evangelicals and Reformed pastors who fear the dangers of ritualistic worship refuse to kneel. You can see that this approach uses fear as the guiding principle of what one should or should not do in worship. The scriptures tell us that faith and not fear should be the guiding principle of worship. It would be more revitalizing and in fact it is quite liberating to approach these questions afresh—say what God says and then let the chips fall where they may.

This little book on worship is an attempt to do just this. I attempt to tackle a handful of questions about worship by faith and not fear. I happen to be a Presbyterian from a committed reformed theological perspective. However, one of the most basic commitments that I take as a Christian is that the scriptures are my ultimate authority. Thus, I hope to approach the subject of worship from this very perspective. Join me in an exciting and hopefully refreshing study of worship.

CHAPTER 1

What is Worship?

WORSHIP IS AN EMBODIED experience, and it was this way from our creation as hungry beings. Worship and hunger are intimately related. Our creation as embodied beings include physical hunger that is basic to what it means to be human and also intimately connected to worship. How is hunger related to worship?

Hunger provides us a glimpse of the human condition which is the context for embodied worship. According to Alexander Schmemann, "Man is a hungry being, but he is hungry for God. Behind all the hunger of our life is God."[1] We are created with an essential hunger for God and because of the centrality of worship in feeding this hunger, we are what James K.A. Smith describes as "liturgical animals," creatures who can't *not* worship and who are fundamentally formed by worship practices."[2] Hunger for God is central to what it means to be human, and embodied worship is essential to feeding this hunger. This is partly why Daniel I. Block can assert correctly, "to be human is to worship."[3]

Early in my Christian life I thought that hunger was perhaps part of the curse. Because it struck me as a weakness, I reasoned that hunger appeared among humans as the result of the Fall into sin. However, now it strikes me with continual wonder when I meditate on the reality that even before the Fall, humans were created hungry creatures. At the center

1. Schmemann, *Life of the World*, 2.
2. Smith, *Imagining the Kingdom*, 3.
3. Block, *Glory of God*, 1.

of this hunger is worship; a baffling reality for many who don't care about eating the Lord's Supper in worship. We should care about hunger and worship because it explains why God masterfully arranged as the essential test of our first parents a test of hunger. God positioned two trees at the heart of Adam and Eve's existence as he challenged them to come to him alone for food. Representing God as the ultimate source of their lives, our first parents were to satisfy their hunger at the tree of life eating with God alone in worship. Their hunger was designed to direct them to God, the source of life. Peter Leithart notes well,

> Our lives are directed by our hungers, and we find rest only when we hunger for the one who opens his hand to satisfy the desire of every living thing more than we hunger for the things in his hands.[4]

Adam and Eve were called to meet with God on what Ezek. 28:14 describes as the mountain of God. This is where they worshipped God. This is where God placed them to fulfill their destiny as worshipping creatures. They were created with a hunger for God that was ultimately fulfilled in eating from the Tree of Life. The interplay of hunger and worship reminds us of what Jesus said in the beatitudes: blessed are those who hunger and thirst for righteousness, for they will be satisfied! This is one of the reasons this book will argue consistently that the sacrament of the Eucharist should be a normal and central feature of every worship service. Our savior also said something amazing about our relationship with him and hunger. Jesus says in John 5:53,

> Truly, truly, I say to you, unless you eat the flesh of the Son of Man and drink his blood, you have no life in you. Whoever feeds on my flesh and drinks my blood has eternal life, and I will raise him up on the last day. For my flesh is true food, and my blood is true drink. Whoever feeds on my flesh and drinks my blood abides in me, and I in him. As the living Father sent me, and I live because of the Father, so whoever feeds on me, he also will live because of me. This is the bread that came down from heaven, not like the bread the fathers ate, and died. Whoever feeds on this bread will live forever.

This should continually remind us that worship is about coming to feast with God in Christ as an embodied experience and not merely a theological/cerebral or emotional experience. In this sense, we need to think

4. Leithart, *Blessed Are the Hungry*, 20.

about the importance of liturgy in worship. James K. A. Smith summarizes it nicely in another way saying, "To be human is to be a liturgical animal, a creature whose loves are shaped by our worship. And worship isn't optional."[5] To be human is to be full of the hunger unique to humanity.

All living creatures are physically hungry, but humans are uniquely hungry for God, and it shows in our instinctive desire for gathering. I was struck by humanity's distinctiveness in this regard because while writing this chapter, I stayed up late with my son to watch the semi-finals of the World Cup. Millions of people all over the world were doing the same thing, but have you ever wondered why? It's because we're human. How does this relate to worship?

Worship as a gathering before God fulfills an exclusively human instinct or hunger for a longing to gather and to share with others in something beyond us—things true and beautiful—God. Human beings are hard wired with a desire to gather together to feed their hunger for truth, beauty and goodness. We do it instinctively as something flowing from our very constitution as humans made uniquely in the image of God.

No other creature on earth is so incomparably suited for this. For instance, have you ever seen a group of dolphins assembling to enjoy and to judge the beauty or excellence of the other dolphins' jumps? We do! Have you ever seen a gathering of bears sitting in bleachers along the river to enjoy and to marvel at the excellence of each other's salmon snatching? Humans do this very thing. Because we are made in the image of God, we gather to watch these kinds of things endlessly in various forms. Have you ever seen cheetahs gathered to watch a race to judge who is the fastest? I assume you have heard of the Olympics. Why is it that humans are the only creatures that gather together at sports arenas, music concerts, churches or wherever we gather in order to observe and to enjoy the beauty of someone or something that is excellent? It's because we are made in the image of God, and we are the only creatures whose basic composition includes a hunger for God that constitutes us as worshipping beings. This is why James K. A. Smith was correct to note that we are unavoidably liturgical.

As humans it's not as if we may or may not worship; worship is not optional. We are designed to know truth, beauty, and goodness—we hunger for it—it's deep within our very being—we have been designed for it and we can't escape it. This is why worshipping God meets our deepest

---

5. Smith, *You Are What You Love*, 23.

needs as human beings. It's also why worship is our highest and most noble activity, and why we should give serious consideration to the nature and purpose of worship. Unlike Aristotle's description of man as a featherless biped, Schmemann describes a human being as, "a worshipping being, *homo adorans*: the one for whom worship is the essential act which both posits his being and fulfills it."[6]

The fall into sin was fundamentally about worship. As noted above, it was also framed in the obviously embodied experience of eating. In the fall, Adam and Eve rebelled against God as they attempted to worship in their own way, which plunged humanity and the world into its present sinful estate. You should also notice that their worship and service to God was an unavoidably embodied one. They hungered for God and the test was the embodied activity of eating. The agonizing reality for Adam and Eve and for us is that the fall did not change this essential hunger for God or the basic need to worship. Though misdirected and poisoned by sin we are no less liturgical and no less hungry after the fall than before it. Even though due to the fall we are selfish and sinful we are still hungry, and we still need to worship. As sinners who need God's reordering love, worship becomes an even more central issue for our lives.

As sinners, we need worship to disciple us; godly worship reshapes our misshapen affections away from sin and towards their proper ends in God. In worship we experience the best of what it means to be human, and we are redirected to the source of our life: God. We eat and drink with God in worship, we listen to him speak to us, we speak back to him, we raise our hands, we shout amen, we kneel, we pray, we cry, we laugh, and we sing. We do what God created us to do as embodied beings: glorify him and enjoy him![7] Let this sink in! Many people think that we worship so we can get the spiritual energy we need to go out and do the really important things, but it's actually the other way round. Worship is why we are here—it's why we exist. In fact, worship is so essential to our purpose as humans that *it's the reason for all the other things we do.*

As a missionary I love John Piper's declaration, "missions is not the ultimate goal of the church. Worship is. Missions exists," says Piper,

---

6. Schmemann, *Life of the World*, 118.

7. Many readers will recognize this sentence as a virtual quote from the famous *Westminster Shorter Catechism*, which asks in the first question—what is the chief end or primary purpose of man? The answer is to glorify God and to enjoy him forever.

"because worship doesn't. Worship is ultimate, not missions because God is ultimate, not man."[8] In a similar vein, John Frame writes,

> *In one sense, worship is the whole point of everything.* It is the purpose of history, the goal of the whole Christian story. Worship is not one segment of the Christian life among others. Worship is the entire Christian life, seen as a priestly offering to God. And when we meet together as a church, our time of worship is not merely a preliminary to something else; rather, it is the whole point of our existence as the body of Christ (emphasis mine).[9]

Defining Worship?

Since worship is so central to life, then what do we mean when we talk about worship? In English the word worship, is derived from the Saxon/Old English 'weorthscipe' or 'weordhscipe.' In its simplest form, it basically means to ascribe worth to something or to someone. To worship someone or something is to ascribe a quality of worthiness connected to a deep respect or reverence for the object of worship. True worship is always motivated by a reverence and a respect that is generated from a genuine attitude of the heart: sincerity. In other words, genuine worship has nothing to do with ascribing worth or worthiness in a perfunctory or false way, but as a sincere act of reverence.

If we look at some dictionaries for a definition of worship, we find that while they vary a bit, they tend to point us to the idea of honor and respect for something or someone who is superior. In organized public worship this includes honor and respect connected to specific acts of worship such as prayer, praise, etc. *Webster's Dictionary* of 1828 is helpful because it indicates that worship involves extravagant love and extreme submission. The idea of passionate expressions of love linked with submission helps to move us closer to the idea of worship that God provides in the Holy Scriptures. A dictionary is a good start, but as Christians we find the most important definition of worship in the Holy Scriptures.

In the scriptures the words for worship include everything a dictionary mentions but the Scriptures add an important embodied dimension. Scriptures don't merely say to ascribe intellectual/theological things to God. The difference is that in the Scriptures the words for worship always

---

8. Piper, *Nations Be Glad*, 15.
9. Frame, *Worship in Spirit and Truth*, 11.

provide vivid pictures of embodied postures and activities directed to God (commonly called liturgies). Both of the two primary Old Testament and New Testament words that are translated as worship could also be translated literally to bow down, to fall face down, or to kneel. This should strike us as quite amazing. Ironically, even though millions of scripture-loving Christians never kneel in worship, the posture used to define/describe worship is kneeling. Everything about biblical worship is embodied and yet most Protestant Christians in America never actually worship God using this obviously biblical and very basic posture.

The most prominent Hebrew word in the Old Testament, *shachah*, can mean bowing down as one kneels down before a king or before royalty. In the ancient near east this might even have meant falling down on one's knees and touching one's forehead to the ground. In the New Testament the most commonly used Greek word, *proskuneo* also means to fall down, to kneel before or even to bow down in order to show extreme submission—like a dog falls down in humility before his master. This is the word Satan used when tempting Jesus to bow down to worship him in Matt. 4. If the very word for worship means to kneel or to bow down, why don't more Christians kneel when they worship—especially ones who say they trust the Bible? This is no small matter.

Another important Greek word used in the New Testament is the word *latreo*. This word is connected to what we already saw in Rom. 12:1 it's associated to the idea of rendering an act of religious service such as bringing a sacrifice, or an offering, etc. This is liturgy—the activity or service of worship. All worship is liturgy and all Christians "do" something in worship which means whether it's good or bad—all Christians have a liturgy.

The scriptural words for worship are active words that include the body. This is why John Frame rightly maintains that "worship is active. It's something we do . . . we can see that worship is far different from religious entertainment. It is always to be understood as an embodied activity. In worship we are not to be passive, but to participate."[10] The bodily postures in the scriptures indicate that worship involves showing honor, reverence and respect for God who is superior. Rom. 12:1 as we already explained requires this honor and respect to be embodied.[11]

---

10. Frame, *Worship in Spirit and Truth*, 1.
11. See this book's Introduction for more.

Ps. 96:7-9 provides an example describing how we ascribe to God the glory due to him as God in worship:

> Ascribe to the LORD, O families of the peoples, ascribe to the LORD glory and strength! Ascribe to the LORD the glory due his name; bring an offering, and come into his courts! Worship the LORD in the splendor of holiness; tremble before him, all the earth!

This Psalm as well as many other portions of the scriptures speaks to the *duty* of worshiping God alone as the true God. Not only the duty of worship but the destiny of worship. Destiny here is connected to the ultimate aim of all creatures worshipping God. Ps. 148 captures this idea magnificently.

> Praise the LORD! Praise the LORD from the heavens; praise him in the heights! Praise him, all his angels; praise him, all his hosts! Praise him, sun and moon, praise him, all you shining stars! Praise him, you highest heavens, and you waters above the heavens! Let them praise the name of the LORD! For he commanded and they were created. And he established them forever and ever; he gave a decree, and it shall not pass away. Praise the LORD from the earth, you great sea creatures and all deeps, fire and hail, snow and mist, stormy wind fulfilling his word! Mountains and all hills, fruit trees and all cedars! Beasts and all livestock, creeping things and flying birds! Kings of the earth and all peoples, princes and all rulers of the earth! Young men and maidens together, old men and children! Let them praise the name of the LORD, for his name alone is exalted; his majesty is above earth and heaven. He has raised up a horn for his people, praise for all his saints, for the people of Israel who are near to him. Praise the LORD (Ps. 148:1-14)!

This beautiful Psalm points us to the duty of worship and to the destiny of worship. This is our purpose and the purpose of all creatures great and small, rational, and irrational, visible and invisible—everything and everyone will worship God—it is the destiny of all creation. If we keep this powerful idea in mind, then we would more likely understand the importance of why it would be natural to kneel in the presence of God.

When one is discussing worship, theology matters, and good theology often runs counter to our own desires: this is a rather critical point that we will address throughout this study. It may also answer the question as to why the posture of kneeling is ignored in worship even though it expresses the primary meaning of worship.

It is my sincere hope that Christians everywhere and Protestants in particular will undertake a serious, renewed consideration of worship, particularly the importance of liturgy and posture in worship as derived from the Scriptures. This should resonate with Protestants because though it's sometimes overlooked the origins of the Protestant Reformation were driven in large part over the issue of worship.

Many reformers were actively resisting what they perceived to be superstitious and false worship. John Calvin, for instance, broke with his former French classmates and one scholar argues persuasively that a major focal point changing young Calvin's mind was the question of worship.[12] Thoughtful and reformed-minded Christians of Calvin's day confronted deeply rooted superstitions in the use of statues, relics, and images of all kinds. They called this kind of superstitious worship idolatry. As Calvin and other thinkers took sin and corruption seriously, they connected it to the issue of idolatry in worship.

> As the corruption of man's proper relationship with God, the problem of idolatry assumes a key position in the thought of Calvin. In fact, Calvin's attack on idolatry is an attack on the corruption of all religion, it is an involved defense of the truth of the Gospel against its antithesis. The significance of this defense cannot be underestimated, since it lays bare many of the central points of Calvin's theology.[13]

Idolatrous worship or false worship is essentially turning worship inside out and worshipping the creature rather than the creator or worshipping the creator in a way that God does not want. Human beings have a sinful tendency to say they are worshipping God while turning the liturgy or activity of worship towards themselves. Thus, worshipping the creature rather than the creator. This is basically what Cain did in opposition to Abel.

Calvin was right to identify improper worship as idolatry. Idolatry flows from our sinful nature and situates sin as one of the most serious considerations when studying worship. Our God-created design to worship him has been perverted in the Fall, and though we can't change the deep hunger in our souls as image bearers, sin has caused us

---

12. See Eire, *War Against Idols*, 195.
13. Eire, *War Against Idols*, 196.

to pervert this hunger and to direct it to someone or something other than God—usually back to ourselves. We still have a hunger and thirst for truth, beauty, and goodness, but sin has twisted and perverted it. In tackling the subject of idolatry in worship, however, Calvin did not reject liturgy per se.

We need thoughtful liturgy in worship because in doing so we are not only glorifying God but simultaneously redirecting and reshaping our own sinful lives away from idolatry and from ourselves and unto our savior, Jesus Christ. Calvin put it like this:

> Let us now see what is meant by the due worship of God. Its chief foundation is to acknowledge Him to be, as He is, the only source of all virtue, justice, holiness, wisdom, truth, power, goodness, mercy, life, and salvation; in accordance with this, to ascribe and render to Him the glory of all that is good, to seek all things in Him alone, and in every want have recourse to Him alone . . . renouncing the world and the flesh, we are transformed in the renewing of our mind, and living no longer to ourselves, submit to be ruled and actuated by Him. By this self-abasement we are trained to obedience and devotedness to his will, so that his fear reigns in our hearts, and regulates all the actions of our lives.[14]

If he is correct that worship is to "train" us in obedience and love, then *worship is the most important form of Christian discipleship,* which is why we should think carefully about liturgy and posture in worship. In worship God is training and teaching us that we are not God, but creatures. Worship profoundly instructs us that God is the creator and we are his humble creatures. This fundamental reality helps to orient our whole lives and order what sin has so badly disordered.

As noted already, the scriptures speak of worship not merely as thinking reverent thoughts about God, but as an embodied activity directed to God. In Rom. 12:1 and in Ps. 96 we see God's people speaking (ascribing perhaps even singing). We see them bringing an offering and trembling as they kneel before him. These are incarnate, liturgical activities—kneeling, speaking/singing, bringing an offering, etc. These actions involve postures appropriately connected to them. I want to emphasize that our posture in worship is as much a part of worship as the disposition of our heart especially because some people popularly think that worship is merely a matter of the sincerity of the heart alone.

14. Calvin, *Necessity of Reforming Church*, 17.

When discussing the importance of kneeling in worship, one of my friends once said, I won't kneel outwardly because it's too liturgical, but I'll be kneeling in my heart. I still laugh when I think about this because I'm not sure what on earth anyone could mean by this. I can see how someone could have an outward bodily posture of kneeling while remaining stubborn in his heart. I can even see that someone may force you to do something outwardly while your heart is not in it. But I have yet to figure out what the opposite means. How does one willingly kneel in his heart when the heart has no legs? How does one drink wine with his heart? We are embodied beings with flesh and blood and bones. When we worship God, if we can do so, he expects us to bend our knees literally, raise our hands literally and open our mouths literally—yes even to eat and to drink the bread and wine that he offers to us in Holy Communion. Of course, all of these postures are done in sincere faith, but they are done none the less.

Worship is an activity that engages us as incarnate beings, which should innately point us to humanity's constitution—we are embodied beings. When Jesus said that we must worship him in spirit, he did not mean without our bodies. He meant in Christ and by the power of the Holy Spirit. We don't engage the heart or soul isolated from our bodies as if we could somehow stop being human and become like angels in worship. God himself doesn't want this if for no other reason than he tells us to eat and drink in remembrance of him. You can't eat and drink with your soul alone.

To worship as incarnate human beings means that we engage the body and the soul together. In fact, to engage the body is to instruct the soul because they cannot be separated. Worship involves concrete, tangible gestures and/or actions (liturgy)—not heart thoughts alone— whatever a heart thought might look like. This relates to the earlier scriptural word from which we get our English word, liturgy. Liturgy is simply the activity of worship, which means that everyone has a liturgy; the question is do you have a good one. Do you have a liturgy that redirects your misaligned heart back to God? Do you have a liturgy that reorders the constant disorder in your life?

As sinners we are inclined to serve ourselves and to create idols that support our disordered affections, which originate from sin and self-love. To make matters worse every day throughout the whole week we have these sinful inclinations reinforced as we engage in all kinds of cultural practices (what some have called cultural liturgies) that misshape and misdirect our affections. Perhaps a reality that is often never considered is the powerful way in which our culture shapes and forms us in ways often imperceivable. This is why we need embodied worship as a central part of our lives—to reshape and to reform us towards God.

Many little children in America grow up as unwitting consumers. They are pushed around in a grocery cart through acres of various foods and goodies in the grocery store. If it's a big chain store they move through aisles of items stacked twenty feet high. They enter the store as automatic doors require nothing but your presence to open them. In the summer you're greeted with a gush of fresh cold air. The produce section has hundreds of fruits and vegetables from all over the world arranged beautifully for your consideration and selection. Pleasant grandmother like women offer free samples of delicious tidbits. When mom takes her child to the cereal aisle to look for breakfast treats, she begins to stroll down a vast section of chocolatey, sugary, candy-shaped goodies complete with a super-hero toy inside the box, the child never realizes that his/her life is being shaped as a self-centered consumer.

Everything in almost every way is designed to alert the consumer that he/she is the center of a world which is here to be consumed like fruit loops and candy. In many places in the world a child may grow up not knowing if he/she will eat for a day during the dry season, but in the luxurious world of America and the west children breathe in the air of a luxurious, consumer world in which their phones and gadgets are required to entertain them with the latest and greatest movies, games, and social media that they expect to have at their fingertips—all the time. Please don't think I'm blaming parents for the world in which they live, but something needs to counterbalance the all-consuming consumerism that is like the air we breathe.

James K. A. Smith nicely summarizes how consistent worship practices retrain and reshape our lives back to our creator and redeemer. He notes:

> Christian worship, we should recognize, is essentially a *counter*formation to those rival liturgies we are often immersed in, cultural practices that covertly capture our loves and longings, miscalibrating them, orienting us to rival versions of the good life. This is why worship is the heart of discipleship.[15]

---

15. Smith, *You Are What You Love*, 25.

This is a profoundly important point because if worship is at the heart of discipleship, then it is at the heart of the mission of the church as outlined in the Great Commission in Matt. 28. Many churches have not only failed to teach this, but they have also missed this point entirely. For instance, worship should not be structured around the interests and desires of unbelievers (or believers per se)—worship is discipleship and therefore structured around God and his ordinances. Worship should not be fashioned to satisfy us, although nothing satisfies us more than true worship. Rather, worship should be structured to shape our tastes, our affections and the entire direction of our lives making worship the most foundational activity in life.

Informal and Formal Worship

Before one has a serious discussion about worship it's also important to distinguish between informal and formal worship as taught in the Scriptures. You may wish to speak of the distinction as between public and private or official and unofficial, or even call it corporate worship. Many people fail to make this distinction or refuse to acknowledge that there is a difference between informal and formal worship. First, we can see that God wants our whole lives to be liturgy or acts of worship from the following verses:

> I appeal to you therefore, brothers, by the mercies of God, to present your bodies as a living sacrifice, holy and acceptable to God, which is your spiritual worship (liturgy). (Rom. 12:1)[16]

> Praying at all times in the Spirit, with all prayer and supplication. To that end keep alert with all perseverance, making supplication for all the saints. (Eph. 6:18)

> So, whether you eat or drink, or whatever you do, do all to the glory of God. (1 Cor. 10:31)

God wants our whole lives to be liturgical: to be acts of worship directed to him. Everything we think, everything we say, and everything we do must be done for the glory and honor of God as liturgies/activities of worship. However, it also doesn't take much searching of the same scriptures to notice that there are public meetings or gatherings of worship, and these

---

16. I've added the word, liturgy as a more literal translation of the word, *latreo* or act of worship.

are different from the way we worship in our daily lives as individuals or families. We engage in private activities offered to God as worship, but not all of them should be done in public meetings.

Yes, says the student of worship, but what's the difference between informal, private, personal acts of worship and formal, public worship? Why can't we get just as much from private devotions and/or a small group who wants to "worship" at home as we can get from going to an official church service. In fact, before I left for Africa many American Evangelical churches were virtually obsessed with the idea of house or home churches at least in part because these little groups, so they said, allowed people to worship God more personally and without the impersonal structures of "religion." Religion in this sense is used as a pejorative word (usually for liturgy). Private vs. public/formal worship is a significant distinction and it makes a very serious difference in your approach to God particularly in public worship. Again, this is why theology matters.

First, the church did not fabricate the idea of formal worship for its own benefit. Many people act as if the church made up the idea of corporate worship so as to bring the church and her leaders more power. However, this distinction of formal worship as marked out as an official meeting/gathering with God, is taken from the scriptures themselves. When you look, for example, at a gathering or an assembly to meet with God you find that the idea of corporate worship is almost obvious. In fact, the scriptures use specific words for official meetings or gatherings before God. Hebrews warns us not to miss worship services or the gatherings called by the church when it says, in Heb. 10:24,

> And let us consider how to stir up one another to love and good works, not neglecting to meet together, as is the habit of some, but encouraging one another, and all the more as you see the Day drawing near.

At first glance you might ask what is so important about "meeting together?" However, the word for meeting together is a precise Greek word that specifies an official gathering or assembling together. The word in verse 25 is the word, *episunagoge*, to assemble together or to gather together in an official capacity: in this case for worship. The root word, *sunagoge*, is almost the same as our Anglicized version in English, synagogue, which generally refers to a Jewish gathering for worship.

This is an actual, literal meeting of people—not a televised meeting online or "meeting" via a computer. This passage reminds us that there is actually something necessary and encouraging about meeting with other believers in an embodied meeting. Recently as the corona virus pandemic swept through the world, governments everywhere shut down worship gatherings. We all experienced the amazing way we felt when we were finally able to meet again in an actual or real worship service versus the virtual service that many governments around the world told us should satisfy our religious needs.

As things opened up after COVID-19 lockdowns, I remember the first time I was able to meet with other believers in a church building for worship and I remember almost crying when I sang together with other actual people. I felt their presence in their songs, and I experienced them as we sang and praised God together. The actual, embodied gathering of real people is something that cannot be satisfied by meeting online.

Here is where a look at the Old Testament provides some roots and context for the importance of formal worship gatherings. In the Old Testament God officially gathered his people to come before him and to meet with him or to assemble before him. These gatherings had some basic characteristics. First, there was a divine call to assemble before him that came through an ordained leader. God summoned his people to meet with him as we see for instance in Exod. 19:10,

> the LORD said to Moses, "Go to the people and consecrate them today and tomorrow, and let them wash their garments and be ready for the third day. For on the third day the LORD will come down on Mount Sinai in the sight of all the people.

God designated a place for them to meet where he would manifest his special presence with them. Sinai was one of the most powerful places where God met his people on the mountain. Mountains were common places where God would come down to meet with his people. In fact, after the tabernacle settled on Mt. Zion, Jerusalem and more pointedly the temple became the specific Old Testament place where God met with his people.

Worship in the Old Testament began in the Garden of Eden and after the Fall into sin, worship continued with animal sacrifices. Cain and Abel worshipped in special meetings with God at special times and at special places. Noah worshipped, Abraham worshipped, and they all met with God in special places at special times with blood sacrifices. Worship was increasingly formalized in redemptive history and developed seriously with the Exodus of Israel from Egypt (Exod. 3:12,18). When God called Israel out of Egypt it was with a promise connected to worship. Israel was a nation called out by God. Notice they were not called out and saved per se, but they were called out/saved in order to gather in God's special presence for worship. This special presence was spoken of as God's dwelling place or his sanctuary. Note Exod. 15:13 & 17,

> You have led in your steadfast love the people whom you have redeemed; you have guided them by your strength to your holy abode . . . You will bring them in and plant them on your own mountain, the place, O Lord, which you have made for your abode, the sanctuary, O Lord, which your hands have established.

God promised to dwell with them and meet with them with his special presence in the tabernacle and eventually in the temple worship. Along with the temple God also created an intricate system of worship. Aaron and his sons served as priests and the Levites were connected to this system of worship performing all kinds of liturgical service. There were specific days and festivals when God's people were called to come to him in the temple and the ordained ministers led the gathering before God.

Worship in the Old Testament developed into a rather elaborate affair that was intimately linked to the sacrificial system. New Testament worship changes dramatically because Jesus fulfills and replaces the entire sacrificial system and all the ceremonies associated with it—the tabernacle and the temple, and all the ceremonies attached to them. The Westminster Confession of Faith XIX.3 speaks of this at least in part in the following:

> Beside this law, commonly called moral, God was pleased to give to the people of Israel, as a church underage, ceremonial laws, containing several typical ordinances, partly of worship, prefiguring Christ, his graces, actions, sufferings, and benefits; and partly, holding forth divers instructions of moral duties. All which ceremonial laws are now abrogated, under the New Testament.

Hebrews is critically helpful for this idea. Hebrews teaches us that Jesus has fulfilled and replaced the entire apparatus of Old Testament worship as it related to the sacrificial and ceremonial system. This means that all of the Old Testament ceremonies and ordinances that patterned or prefigured Jesus Christ are no longer part of New Testament worship, but they are fulfilled in Christ. Since Christ instituted the Lord's Supper, we still have blood sacrifice at the center of our worship, but it's a celebration of Christ's blood, not the blood of bulls and goats.

In fulfillment of the Old Testament priestly order and sacrifices Jesus has become our great high priest who has offered himself once for all for us (Heb. 7:27). Because Jesus' blood fulfills and replaces the Old Testament sacrificial system, we no longer include any of the ceremonial ordinances in New Testament ordinances (Heb. 9:12–14; 10:1–4,10,11–18). Other specific ordinances, such as incense, priestly head wear, styles of robes, and the entire priestly order of the Old Testament system is fulfilled in Christ, but the basic elements of worship such as prayer, praise, and preaching that are not specifically shaped by the ceremonies of the Old Covenant remain important parts of New Testament worship.

Likewise, New Testament worship changes the place or location of worship. The location of worship changes in New Testament because Christian worship occurs as God meets with his people not in a specifically designated geographic site, but as he meets with them wherever two or three are "gathered" or assembled for worship in his name in the church through the Holy Spirit. In the Old Testament God ultimately required his people to meet him at the temple. In the New Testament worship takes place in any geographic location, in building or under a mango tree or wherever two or three are officially gathered to meet with God.[17]

Old Testament Israel was a worshipping community with the tabernacle at the center of their culture and eventually the temple replaced it and was also situated as the center of life for the faithful. Prior to the coming of Jesus, the temple and all of the ceremonies connected to it were central to official assemblies of worship before God. Now, however, the scriptures describe Christ as the center. He has entered into the holy of holies once for all (Heb. 9:11–14). Jesus is at the center of New Testament worship and in Christ all the Old Testament ceremonies have been fulfilled. This doesn't mean that New Testament worship should be some kind of informal chaos. In fact, New Testament worship continues to be an official gathering before God through Jesus Christ, but without the Old Testament patterns, which pointed to Christ.

---

17. In Deut. 4:10 God calls an "assembly" or gathering to meet with him. Three times in Deuteronomy Moses refers back to this experience as "the day of assembly" (Deut. 9:10; 10:4; 18:16). This day of assembly (Hebrew word *qahal*) became something of a prototype of all subsequent gatherings or assemblies. This is the pattern used multiple times in the Old Testament and acting as a pattern for New Testament worship.

In the context of an official church gathering we hear Jesus promise his special presence for official meetings in Matt. 18:19–20.

> Again I say to you, if two of you agree on earth about anything they ask, it will be done for them by my Father in heaven. For where two or three are gathered in my name, there am I among them."

First, let's remind ourselves that the phrase "two or three" is language that we might call Deuteronomic language of the courtroom (Deut. 17:6; 19:15). This is the language or phraseology of a courtroom setting. This is connected to the idea of an official meeting or assembly, which is why we also observe that the word gathered in Matt. 18:20 is derived from the basic word, synagogue, which like the word in Heb. 10:25 indicates an official, formal assembly in the presence of God.

Another important characteristic of worship services like the ones described in the Old and the New Testament is that they take place in the presence of God at his altar as a gathering characterized by sacrifice and feasts. One author correctly notes,

> Christian worship—that is, the gathering of the church as church—is the culmination and completion of this ages-long pattern of God calling his people to his dwelling place. This biblical motif of divine-human assemblies has a special character that distinguishes it from other gatherings, such as Bible studies, prayer groups, and Sunday school classes.[18]

This accounts at least partly in why we see amazing and unique promises to the church in Matt. 16:18–19.

> And I tell you, you are Peter, and on this rock I will build my church, and the gates of hell shall not prevail against it. I will give you the keys of the kingdom of heaven, and whatever you bind on earth shall be bound in heaven, and whatever you loose on earth shall be loosed in heaven."

The binding and loosing imagery used in Matt. 16 is connected to the special character of the church as a "gathered" body in Matt. 18:18–20.

> Truly, I say to you, whatever you bind on earth shall be bound in heaven, and whatever you loose on earth shall be loosed in heaven. Again I say to you, if two of you agree on earth about anything they ask, it will be done for them by my Father in

---

18. Kineer, "Worship More Than a List," para. 13.

heaven. For where two or three are gathered in my name, there am I among them."

The very same language is used in both passages, and we need to keep them together because of the unique and powerful character of the church of Jesus Christ as a gathered community. The church is the only institution given the amazing promise that the gates of hell will not prevail. Notice this is to the church as the "gathered" body of God—the church as a worshipping community. This kind of clearly embodied gathering of actual people together in worship is not something that can be done online or at a virtual "meeting."

Please don't pull the supposed Protestant trump card arguing for the "priesthood of all believers." While it's true that we can go directly to God through Jesus, our great high priest, this doesn't mean that God has abolished all order or hierarchy in the church. He has not! The apostles had authority in the church more than un-ordained leaders or what we call laymen.

God has ordained clergymen with specific qualifications (see I Tim. 3:1–7). Titus 1:1–9 outlines similar qualifications making it clear that ordination of pastors and elders is not the invention of the church, but God created a hierarchy of leaders with specific qualifications. The Old Testament priests and all the ceremonial rites and rituals are fulfilled in Christ, but this doesn't mean that the church is without leadership. Today ordained pastors lead us in worship in the New Testament by God's own design.

Because the scriptures themselves use the language of a courtroom, I think the best illustration of formal worship can be compared to that of a courtroom today. A throne room might be even better, but in an age of democracy few of us have ever experienced a throne room or a meeting where a king gathers his subjects together before him in order to address them and for them to address him as well. Many people, however, are still familiar with the beauty, order, formality and yes, the hope of justice found in a courtroom.

The last traffic ticket I received was one that I decided to contest in court. It was a long shot (and I actually did get the fees waved), but I decided to see a judge in court. When I arrived, I was struck by how the architecture of the courtroom called me to attention. The massive wooden doors, and the design of the room made me feel that I had entered a different kind of place; this was a serious place that called for reverent attention.

I remember the bailiff who walked around in front of the courtroom was visibly upset as he roughly told a disheveled young man, "Take off your hat son, you're in a courtroom." He said it as if everyone knew that when you were in a courtroom, you were supposed to act accordingly. You had to show the kind of respect for protocol, posture and actions that are expected in a courtroom. The young man immediately pulled off his hat, tidied his long hair and sat up straight as if he had come to attention. Many of us older folks laughed quietly or to ourselves, because we knew that this young man looked like he was in serious need of what my dad used to call "an attitude adjustment," and from the sound of the bailiff, he was about to get it!

I looked around at the scenes on the walls and ceilings and knew very well that this was a place of justice; a sobering place where guilt and innocence were determined. For some people this courtroom was a place of life and death. It was a serious setting where everyone in the room knew that they were going to face the judge in order to settle their affairs before him. For me the scene was both sobering and hopeful at the same time—after all, I thought if I could meet the judge and plead my case, then perhaps I would be declared innocent. This made for a context in which certain ideas sometimes improperly set in opposition are put together: reverence and joy or sobriety and hope, etc.

When it was time for the court to begin its session, the bailiff walked to the front, opened the door, and instructed us all to stand. "All rise," he said, "the honorable judge 'so and so' was presiding. This was an authoritative call for all of us to recognize that the official meeting of the court was now about to begin because the judge was coming. We stood to attention as the judge entered the room dressed in a black robe, the judge sat down in the official judge's seat, and we waited for him to speak to us. "Please be seated," he said, "this court is now in session." We sat down and again waited for the judge's direction.

I love this scene as something of an introduction to the idea of a formal meeting with our God because when God calls us to worship, he expects us to meet with him as the just judge of all the earth. He expects us to come with reverent attention because he is the King of all kings, creator of heaven and earth, the sovereign, the only true and living God. He is a holy God like no one and nothing else in heaven or on earth who meets with us in worship, and we should be aware of it. At the same time as we will see in this study. This powerful God is also the merciful and forgiving God who sent his son, Jesus Christ to save sinners because he is a God of love. What a great combination to consider when coming to worship; reverence and awe combined with immeasurable joy and praise.

This is a helpful illustration of at least part of the scriptural idea of formal worship, and it's also something that we desperately need to rediscover—the idea of an official, formal gathering of God's people to meet with the judge of all the earth. It's a notion that comes from the scriptures. It seems to be an idea that is lost to modern worship practices, especially reverence and awe.

The very first church buildings that Christians began constructing publicly came after Constantine made Christianity a legal religion in the Edict of Milan in 313AD. These buildings had an architectural theology of worship that matched their use. It appears that the first church buildings were patterned after the Roman Basilica. The Basilica was a building serving multiple purposes, but acting primarily as a courthouse, meeting hall or council chamber—especially for formal occasions.

One of the best-known Basilicas is sometimes called the Basilica of Constantine in the ancient Roman Forum. Originally, it had a grand, but welcoming entryway that opened into a large, long hallway called a nave, which led to the eastern end to which it pointed where there was in the original basilica a colossal statue of Constantine. In the Christian Basilica the nave led those who entered to an eventual meeting with the greatest emperor the world had ever known, Jesus Christ. Churches followed this pattern and later decided that the entry faced west while leading those who entered to the eastern end where the ordained pastors led the people to meet with God.

At the eastern end was the place where the table of Holy Communion offered the people of God an opportunity to fellowship with their great prophet, priest, and king. It appears that for some time churches were situated so that the priest was facing west in such a way that reminded the people that the direction of their worship pointed then to the hope of the final resurrection and ultimate coming of Jesus. They people faced east or towards the orient, from which we still use the phrase oriented. It's a powerful idea in worship because even today we should orient our whole lives towards God in worship—and worship reorients us towards God. The architectural design of the church contained in it a theology of reverence and awe and also grace. This sense of reverence and awe is lacking in today's church both in architecture, but more importantly in practice.

Reverence and awe are often missing today because the central idea of promoting God's glory alone is missing. We often forget that though worship is discipleship, its primary purpose is the glory of God. The glory of God should always be the driving and defining factor when thinking about worship. We don't come to God in worship hoping that he will reward us in some way by giving us back a blessing in response to our coming to him. No, we come to him from duty, love and by faith to his call to worship.

Here I agree with John Calvin that any kind of worship that does not seek the glory of God primarily is a kind of idolatry. Calvin is helpful because he speaks of sinful human beings as having a heart that is an idol-making factory. By this he doesn't merely speak of statutes and pictures. Rather as one scholar notes, Calvin finds the origin of idolatry in man's effort to domesticate God and tailor religion to his own desires.[19]

A very critical reason that popular worship today is not characterized by reverence is because a theology of God and sin is very, very weak. Some have the joy part of worship down to a science because the "worship leader" is shouting to us that we are celebrating Jesus. They flash spotlights, play the guitar, and beat the drums while people shout and clap their hands having entered a virtual rock-n-roll concert for Jesus. They have a lot of fun, but somehow the idea that they are meeting with the mighty creator and righteous judge of all the earth has been almost entirely lost.

Yes, I know that at a few psychologically critical times the "worship leader" dims the lights, lowers the music and whispers some gentle words about Jesus' love, and how it heals our brokenness, but still, he gets us nowhere near the idea of reverence and awe. This is contrary to the basic idea of worship. In worship we should be full of respect, admiration and wonder that God wants to meet with us. God as creator and redeemer is the only one to whom belongs all glory, honor, and praise and the reality of meeting with our creator and redeemer should be an overwhelming experience.

I recall once in my life when I was at a political rally and the candidate and soon-to-be president was George H.W. Bush. I was in the front of the line with thousands of people and as Bush walked by, the secret

---

19. Eire, *War Against Idols*, 209.

service who I knew full well had machine guns under their coats, were watching all of us, then he stopped, reached over and shook my hand. Ha, I turned to my friends and couldn't suppress the smile. What a great moment! One of the most powerful people in the whole world reached out to me and shook my hand. I never really cared for Bush that much, but I had to admit that when the future president of the United States shook my hand, I was honored. Allen Ross speaks to this saying,

> Our attention to the Lord must not be an ordinary part of life; our worship of him should be the most momentous, urgent, and glorious activity in our lives. But we rarely see the splendor, the beauty, and the glory of worship because we are not drawn out of our world enough to comprehend this God of glory; consequently, our worship is all too frequently unexceptional and at times irrelevant . . . He is the inconceivable and incomprehensible source of all existence; he is the invisible majesty who reigns on high. This God we claim to know is the one before whom thousands upon thousands of angels and archangels stand, never ceasing to laud and praise him as the holy and glorious majesty. This Lord merely speaks, as he did at creation, and myriads of angels wait to carry out his will. He is completely unique, truly glorious and incomparably holy—there is no one like him, anywhere, at any time. And there is no measure of the magnificence and beauty of his holiness, for all his works are amazing, good, and glorious. And we say we know him![20]

What an amazing aspect of worship. If any of us were ever asked to join the president, the prime minister, or a leader of our nation for a meal and conversation, we would be pretty amazed—rightly so. Presidents and politically powerfully people don't have time to hang out with common folks like most of us. They are influential leaders with the weight of the world on their shoulders and they are concerned usually to meet with other great dignitaries in order to deal the world's problems. Imagine how profoundly stunned we should be that the creator of the universe, the king of kings and Lord over all lords is not only willing to meet with us, but he actually desires to meet with us. He wants to draw near to us and when he calls us to himself, he tells us that he loves us and that we matter to him. This is why many churches rightly begin their services with the minister speaking an apostolic greeting and a call to worship. As we think about embodied worship, we might

20. Ross, *Recalling the Hope of Glory*, 36.

consider envisioning the minister with his hands raised (palms facing the people) and the people also standing with hands raised (palms upward) as they receive the blessed welcome of God.

In worship God reminds us that he loved us so much that he sent his only son Jesus Christ to die for us. He also wants to hear from us. This should be equally hard to conceive—why would God want to hear from us!! He wants to hear if we hurt, if we are sad, if we are discouraged; he wants to hear from us because he cares for us. The sovereign creator of the world wants to meet with us, and he loves us. This should be a central idea that humbles us with reverence and awe while simultaneously filling us with the greatest feelings of love and satisfaction. Meeting with God satisfies our deepest longings for significance as humans—it feeds our deepest hunger as humans. Every worship service should cause us to stagger with wonder that God loves us. Likewise, the structure of the liturgy should reflect this reality.

Worship as Warfare

This last point in this chapter is a neglected yet important one: worship as warfare! This is central and so profound, yet incredibly overlooked. I want to push this notion into the conscience of believers: worship as warfare. We need to understand the radical character of a Christian "gathering." Worship reorients our lives to their ultimate destiny, which is to live in the presence of God forever. This was our purpose in the original creation, and this is our purpose in Christ.

When we worship, we experience the glorious meeting of the heavenly realms and the earthly realms. God created the heavenly realms full of angelic worshipers and in formal worship we pattern our meeting with God after these heavenly worshipers—who Isaiah 6 describes as crying out "holy, holy, holy, the Lord God almighty."

Worship is where God in Christ reveals himself as the ruler of the heavenly realms where he is the ruler of heaven and earth, but in worship we see the heavenly and the earthly realms interface in mysterious and profound ways. In Worship we experience the opening up of the heavenly realms as described in Isa. 6 and Rev. 4 where the angels in heaven are constantly worshipping God. In Christ, this heavenly worship is brought to down our realm as heaven comes to earth.

WHAT IS WORSHIP?

Our assembly to worship the only true and living God through Jesus Christ is a radical, "political" act. It is an act of defiance to any authority who may claim rule over us. Worship is the gathering of warrior saints! Listen to Oliver O'Donovan's insight when speaking of Israel's gathered character in the Old Testament.

> The link which ties the exercise of Yhwh's kingly rule to the praise of this people is that as the people congregate to perform their act of praise, the political reality of Israel is displayed. 'To you belongs praise, /Elohim, in /Zion . . . to you shall all flesh come' (Ps. 65:1f) The gathering of the congregation is the moment at which the people's identity is disclosed (as in the late Ps. 149 the distinct identity of the warrior-saints (*Hasidim*) is seen in the fact that they have their separate assembly of praise). Hence, the importance of "gathering," both on annual pilgrimage and in a final and complete return from exile, to the hopes of the post-exilic community: 'Gather us from the nations,' (Ps. 106:47) *The community is a political community by virtue of being a worshipping community*; while the worship of the single believer, restored from some affliction and desiring to thank God, must, as it were be politicized by being brought into the public arena of 'the great congregation' (Ps. 35:18; 40:9f) Otherwise, the poet says, Yhwh's righteousness, faithfulness, salvation, love and truth would be 'hidden' and 'concealed' (Ps. 40:10) (emphasis mine).[21]

By definition Christian worship is a political proclamation that there is no authority in heaven or on earth that is greater than the true King, Jesus Christ. As part of this proclamation God's people remind themselves and the whole universe that God is king of all. In worship we are drawn into the heavens, and we are called to the future that belongs to us in Christ.

In this sense and in a context of political rulers who claim ultimate authority in our lives worship is an act of revolution. Yes, worship is a declaration of revolution against all earthly authorities who claim to be gods in our lives. This is why in ancient Rome Christians were allowed to maintain a belief that Jesus was one god among many others. Yet, the moment a Christian refused to swear allegiance to the gods of the age and claimed in worship that there is only one, true and living God their liturgies became acts of revolution.

At a certain point Caesar did not mind placing Jesus in a group of other gods under his ultimate command, but when Christians worshiped

---

21. O'Donovan, *Desire of the Nations*, 47.

God as the ultimate sovereign in heaven *and on earth* it was a direct threat to his claims and as such worship was an act of revolution. In this sense earthly autocrats have always understood genuine Christian worship as a revolutionary act. This is why true Christian worship has often been rightly considered revolutionary—Christian worship is an official declaration against all tyrants—earthly and heavenly. It is a public declaration that we are free people with only one ultimate ruler, King Jesus.

Worship declares war against all forms of tyranny. Our minds may rush to political tyrants, but cultural tyranny should also be in view. Any aspect of our culture which claims ultimate allegiance in our lives against the true of claims of King Jesus is prohibited in Christian worship. This includes a disposition to see ourselves primarily as consumers rather than servants of the living God. This includes the cultural obsession to see ourselves primarily as in need of constant entertainment. This includes cultural pressure to place our own will at the center of our existence. If Jesus is Lord, then worship declares us to be liberated from all forms of tyranny: political and cultural.

Worship reminds us, and the watching world, that God has become our God in rescuing and redeeming us from sin and Satan. When we praise God for our salvation, we thank him for his victory over our enemies who once held us under their oppressive authority. In the Old Testament God's salvation of his people had a military quality. The same is true in the New Testament. So, Paul speaks of salvation as being "rescued" from a foe. In Col. 1:13–14, he says,

> He has delivered us from the domain of darkness and transferred us to the kingdom of his beloved Son, in whom we have redemption, the forgiveness of sins.

This is aggressive, military imagery of God's engagement with the forces of darkness. Later in Colossians Paul continues,

> And you, who were dead in your trespasses and the uncircumcision of your flesh, God made alive together with him, having forgiven us all our trespasses, by canceling the record of debt that stood against us with its legal demands. This he set aside, nailing it to the cross. He disarmed the rulers and authorities and put them to open shame, by triumphing over them in him (Col. 2:13–15).

This is more powerful than someone being grateful that they accepted Jesus into their heart as their personal savior. Rather, this is an authoritative act of God to rescue his people and judge their enemies. Yes, in worship we declare that God is the supreme justice and that one day he will judge all people everywhere who refuse to bow their knees to his majestic authority. We sing about this especially when we sing the Psalms in worship.

The righteous judgment of God is part of what we proclaim when we sing and praise God for our salvation. This is an offensive undertaking for many people. It becomes even more aggressive because when we worship God, we ask him to defeat his enemies and rule over the whole earth. When God's people worship him rightly his glory is manifested—this is what we need, and this is what we should want. This is what the world needs as well. In worship we ask God to shape our deepest affections according to his own holiness and to shape the affections of all people. Worship is a universal proclamation that Jesus is King.

Those who have been saved and rescued from the forces of darkness are anxious to come to God in worship and offer him whatever he wants. They long to pray to him. They long to praise him. They long to listen to his word and to obey him. They are so overwhelmed with what Paul calls the immeasurable power of God that they are willing to offer more than a tithe—they come to meet with their king to offer him themselves, and when they do this, God loves to meet with them.

God's people fall down before him as in ancient depictions of warrior knights who bow before a king and pledge their allegiance in life and in death. We bring our offerings to God in worship just like the ancient peoples brought tributes to their emperor recognizing his rule over them. God is so pleased at the obedient responses of his loving children that he promises his special presence and he responds with divine power to their worship. Worship entails God's people coming to him and offering themselves as living sacrifices—God loves this so much! God loves faithful obedience in worship, and he blesses it.

When we pray the Lord's Prayer it also includes the element of warfare in it. For instance, in two petitions we request God to bring his kingdom here on earth just as it is in heaven. This means that such prayers and praise in worship involves militant activity. This is not literal militance on our part, but spiritual militance that God translates into literal activity on earth—he hears, and he responds—and when he responds, things on earth change. A simple and clear explanation of this kind of prayer is found in the Westminster Shorter Catechism:

Q. 102. What do we pray for in the second petition?

A. In the second petition, which is, *Thy kingdom come,* we pray, that Satan's kingdom may be destroyed; and that the kingdom of grace may be advanced, ourselves and others brought into it, and kept in it; and that the kingdom of glory may be hastened.

Q. 103. What do we pray for in the third petition?

A. In the third petition, which is, *Thy will be done in earth, as it is in heaven,* we pray, that God, by his grace, would make us able and willing to know, obey, and submit to his will in all things, as the angels do in heaven.

This is related to kingdom warfare against God's enemies and it's central to worship. We pray like this; we sing like this; and we preach like this. Our worship puts us on God's side of a war with the forces of darkness and our worship is the most powerful part of this war.

The coming of God's kingdom is not accomplished through ordinary earthly means. Worship, for instance, is not the meeting of a political party. While it's perfectly proper for Christians to engage in ordinary political processes—and God uses these for good. Christians, however, should never imagine that God's kingdom comes simply by lobbying our legislatures, electing a better president, or changing the justices on the Supreme Court—the actual way things change on earth though mysterious to us is by means of worship. In prayer and in praise in the context of corporate worship we look up to the real supreme court in heaven, to the great judge, Jesus Christ. We do this most powerfully in corporate worship.

We can see a pattern in the Old Testament where humble worship is a common means by which God saves his people and defeats his enemies. One very powerful example is 2 Chr. 20. Here King Jehoshaphat is surrounded by overwhelming numbers of enemies who seek to destroy God's people.

> After this the Moabites and Ammonites, and with them some of the Meunites, came against Jehoshaphat for battle. Some men came and told Jehoshaphat, "A great multitude is coming against you from Edom, from beyond the sea; and, behold, they are in Hazazon-tamar" (that is, Engedi). Then Jehoshaphat was afraid and set his face to seek the Lord, and proclaimed a fast throughout all Judah. And Judah assembled to seek help from the Lord; from all the cities of Judah they came to seek the Lord. (2 Chr. 20:1–4)

The story continues with a spine-tingling victory for God, which is directly linked to Israel's praise and worship. In response to worship and praise, God confuses his enemies and destroys them. Scriptures tell us that it took three days for the people of God to collect the bounty from a battle they never physically fought. What a great story of the power of worship! Is this not like the battle against Egypt? Didn't God's people plunder the land of Egypt leaving in military formation after never having raised any weapon except the weapons of prayer and praise!

When we praise God in worship, for instance, using the Psalms, we find them packed with references and calls for God to scatter his enemies and defeat his foes. We should preach this in worship, pray for this in worship and praise God like this in worship. The New Testament also encourages us to long for the same thing most especially since we now worship him in the power of the resurrection from the dead.

This is why Paul puts the church central to history itself in the unfolding warfare here on earth. Paul outlines it beautifully in Eph. 1:19-23.

> And what is the immeasurable greatness of his power toward us who believe, according to the working of his great might that he worked in Christ when he raised him from the dead and seated him at his right hand in the heavenly places, far above all rule and authority and power and dominion, and above every name that is named, not only in this age but also in the one to come. And he put all things under his feet and gave him as head over all things to the church, which is his body, the fullness of him who fills all in all.

In corporate public worship the church experiences what Paul is describing. We assemble before the throne of our king and humbly but sincerely beg him to put his enemies under his feet. In worship by faith and in the Holy Spirit God opens the heavens for us to meet with him before his throne. Worship is like ascending the mountain of God to meet with him as he comes down to touch the mountain and dwell with us. The angels join us in this kind of worship as well. We have a few amazing examples in the scriptures where we get a glimpse into the heavenly realms during worship.

When the church gathers in worship to meet with God through Jesus Christ it not only officially meets here on the earth, but there is a supernatural dimension that as it were opens heaven to us as his people and allows us to ascend the mountain of God joining with the angels in heaven in worship. So says Heb. 12:22-24.

> But you have come to Mount Zion and to the city of the living God, the heavenly Jerusalem, and to innumerable angels in festal gathering, and to the assembly of the firstborn who are enrolled in heaven, and to God, the judge of all, and to the spirits of the righteous made perfect, and to Jesus, the mediator of a new covenant, and to the sprinkled blood that speaks a better word than the blood of Abel.

In Christ we have the culmination of all the mountains of God on which God's people worshipped him. Surely this was part of what the woman at the well was considering when she mentioned various mountains to which people have been directed for worship. Adam was expelled from the mountain of Eden and the presence of God. However, God continued to meet with his people in worship such as Noah on Mt. Ararat, Moses on Mt. Sinai, and of course the temple on Mt. Zion. All these earthly mountains were pushing us forward to the coming of Christ to the earth where we would meet with him on the heavenly Mt. Zion by the power of the spirit of God as described in Heb. 12.

In Christ we worship God in spirit and in truth as Jesus himself said that true worshipers would do. This is spiritual worship helping us to see worship as warfare, but not exclusively so. This is a powerful though limited aspect of worship. We don't come primarily to request him to destroy things or command him to move mountains. Rather, we worship God as a duty and as an act of humble, faithful, loving, obedience. This means we kneel down asking for forgiveness, we raise our hands in humble praise and thanks that he does forgive us through Jesus Christ, and we listen to him speak to us in his word as well as seal this relationship with sacraments such as a Lord's Supper/Eucharist. When we come as his humble suppliants, he is pleased to hear us, bless us and reign down fire on his and on our enemies. In this sense, worship is more powerful than we may have ever imagined, and it calls us upward and forward to the glorious time when the veil of heaven will be completely removed, and all will be made right.

Worship as warfare is one of the most profound, supernatural activities that we will ever experience. When the church meets God in public/formal worship the heavens open, God comes down to meet with us and we by his Holy Spirit ascend into heaven through Christ to meet with God on his Holy Mountain. We worship him as we join with the angels in heaven. One very wonderful passage like this is found in Rev. 5:6–14.

And between the throne and the four living creatures and among the elders I saw a Lamb standing, as though it had been slain, with seven horns and with seven eyes, which are the seven spirits of God sent out into all the earth. And he went and took the scroll from the right hand of him who was seated on the throne. And when he had taken the scroll, the four living creatures and the twenty-four elders fell down before the Lamb, each holding a harp, and golden bowls full of incense, which are the prayers of the saints. And they sang a new song, saying, "Worthy are you to take the scroll and to open its seals, for you were slain, and by your blood you ransomed people for God from every tribe and language and people and nation, and you have made them a kingdom and priests to our God, and they shall reign on the earth." Then I looked, and I heard around the throne and the living creatures and the elders the voice of many angels, numbering myriads of myriads and thousands of thousands, saying with a loud voice, "Worthy is the Lamb who was slain, to receive power and wealth and wisdom and might and honor and glory and blessing!" And I heard every creature in heaven and on earth and under the earth and in the sea, and all that is in them, saying, "To him who sits on the throne and to the Lamb be blessing and honor and glory and might forever and ever!" And the four living creatures said, "Amen!" and the elders fell down and worshiped.

CHAPTER 2

What does God want? or Principles for Worship

AFTER DEFINING CORPORATE WORSHIP, we naturally ask the question: what should we do in worship? This question has provoked a lot of disagreement and controversy. Some people have called this controversy the worship wars. Worship wars, however, are not new to modern times. In fact, immediately after the Fall into sin the very first struggle between Cain and Abel was a conflict over worship. God accepted one man's worship and rejected the other ones, which led to violent conflict. This was the first great worship war in history, and it's been happening ever since the Fall.

The story in Gen. 11 and the Tower of Babel also have worship at the center of the struggle. We call it the story of the Tower of Babel but in fact the people were actually building a city or culture with a Tower in the center of the city around which they gathered for worship. Whether we're thinking about Cain and Abel or the Tower of Babel, it's important to see the connection between worship and culture because they are inseparable as the phrase goes—*lex orandi, lex credenda*—the rule of prayer/worship is the rule of belief.

The tower of Babel for example, represented a new, man-centered worship that was the heart of their culture. This illustrates for us the earlier point we noted about the image of God in man and the necessity of worship. Because humans are made as worshipping beings, from the very beginning of human history worship is the central cultural activity from which all other aspects of culture grow as from a root. Worship offers us a principle for life mentioned earlier: as goes worship, so goes the culture.[1] The story of Cain and Abel tells us about two very diverse cities or ways of living that began to develop from worship. This is yet another reminder that no theological subject is more controversial, more divisive, and yet more critical than worship.

So what do we do? If worship is central to culture and if worship has been terribly divisive, then how can we tackle this subject so that we bring unity and clarity instead of conflict and division? First, we need to agree on some guiding principles. The easiest guiding principle of worship could be stated simply in the following: *do what God wants*.

At the risk of oversimplifying, Cain brought God what Cain wanted and then he expected God to be happy with it. This turned things upside down. Abel on the other hand, worshipped God by faith and offered God what God wanted: the blood sacrifice necessary for the forgiveness of sins. Abel offered what God wanted and he did so by faith. In worship if we want to approach the true and living God who is holy, we will do what he wants us to do; not what we want to do. This sounds so simple that it's almost too easy, and yet this is *the* challenge before us.

For many of my readers, the following may seem obvious and perhaps even pedantic. If you're even slightly aware of modern worship practices especially among Evangelicals, then you know that following this simple principle would eliminate a driving and shaping factor for much of worship in modern times. We could summarize modern Evangelical worship as entertainment. In his book on worship John MacArthur outlines some of these trends in American Evangelical worship. For example, one pastor who loved country music decided to have a church service that was themed, "God's Country Goodtime Hour." Another church from the south appropriately themed their "worship" after a circus. They proudly advertised saying,

---

1. This is important since our word culture, which loosely means a way of living comes from the word, cultus, which is related to worship. In the history of redemption, the scriptures are constantly pushing us to connect worship and culture as two sides of the same coin. The cultus or worship practices of people groups most certainly produce the ways of living of these same tribes/people groups or cultures.

See Barnum and Bailey bested as the magic of the big top circus comes to The Fellowship of Excitement! Clowns! Acrobats! Animals! Popcorn! What a great night![2]

This problem is an old one in American church history. As early as 1844 one theologian lamented some of the problems with Protestant worship in America. He said,

> What great evils result from the loose and informal manner which in many congregations, the services of the sanctuary are conducted... With some the sermon is regarded as the only important part of public worship. The prayers are of little account, except as appropriate solemnities—the shorter, the better—to compose the mind and prepare it for the performances of the pulpit; and at best as suitable forms of invocation for the divine blessing upon the exercises of the occasion. Farther than this, they have no special interest for them. As for the choral performances, they are estimated according to their musical merits, and have place, as agreeable interludes, for the entertainment of the hearers in which they are scarcely expected to take part.[3]

What started as an informal style of religious entertainment led to the strange situation we have today. For instance, the same church mentioned above not surprisingly staged a service in the form of a pastoral wrestling match. They hired professional wrestlers to train their pastors how to throw each from the ring, pull hair, and kick shins without actually hurting each other.[4] While this must have been rather entertaining, none of it comes even close to capturing the nature of scriptural worship. Furthermore, this kind of crass showbiz lowers the pastors to little more than clerical clowns. Actually, this is an overly inflated title because most of them wouldn't have the qualifications for which we should include the word, clerical—they're just clowns.[5] Worse yet, they are clowning around with something that God takes very seriously.

Approaching worship in such a manner is not only infantile and adolescent, but it is offensive to God and morally corrupting for those who attend it. Even if they love it, it still has a degrading effect on them

---

2. MacArthur, *Worship*, 27.
3. B.C.W. "Public Worship," 296.
4. MacArthur, *Worship*, 28.
5. The word, clerical has deep roots in classical culture relating to a minister's role as a well-trained servant of the church and culture who was one of the few well-qualified people steeped in Latin, logic, and literature.

in ways that too many leaders ignore and that many people don't even recognize. It feeds a self-centered, individualistic, consumeristic view of life. One thinker, for instance, says,

> If we position worship as a form of Christian entertainment we shape Christians who consume worship as a product; Christians that move from one worship "high" to the next, chasing one stimulating event after another; Christians that assess how good the worship was by how fuzzy it made them feel; and Christians that will leave one congregation for another with little hesitation if a more entertaining gathering springs up in another church. But this kind of worship is, at rock bottom all about me, and God is approached as if he were under some obligation to keep my happy. He is my drug of choice, but if he gets boring, I'll move on.[6]

Another problem with the idea of entertainment in worship is that it leads to an obsession with "creativity," originality, and sincerity, pushing them ironically to a very below average and unoriginal kind of worship that we might call "pop culturish." In a rush to be relevant and original, they are not original at all. Their entertainment style of worship usually becomes what we might call a "cheesy," a plagiarized version of pop culture complete with pastoral skinny jeans and cool haircuts. With such an obsession for the trendy, it still amazes me how "popular" Christian worship practices always seem to be about five or ten years behind the latest in genuine pop culture practices. It could be something like the adage that someone obsessed with originality will never be original. This seems to be true in many contemporary worship practices.

Beyond the criticism of "cheesy," unoriginal, and pop-culturish, how do we know whether or not God wants this kind of worship. While we may be quite amused with religious clowns and line dancing in the place of traditional worship, a more powerful question would be—is God similarly amused; and if so, how would we know? It's actually not a mystery—he tells us in his word! God has already told us what he wants us to do in worship in many ways and in many places. He also reminds us in other places in the scriptures that we are not to add to nor take away from what he says. See Deut. 12:32:

---

6. Walker and Parry, *Deep Church Rising*, 98.

"Everything that I command you, you shall be careful to do. You shall not add to it or take from it.⁷

Imagine how much chaos and division we could avoid if we did only what God wants us to do! This won't answer all of our queries about worship, and we won't suddenly have all the solutions to every question but imagine how many we could solve in one fell swoop! If we only did in worship what God has clearly commanded us to do in worship, we would at least know that we are doing what God wants—and this is a fundamental place to start.

Such an approach to worship is what theologians call the regulative principle of worship. The sixteenth century French reformer John Calvin was one of the first to articulate it in the following way:

> the rule which distinguishes between pure and vitiate worship is of universal application, in order that we may not adopt any device which seems fit to ourselves, but look to the injunction of Him who alone is entitled to prescribe . . . such is our folly, that when we are left at liberty, all we are able to do is to go astray. And then when once we have turned aside from the right path, there is no end to our wanderings, [*add here clowns and cowboys*] until we get buried under a multitude of superstitions [*add here bowing to crosses and praying to saints*]. Justly, therefore, does the Lord, in order to assert his full right of dominion, strictly enjoin what he wishes us to do, and at once reject all human devices which are at variance with his command. Justly, too, does he, in express terms, define our limits that we may not, by fabricating perverse modes of worship, provoke His anger against us. I know how difficult it is to persuade the world that God disapproves of all modes of worship not expressly sanctioned by His Word.⁸

We should do what God wants us to do; nothing more and nothing less. If God has not told us to do it, then we should not do it. Otherwise, how do we know he wants it done in worship? Sometimes we may see the principle put it in the following way: what God has not commanded is forbidden. The Westminster Confession of Faith says it with even more clarity.

> The acceptable way of worshipping the true God is instituted by himself, and so limited by his own revealed will, that he may not be worshipped according to the imaginations and

---

7. See also, Deut. 4:2; 2 Tim. 3:16–17; Rev. 22:18–19.
8. Calvin, *Necessity of Reforming Church*, 17–18.

devices of men, or the suggestions of Satan, under any visible re presentation, or any other way not prescribed in the holy scripture. (WCF XXI.1)

If we return to thinking about the courtroom as an adequate illustration of formal worship, then we can appreciate how a God-directed dialogue could occur in worship: one that is God-centered and full of blessings for his subjects. In a courtroom everyone understands that though a dialogue occurs, it's one that the judge initiates and directs. It's also the kind of conversation and dialogue that you would expect with a judge. After all, if we were going to meet with an important person such as a king or queen or the president of a great nation, we would never imagine doing what we want to do without regard to the expected protocol, manners, and interests of our esteemed host. I imagine that if we were invited to meet with her majesty, Queen Elizabeth II that we would not only be happy to follow the expected behavior among royalty, but in order to respect her and not to offend her or look ignorant to the surrounding nobility we would try to learn everything that we could learn about greeting and speaking to the queen. Why should it be any different with God? He is much more important than a queen, a judge, or a president here on earth. Why would anyone treat God with less respect than a human ruler?

If we respected this approach, it would not only please God, but it would also bring us much closer with other Christians who are also willing to follow this simple outlook. This brings glory to God and unity among fellow believers. Unfortunately, many Christians use a different principle when coming to God in worship; they do anything they want to do so long as they believe that God has not forbidden it. This is a looser approach, and one that appeals to many Christians around the world from various traditions. It could be described as the normative rather than the regulative principle. Basically, it could be summarized in the following: whatever God has not forbidden is acceptable.

The normative principle also supports the idea that we should do what Scripture commands: it includes for example the basics of preaching, praying, and singing praise. However, it adds things that the scriptures do not add, which is a recipe for division and strife—and worse for angering God! People who follow this approach for instance, might illustrate a biblical principle using a skit or a movie clip. They might add drama for children or even puppet shows and finger painting to illustrate something in worship. Or for the more traditional they might carry crosses, sacred objects or swing incense throughout the building while making the sign of the cross. Unless the scriptures explicitly forbid something, then they feel free to add it. In fact, for many folks today; the more creative the better!

Without any scriptural warrant, I have even heard people describe worship as our "creative" response to God. This is especially popular among self-described "Evangelicals" in America. The telling qualifier is the word, "creative." "This seems to suggest," says Simon Chan, "worship is largely a human construct, something worshipers do creatively."[9] If this is true than worship is something that is basically man-created rather than God-created. This guiding principle is essentially why so much of worship today is man-centered rather than God-centered. After all, if worship is our creative response to God, then worship is principally about us rather than God. What a strange deviation from the scriptures and what colossal misjudgment! It may indicate that we actually love ourselves more than God and our worship reflects this painful reality. G.K. Beales says, "What people revere, they resemble, either for ruin or restoration."[10] There may be no better place to witness this idea than in worship practices.

A man-centered approach not only misdirects worship away from God, but it tends to create division among Christians. For instance, what happens if someone's creativity comes into conflict with another person's tastes or with someone else's desires in worship—division and fighting! If worship is our creative response to God, then who should be the judge of what we ought to include or what we ought not to include in worship?

How then do we know what to do in worship? Unfortunately, many leaders use the tried and true test of popularity to determine what to do. I recall my grandma's painful experience when she realized that the church, she had been attending for more than forty years called a new pastor who determined that what he needed to do was to change everything in order to revitalize the church and make things more "relevant." As a side note or as a basic rule of thumb, whenever you hear a "pastor" start talking about making everything "relevant," then run from this guy as fast as you can run.

---

9. Chan, *Liturgical Theology*, 13.
10. Beale, *We Become What We Worship*, 15.

WHAT DOES GOD WANT? OR PRINCIPLES FOR WORSHIP

My Granny sat helplessly as the new pastor fired up the rock band and ditched all the "outdated" hymns. It was as if her church was being pulled right from under her feet. Never mind that she had taught Sunday school faithfully for more than twenty years and she had supported this church for decades of her life. Never mind that she was happy to sing new songs if only a few hymns could have been kept—and perhaps if someone would turn down the volume so that she didn't physically quake every time the speakers hit base notes—you could literally feel the base shake through your body. Still the pastor pressed forward with his own worship agenda to bring "new life" to the church. He stopped preaching through books of the Bible and replaced it with his own version of topical preaching. But why not? What should be the standard for worship?

Creativity may be quite entertaining to large groups of people, but is it really what God wants? Loudspeakers and wrestling matches are great for entertainment, but we still have not addressed the central question as to whether or not God wants his worship to be a center for entertainment! Again, at the risk of oversimplification, if worship is to be pleasing to God, then we should do what he wants us to do, not what we want to do. Worship should be God-centered, not man-centered.

> Worship is the supreme and only indispensable activity of the Christian Church. It alone will endure, like the love for God, which it expresses, into heaven, when all other activities of the Church will have passed away. It must therefore, even more strictly than any of the less essential doings of the Church, come under the criticism and control of the revelation on which the Church is founded.[11]

The standard known as the regulative principle provides the most scriptural and the most practical guide for us to follow because God condemns man-made and man-centered worship.

> And the Lord said: "Because this people draw near with their mouth and honor me with their lips, while their hearts are far from me, and their fear of me is a commandment taught by men." (Isa. 29:13)

This passage describes hypocritical worship, but it also describes worship of God with humanly devised methods. Jesus condemns manmade or unauthorized worship in the New Testament as well as in the Old Testament. Once again, this takes us back to the beginning. God rejected

11. Nicholls, *Jacob's Ladder*, 9.

Cain's attempt to bring what he wanted to bring rather than to approach God by faith with blood sacrifice. Cain needed his sins forgiven to worship God; he did not need to center worship upon his achievements as a farmer or what he preferred to bring to God. This is a principle of worship found throughout the whole of redemptive history. One sobering example is the story of Nadab and Abihu.

Saying that God was not pleased with the creative worship of Nadab and Abihu would be what my old English professor would have called an understatement. Not only was God NOT pleased with the creativity of Nadab and Abihu, their creative use of incense provoked God to anger when they decided to add to what he had not commanded. Lev. 10:1–2 describes their attempt to be creative in worship.

> Now Nadab and Abihu, the sons of Aaron, each took his censer and put fire in it and laid incense on it and offered unauthorized fire before the LORD, which he had not commanded them. And fire came out from before the LORD and consumed them, and they died before the LORD.

I recall the first time I read this story as a boy. To be honest I was a bit horrified that God burned them up with such fury even as they were trying to worship him. There is nothing in the text that indicates they were insincere because sincerity is not the sole measure that God for worship. If they were sincere, then what on earth had they done that was so bad that God decided to burn them to death? At the time I admit that when I first read this story that I thought God's response was a bit of an overreaction. It reminded me of another story related to doing something in God's special presence that he had not commended. This one is found in 2 Sam. 6:6–7.

> And when they came to the threshing floor of Nacon, Uzzah put out his hand to the ark of God and took hold of it, for the oxen stumbled. And the anger of the LORD was kindled against Uzzah, and God struck him down there because of his error, and he died there beside the ark of God.

Here I noticed what I thought was the same thing—that when someone approached his presence God was more than a little bit on edge when it came to dolling out fire and brimstone on poor people who did such small things as adding a pinch of incense or touching the ark to prevent it from falling off the cart. This illustration shows for certain that sincerity alone was not God's standard when approaching his presence. I remember thinking that I was sure happy I didn't live in the Old Testament when God was seemingly so quick to kill people for small things— especially since I was rather easily distracted in Sunday morning worship.

And yet when you step back a bit you realize that he is not killing people arbitrarily, but he is teaching us that he is holy and because he is holy approaching him in a way that he has not commanded is not only *not* acceptable, but it angers him. The presence of God is holy ground and because God is holy, and he expects us to approach him with the kind of reverence and awe for which he is worthy. Again, at the risk of understatement, God shows no interest in our creativity, novelty or ultimately even our sincerity in worship. Of course, he wants us to be sincere, but he wants us to approach him with fear and awe in a way that pleases him, after all, he alone is God. Our worship should recognize this basic reality.

While it's true that the coming of Jesus Christ has opened a new way of worshipping him through the risen Jesus Christ, it is not true that God no longer cares about how we approach him in worship. Worship in the Old Testament was full of specific regulations, and it was quite complex. In Christ the sacrificial and ceremonial regulations have been fulfilled. However, worship in the New Testament though simpler and less complex is still a holy gathering to meet with a holy God. While we marvel at how simple and uncomplicated it is to worship God through Jesus Christ, we should never forget that we are still worshipping God and that we still need to ask the question—what does God want in worship.

Elements and circumstances in worship

Before we continue it may be helpful to notice that the regulative principle can be abused. I have watched some folks use this principle to strip worship of its emotion and joy whilst telling people of all the things they may not experience in worship. I'm reminded of an E. E. Cummings poem which says—I would rather learn to sing from a single bird than to teach a thousand stars how not to dance. Some people use the regulative principle as a way of teaching a thousand stars how not to dance rather than to teach God's people how to sing like a bird.

Sometimes the regulative principle has been used to demand a specific verse for everything we do in worship, which tends to make what some critics describe it as a "wooden" methodology to worship. Peter Leithart remarks,

> In the hands of at least some writers, the regulative principle is, in practice, hermeneutically wooden and theologically Marcionite. It is wooden because an explicit "command" is required for every act of worship, and it is Marcionite because it ignores the abundant Old Testament liturgical instruction in favor of exegeting a few passages of the New.[12]

Perhaps the most important distinction in this matter is division between the things God commands or directs us to do in worship (elements) and the way in which we carry out these commands (circumstances). Knowing the difference between a God-commanded element of worship such as praising him with music and songs and the difference between the circumstances of singing praise as we clap our hands also using a piano, a guitar or drums is not only important, but decisive for maintaining worship's robust fullness as our great offering to God.

What Leithart was alluding to is the problem of using the Bible to exclude what the Bible teaches. When only small, narrow sections of the scriptures are overemphasized, then we may find ourselves using the Bible to exclude the very things the Bible encourages. A few examples might be the very strange traditions which forbid the use of musical instruments in worship. How can you have a tradition which forbids using musical instruments when the scriptures in Ps. 150:3–5 tell us,

> Praise him with trumpet sound; praise him with lute and harp! Praise him with tambourine and dance; praise him with strings and pipe! Praise him with sounding cymbals; praise him with loud clashing cymbals!

Thankfully the "no instruments" approach to singing praise comprises a tiny group of people and makes little sense to most Christians throughout the world and throughout history. Still, we wonder how could some traditions possibly conclude that God does not want us to do something he has directly told us to do in the scriptures? I have marveled with my own tradition of worship among Presbyterians who rarely if ever raise their hands when the scriptures in many places encourage it (1 Tim. 2:8)? While we can't solve all the worship questions and queries, we can strive to study worship from the scriptures so that we can move ourselves and call others to a great unity and power in worship. This will also give us greater liberty and joy in worship. Let's look at the elements and circumstances of worship.

12. Leithart, *Silence to Song*, 15–16.

What is an element?

In simplest form we would define an element of worship as something God has told us to do. The list is small, and it comprises the basics of what most Christians instinctively know they should do in worship. Here is a simple list:

1. The reading (Acts 15:21, Rev. 1:3) & preaching (2 Tim. 4:2) of the Holy Scriptures—this reading could include an apostolic greeting and benediction.
2. Singing praises to God (Col. 3:16, Eph. 5:19, Jas. 5:13 and too many Psalms to list).[13]
3. Praying (Matt. 5:6-9; 1 Tim. 2:1-10).
4. Sacraments of baptism (Matt. 28:19) & holy communion/Lord's supper (Matt. 26:26-29, 1 Cor.11:23, Acts 2:42).
5. The collection of offerings (Gal. 2:10, 1 Cor. 16:2).
6. Public exchanging vows and confession of faith (Rom. 10).

These are what we would call the elements of worship. We could call this the "what" of worship. This list is not too difficult to compile, and we don't find any other things in the Scriptures that God has told us to do in the same way that he has told us to hear his word, pray, praise him, etc.

Circumstances

The previous list of elements we called the "what" of worship, yet we still haven't answered perhaps the more troubling issues of the "how" of worship. The "how" of worship we sometimes call the circumstances of worship. The circumstances of worship are the conditions that determine the best way to worship God within the structure provided by the elements. The circumstances might be the way in which you do the elements of worship. In order to be a circumstance, it should be according to many teachers something that is morally indifferent, which you will

---

13. Notice that the lists of verses are representative; not exhaustive. You could certainly find more verses to support each of the elements of worship. The verses are simply exampling that each element of worship is found directly in the scriptures, they represent what God wants when we meet with him.

sometimes hear referred to by the phrase *adiophora*: things indifferent. Ursinus gives a good list of examples:

> of which kind are the time, the place, the form and order of sermons, prayers, reading in the church, fasts, the manner of proceeding in the election of ministers, in collecting and distributing alms, and things of a similar nature.[14]

In the middle of the 17th century John Owen said essentially the same thing:

> Whatever is of circumstance in the manner of its performance, not capable of especial determination, as emerging or arising only occasionally, upon the doing of that which is appointed at this or that time, in this or that place, and the like, is left unto the rule of moral prudence, in whose observation their order doth consist.[15]

One great example could be prayer. God has commanded us to pray, but he has not said how many times to pray in worship. He has not said when in the order of worship that he wants us to pray. He has not commanded that all our prayers be either written in advance or completely spontaneous. These are the ticklish questions that in many ways form the nub of the controversy.

We could start to tackle this issue with a principle set down in the Westminster Confession of Faith, which says,

> there are some circumstances concerning the worship of God, and the government of the Church, common to human actions and societies, which are to be ordered by the light of nature and Christian prudence, according to the general rules of the Word, which are always to be observed." (WCF 1.6)

The Directory for Worship for the Orthodox Presbyterian Church (I.C.3) also notes,

> The Lord Jesus Christ has not prescribed a set order for public worship; rather, he has given his church a large measure of liberty in this matter.

This does not mean that the circumstances of worship are irrelevant. In fact, embodied worship requires us to consider the circumstances of

---

14. Ursinus, *Commentary on Heidelberg Cathechism*, 820.
15. Owen, see questions 15–19 in *Brief Instruction on Worship*.

worship. How then do we approach worship regarding what is apparently a rather large area of potential controversy?

Again, the scriptures can help us here. Perhaps the clearest example of a guiding principle would be I Cor. 14:40.

> But all things should be done decently and in order.

This passage is one set squarely in the context of questions about worship practices. The guidance God gives is profound. He provides a twofold yet connected guiding principle—do things decently and orderly. What does God mean when he uses the word decently? The word itself is amazingly helpful. According to one theological reference:

> It does not refer here to absence of impurity or obscenity. It refers rather to good order in the conduct of public worship. All things that are done and said in public worship are to be in *harmony* with the becoming and reverent spirit and tone that befit the true worshipers of God. Cf. also Rom. 13:13 ("becomingly"); 1 Thess. 4:12.[16]

This is a powerful Greek word that was also used among Greek thinkers to argue for an integrity and wholeness in one's thought and action. It's related to the word integrity in so far as integrity was used to indicate wholeness. This wholeness is related to a harmony of the parts of worship to the whole purpose (sometimes called the telos or end for which worship was designed) of worship. The purpose of something in its overall design had to have integrity, which also connected it to beauty. As we think about worship, God demands an integrity (a wholeness and fittingness) to the elements and actions of worship that fit harmoniously with the overall telos or purpose of worship.

This means that every element of worship must be studied carefully as to its scriptural meaning and purpose, but also how the aim of the act best fits into the overall purpose of public worship. Every act of worship should be examined as to its place and purpose within the context of formal or corporate worship—particularly—what God wants us to do and how we are supposed to do it as we meet formally with him to worship him. This encourages us to keep thinking of worship as a holy dialogue in a kind of courtroom setting.

The other term that God uses is the word order. Though it has a variety of uses, in the context of worship it indicates the fitting

---

16. Fortune, "Decently," 873.

arrangement of persons, objects or events in their proper places in relation to each other. This is like the first word, decently. It means that each element of worship should be carefully considered as to its nature and purpose in a gathering or an assembly with God. The word helps us to know that whatever we are doing we must understand its theological and therefore logical meaning in worship.

> The Greek New Testament word is related to a Hebrew Old Testament word that can add some insight. The Hebrew verb ʿāraḵ often means setting in layers or rows: e.g., arranging wood or offerings on an altar (Gen. 22:9; Lev. 1:7f, 12; 6:12 [Matt. 5]; 1 Kgs. 18:33; cf. *maʿ arāḵâ*, Judg. 6:26), the bread of the Presence on the table (Exod. 40:4, 23; Lev. 24:8), lamps in the tabernacle (Lev. 24:3f), stalks of flax on a roof (Josh. 2:6). In Job 33:5 ʿāraḵ has the sense of setting forth arguments in a legal case (cf. 13:18; 23:4; 32:14; 37:19). It has a similar forensic meaning in 2 Sam. 23:5, where David praises God for having made a covenant that is "ordered in all things" (*ʿarûḵâ bakkōl*); i.e., its terms are fully set forth. The same verb is used of lining up troops in battle Array (cf. 1 Chr. 12:38 [MT 39], *maʿ arāḵâ* AV "rank"). A chronological sequence of generations is indicated by *tôlēḏôṯ* (Gen. 25:13; Exod. 28:10). Gk *kathexēs* indicates that events are narrated in chronological or logical sequence ("orderly," Luke 1:3; "in order," Acts 11:4). The frequently occurring phrases "in order to" and "in order that" express a causal sequence, and therefore purpose.[17]

Both of these words, decently and in order provide powerful principles for us in worship. Certainly, this should teach us that worship is not something someone does "willy-nilly" on his guitar as the "Lords leads." To the contrary, these two words call for deep consideration and careful reflection—even serious preparation before worship ever begins. Following the principle of what is decent and orderly must be held together with a similar exhortation in Phil. 4:8.

> Finally, brothers, whatever is true, whatever is honorable, whatever is just, whatever is pure, whatever is lovely, whatever is commendable, if there is any excellence, if there is anything worthy of praise, think about these things.

These words draw us to the deepest reflections as they relate to truth, beauty, and goodness. We must think deeply and carefully about

17. Bass, "Order," 613.

what is beautiful and good in worship because we are trying to do what God wants us to do and to do it in a way that pleases him. Thus, we are required to order things in a beautiful and excellent way in worship—glorifying God and blessing his people. Worship then is taking place amid an ongoing historical conversation about what is true, beautiful and good. This is especially important as the world around us increasingly becomes corrupt and indecent pushing us to the need of a safe place where we can go to experience the beauty and goodness of God—worship.

As noted earlier, worship is the church's most important form of discipleship, therefore, we need worship to shape and to form us towards the truth, beauty, and goodness of God. Pastors and elders need to reflect deeply on the structure and content as well as how the content and structure fit together. As such worship drives us away from bad ideas and pushes us away from a subjective/man-centered view of what is decent, orderly and excellent —this is particularly true when giving thought to embodied worship. Ken Myers notes,

> Paul does not say that we should reflect on what we think is lovely, or whatever we feel is admirable. We are to give sustained attention to whatever is objectively true and noble and right. One of the greatest problems with the way popular culture works is that it is so subjective. Praiseworthiness tends to be established by the market rather than by any objective standard.[18]

You may have soaked in the popular notion that beauty is in the eye of the beholder, but worship teaches us something different. Myers in other parts of his book on popular culture makes a salient point that we can't ignore—he asks in multiple ways if it's possible for popular culture to coincide with genuine Christianity. This is an especially powerful question as it relates to worship.

If, as Myers suggests, the quest for novelty and the desire for instant gratification is a constituent part of popular culture, then any church which uses pop culture as a guide for worship will be undermining the most fundamental purposes of worship—which hinges more on the satisfaction of a holy God than the fleeting interests of religious thrill seekers. Myers is tapping into and developing an ancient idea that Calvin articulated in the following way:

> This is the origin of idolatry, that when the genuine simplicity of God's worship is known, people begin to be dissatisfied with

18. Myers, *All God's Children*, 98.

it, and curiously to inquire whether there is anything worthy of belief in the figments of men; for men's minds are soon attracted by the snares of novelty, so as to pollute, with various kinds of leaven, what has been delivered in God's word.[19]

Anyone obsessed with novelty and entertainment will be immediately disappointed with the ancient, traditional liturgies of the church. The basic practices or liturgies of Christian worship force the worshipper to come face-to-face with the ancient, unchanging reality of the one true eternal God—this God has no need to entertain inattentive people on an endless quest for novelty and amusement. Such is not the purpose of worship! What Calvin described as a basic instinct of sinful human hearts has now become a constituent part of pop culture and unfortunately a guiding principle for constructing worship services. Ken Myers asks another penetrating question that would apply to worship:

> The question remains whether popular culture can serve as an able medium of meaning, or whether it is instead a distraction from confronting meaning, as well as meaningless.[20]

Beauty comes from God—God is beautiful, and he expects us to worship him decently, beautifully, excellently and in accord or with an order that he reveals in his Holy word. In his brilliant little book, *Beauty for Truth's Sake: On the Re-enchantment of Education*, Stratford Caldecott mentions that knowing these kinds of principles of virtue and good "will enable us to keep track of goodness amid the moral and social chaos that surrounds us."[21]

Worship that is shaped and guided by what is decent and orderly from God's perspective brings us directly into contact with truth, beauty, and goodness. Worship brings us face-to-face with the triune God of creation and salvation who is himself the source of truth, beauty, and goodness. This requires the church to strive for excellence and to study carefully what it means for something to fit into a place and in a way that is most appropriate to its purpose and in a way that brings the most glory to God. If Socrates was correct to any degree when he said that the purpose of education is to teach us to love what is beautiful then we could say with much more confidence that one of the basic purposes of

---

19. Calvin, quoted in Eire, *War Against Idols*, 209.
20. Myers, *All God's Children*, 64.
21. Caldecott, *Beauty for Truth's Sake*, 12.

worship is to teach us to love the One who is beautiful—God. So, the Psalmist say in Ps. 27:4,

> One thing have I asked of the LORD, that will I seek after: that I may dwell in the house of the LORD all the days of my life, to gaze upon the beauty of the LORD and to inquire in his temple.

I'm convinced that the regulative principle though amazingly helpful in guiding the overall direction of worship to the glory of God, it is not always the deciding factor in many of these kinds of discussions and controversies about worship. The guiding principle from 1 Cor. 14:40 is perhaps more critical when deciding matters in worship controversies and it presents a serious challenge especially for pastors and "worship leaders."

Each element of worship must be investigated as to its biblical nature, character, purpose, and place in formal worship, which means that even after agreeing to the regulative principle, the challenges we face are not simple or easy. It requires thoughtful, rigorous, and deep reflection about the decency, order and beauty of worship and everything in it: most importantly about the God we gather to worship. The rest of this little book will attempt to summarize some of these things in worship.

CHAPTER 3

Praise in Worship

EMBODIED WORSHIP ALWAYS INVOLVES singing praise. According to Psalm 100 God tells us that when we come into his special presence for worship we are to serve or offer him a liturgy singing! Ps. 100:1–5

> Make a joyful noise to the LORD, all the earth! Serve the LORD with gladness! Come into his presence with singing! Know that the LORD, he is God! It is he who made us, and we are his; we are his people, and the sheep of his pasture. Enter his gates with thanksgiving, and his courts with praise! Give thanks to him; bless his name! For the LORD is good; and his steadfast love endures to all generations.

When we worship God, he commands us to sing praises to him. This command is amazing because it reveals how much he loves us. Imagine how great it is that God commands us to do what we already enjoy doing: singing and making music.

We have said already that to be human is to worship. We could also add that to be human is to sing and to make music. You will never observe animals creating a Bach oratorio or composing songs about the tragedy of war, love and especially theology. Crafting music is an aspect of the image of God unique to human beings. This explains why creating and using musical praise in worshipping God is a natural human response to God's goodness and grace, and one worth noting. (I Chron. 16:9; Ps. 33:2-3; Col. 3:16; to name a few). Music is thus central to what it means to be human and central to our worship of God. Martin Luther wrote,

> Music is a vehicle for proclaiming the Word of God . . . The gift of language combined with the gift of song was only given to man to let him know that he should praise God with both word and music, namely, by proclaiming [God's word] through music and by providing sweet melodies with words.[1]

Though some cultures feature music as a more prominent part of life, all people make music. One writer says, "It seems that nothing defines a people like music." He goes on to add, "people are what they sing."[2] This is true of God's people who have always been known as singers. We sing praise to our triune God. We sing thanks to God. We sing of our joy, our sorrow, and we sing about everything to our God. This has always been true, and it finds its most powerful expression in worship.

Music was a central feature of the lives of our forefathers in the faith and we could learn from them. They celebrated and sang while were treading, harvesting their grapes and wine. (Jer. 25:30, Isa. 16:9, Judg. 9:27) They sang when digging, (Num. 21:17–18), cooking (Ezek. 24:3), and sheering their sheep (1 Sam. 25:7–8, 2 Sam. 13:28). Of course, they sang and danced at weddings and at almost every event in life. Scholars of the Old Testament remind us that music and singing lifted the burden of hard work and punctuated the regular features of ancient life but especially the times of celebrations.[3]

It may surprise some people, but music was even an important feature of war. My son plays the Scottish bagpipes, and I can tell you that when you hear him thundering out certain songs you can imagine his pipes roaring with a call to battle! Using trumpets and horns in similar ways Israel also used music as a call to war and to worship (Josh. 6:3–16, Judg. 3:27, 6:34, 7:15–24). Music is one of the most important blessings of our lives and it's a pervasive and unavoidable aspect of our lives, which means we should think carefully about it. One writer notes:

> All cultures are musical by nature. Music is one of God's gifts to man, and back when most of it was homemade, every nation had its songs and styles. In the West, respectable young ladies and gentlemen were expected to play an instrument, or at the very least gather around the piano after dinner. Frontier congregations and community choirs learned *a cappella* sight-singing

---

1. Luther, "Preface to Georg Rhau's Symphonoiaeiucundae," 323.
2. Block, *For Glory of God*, 221.
3. Block, *For Glory of God*, 222.

through shape notes. Work crews, sailors, laundry maids, and street vendors sang. Music was communal and participatory.[4]

If singing is an assumed part of all cultures, it is something that is a necessary element of the life and culture of the church. Of all people, Christians have so many reasons to sing. Therefore, the church always sings! Karl Barth is correct to argue that without singing the church cannot be the church.

> The Christian church sings. It is not a choral society. Its singing is not a concert. But from inner, material necessity it sings. Singing is the highest form of human expression . . . What we can and must say quite confidently is that *the church which does not sing is not the church.* And where . . . it does not really sing but sighs and mumbles spasmodically, shamefacedly and with an ill grace, it can be at best only a troubled community which is not sure of its cause and of whose ministry and witness there can be no great expectation. . . . The praise of God which finds its concrete culmination in the singing of the community is one of the indispensable forms of the ministry of the church (emphasis added).[5]

This is fundamentally true of the nature of the church especially since God commands musical praise in worship. Peter Leithart discusses the powerful imagery of musical praise as God designed it for worship.

> At the tent of David, music dominated worship even more thoroughly. The ark's ascension to Zion was reminiscent of Yahweh's descent to Sinai. At Sinai, the Lord's glory appeared with thunder and lightning, and the people heard "a very loud trumpet sound," which "grew louder and louder" (Exod. 19:16, 19). At Zion, the trumpet did not come from the glory-cloud, but from the people; Israel herself, and particularly the Levites, had become a human glory, resounding with the joyful noise of the angelic host. Led by priests blowing trumpets, Levitical musicians surrounded the ark with a cloud of sound as it was brought from the house of Obed-edom (1 Chr. 15:25–28). When the ark had been set in its tent, David assigned Asaph to head the Levites who were "to minister before the ark continually, as every day's work required" (1 Chr. 16:37), and the context makes it clear that this "ministry" was in song and instrumental music:

---

4. Cheaney, "Everybody Sing!" para. 5.
5. Barth, *Church Dogmatics*, 16.72.4.

PRAISE IN WORSHIP

> [David] appointed some of the Levites as ministers before the ark of Yahweh, even to celebrate and to thank and praise Yahweh God of Israel: Asaph the chief and second to him Zechariah, then Jeiel, Shemiramoth, Jehiel, Mattithiah, Eliab, Benaiah, Obed-edom, and Jeiel, with musical instruments, harps, lyres; also Asaph played loud-sounding cymbals, and Benaiah and Jahaziel the priests blew trumpets continually before the ark of the covenant of God. (1 Chr. 16:4–6)[6]

God wants musical praise in worship, and it's also an aesthetically lovely and emotionally beautiful experience for us. Imagine how kind God has been to us that he wants us to enjoy singing praise to him, which is something we naturally enjoy!

Singing and musical praise have always been the natural response to any encounter with the glory of God. Think of creation; think of the angels who sang at the birth of Jesus in Luke 2, etc. The natural response to any meaningful and particularly to a saving encounter with the true and living God is musical praise! You can see this throughout the scriptures. One of my favorites is Miriam's song. After escaping from the Egyptians and crossing the Red Sea, the people of Israel sang a song to the Lord (Exod. 15). As already noted, singing was part of Israel's formal worship in both tabernacle and temple (1 Chr. 6:31-32, 16:42). The Psalms bear rich testimony that in joy and in sorrow, in happiness and in lament, God's people sang with their voices to God. Jesus himself sang the psalms with his disciples (Matt. 26:30). The New Testament is filled with singing so much that one scholar notes,

> The New Testament begins and ends with outbursts of song. The birth of Jesus brought about the first outburst—four songs recorded in the first two chapters of Luke. Mary sang the *Magnificat* (1:46–55), Zechariah the *Benedictus* (1:68–79), Simeon the *Nunc dimittis* (2:29–32), and the angels sang, "Glory to God in the highest, and on earth peace among those with whom he is pleased" (2:14). The second outburst occurs in Revelation: there the song to the Lamb is picked up in ever-widening circles until the whole cosmos has joined in.[7]

We are blessed to have the gift of music and we are even more blessed that God wants us to praise him with songs and music in worship. I say this because I'm convinced that music is like some kind of divine magic. Yes,

---

6. Leithart, *From Silence to Song*, 55.
7. Stapert, *New Song for Old World*, 14.

music is like magic because it has the kinds of enchanting qualities we often ascribe to magic. For instance, like a magic carpet in Persian legends music has transportive qualities that enable us to fly away. In the case of worship, music transports us simultaneously back into history with the saints of old and into heaven with eschatologically transportive powers where we participate with the angels and saints in heaven in worshipping God with songs of praise—yes, music is like magic. Speaking about the depth and brilliance of the Psalms, Geerhardus Vos states,

> The Psalmist sometimes succeed in transporting themselves into the midst of the joy and blessedness, wherewith Jehovah himself contemplates the consummate perfection of his work. This faculty for entering into the inner spirit of God's own share in the religious process represents the highest and finest in worship."[8]

Music is like divine magic and a blessed gift from God for worship. A popular song writer, Yip Harburg, once quipped, "words make you think a thought; music makes you feel a feeling; a song makes you feel a thought!"[9] Martin Luther, the father of the Protestant Reformation, who wrote hymns for his church which became world famous, adds the following:

> Next to the Word of God, music deserves the highest praise. She is a mistress and governess of those human emotions . . . which control men or more often overwhelm them . . . Whether you wish to comfort the sad, to subdue frivolity, to encourage the despairing, to humble the proud, to calm the passionate or to appease those full of hate . . . what more effective means than music could you find.[10]

More and more research is suggesting what the ancients already knew: music helps to alleviate emotional symptoms for people experiencing serious suffering. The story of David playing music to soothe King Saul's angry soul reveals that our forefathers didn't need a scientific study to know the power of music (I Sam. 16:14–23). Today music is used for dementia, Alzheimer and other neurocognitive disorders that

---

8. Vos, *Pauline Eschatology*, 341. This particular point comes from an insightful chapter entitled, "The Eschatology of the Psalter," which is filled with rich theology that helps with the subject of praise in worship.

9. Smith, "Music, Singing, and Emotions," 469.

10. Luther, "Preface to Georg Rhau's Symphonoiaeiucundae," 323.

affect people in ways that leave them feeling anxious, frustrated, and uneasy. Music has a kind of medicinal quality, and I would add a magical capacity to help people feel happier and more peaceful.[11] Writing on worship, one author says,

> At levels deeper than most of us can explain, music communicates our values, anchors our feelings and expresses our hearts.[12]

I have always been amazed when I hear a certain song on the radio that transports me to another place and time. Listening to some songs, I suddenly feel like I have been carried back to seventh grade when I first heard the song. When I hear some songs from the band America, I recall riding in a white 1967 Thunderbird with the windows down and watching with joy as the outside scenery moved faster and faster. The wind blew, the music played, and I remember feeling so good. Other songs have a similar affect; they seem to "take me back" to a time or to an experience as if the music is transporting me back like a musical time machine—music is like magic that engages the deepest parts of our souls. It has a mysterious quality, which is at least part of the reason why God wants music to be a central element of our worship to him—he wants to touch our souls deeply in a way that the fine arts like music can do so beautifully.

"Ahh," says the stern believer, "we don't want an overly emotional worship service." Some people fear the powerfully emotional components of music. Some don't want people's emotions to be too charged up or they don't want people to become too passionate. However, if God doesn't want us to become emotional and passionate in worship, then why does he command us to praise him with songs? In the scriptures, why does his praise involve shouting, clapping hands and dancing? Fearing the emotional aspects of music is a very awkward and even unwitting position to take since music is inherently emotive. Music is emotional by nature. It is designed to provoke feelings and if it doesn't provoke its desired emotive response of the musician, then it's not good music. God wants good music in worship!

This presents a challenge whereby the adage "don't throw the baby out with the bathwater" can guide us. Music should be used to provoke emotions but not aimless passions. In worship God want us to be so moved emotionally that sometimes we cry out, literally in tears. He wants

---

11. Asprou, "Music for People with Dementia."
12. Chapell, *Christ-Centered Worship*, 296.

us to be moved with the deepest love for him as we sing, clap, and raise our hands. Sometimes our whole being should as it were shake with emotion as we respond with love for our savior.

It's important to note that in the scriptures the emotions of good praise music are linked with good theology. God tells us specifically that praise music is to be informed with theological, gospel influence. Ephesians and Colossians speak directly to this idea.

Eph. 5:18–21:

> And do not get drunk with wine, for that is debauchery, but be filled with the Spirit, *addressing one another* in psalms and hymns and spiritual songs, singing and making melody to the Lord with your heart, giving thanks always and for everything to God the Father in the name of our Lord Jesus Christ, submitting to one another out of reverence for Christ (emphasis added).

Col. 3:15–17:

> And let the peace of Christ rule in your hearts, to which indeed you were called in one body. And be thankful. Let the word of Christ dwell in you richly, *teaching and admonishing one another* in all wisdom, singing psalms and hymns and spiritual songs, with thankfulness in your hearts to God. And whatever you do, in word or deed, do everything in the name of the Lord Jesus, giving thanks to God the Father through him (emphasis added).

Paul tells us that our musical praise should be directed to the glory of God, but he also notes that it should be congregational. There is a very significant horizontal/covenantal character to praise songs that he says should stir each other up to love and good works in Christ. This is what we would call congregational singing. We have already stated that the scriptures use the word "gathering together" for a worship assembly. The following passage is teaching us that worship assemblies are places to stir each other up to love and good works.

Heb. 10:24–25

> And let us consider how to stir up one another to love and good works, not neglecting to meet together, as is the habit of some, but encouraging one another, and all the more as you see the Day drawing near.

I Cor. 14:26 is similar:

> What then, brothers? When you come together, each one has a hymn, a lesson, a revelation, a tongue, or an interpretation. Let all things be done for building up.

Paul argues that everything we do in worship should be done to build each other up—to edify. This includes musical praise in what we sometimes call a hymn. The horizontal or congregational angle of musical praise in worship has theological aims for the congregation that are supposed to teach, to admonish, to instruct, to encourage, and much more. The "one another" aspect of this kind of praise is covenantal, communal, or congregational and the "teaching" aspect is theological. God joins them together as a divinely designed package/gift for praise music in worship.

According to Col. 3:16 this is the kind of singing that is a divine ordinance by which Christ dwells richly in us. This is amazing! Paul teaches us something about the power of music as it is connected to the theology of the gospel in the context of a gathering or a congregation of believers. We should harness the power of musical praise to the glory of God's great grace together. We do this hoping that God's people would be moved to love him so deeply that as they sing praise to him and sing to one another it helps to move our fellow believers to live and yes even die for him. This kind of praise is connected to the power of music and is most appropriate for worship. Singing well and living well are linked together. Singing praise is supposed to encourage godly living. The great St. Augustine reminds us:

> Do you want to sing and play psalms? Then not only must your voice sing God's praises but your actions must keep in tune with your voice. After you have been singing with your voice you will have to be quiet for a while, but sing with your life in such a way that you never fall silent . . . Sing with your voice, then, to edify and encourage yourself and others by the sounds that appeal to the ears, but do not let your heart be dumb or your life be silent.[13]

There is a dynamic to this kind of musical praise. Christians sing praise to the Lord because they are thankful, and their singing stirs up more thankfulness. James 5:13 says, that if we are thankful, then we should sing praise! Happy people who have experienced the joy of salvation sing praises of thankfulness.

---

13. Quoted in Stapert, *New Song for Old World*, 3.

Rob Smith argues, "The simple message here is this: where there is salvation there is joy and where there is joy there is singing."[14] Believers know God and they sing in praise about him because he makes them thankful, happy people. This is one of the great reasons Christians sing: to cultivate thankful, happy lives as we live for God's glory. God tells us to sing to produce "thankfulness in your hearts to God" (Col. 3:16; Jas. 5:13). He reiterates the very same thing again in Ephesians 5:20 telling us to sing giving thanks always. There is a mysterious dynamic. Singing praises to God from a joy-filled life also cultivates a thankful soul. The devotional writer, William Law outlines this idea beautifully saying,

Just as singing is a natural effect of joy in the heart so it has also a natural power of rendering the heart joyful . . . There is nothing that so clears a way for your prayers, nothing that so disperses dullness of heart, nothing that so purifies the soul from poor and little passions, nothing that so opens heaven, or carries your heart so near it, as these songs of praise.

> They create a sense of delight in God, they awaken holy desires, they teach you how to ask, and they prevail with God to give. They kindle a holy flame, they turn your heart into an altar, your prayers into incense, and carry them as a sweet-smelling savor to the throne of grace.[15]

This means that God uses music to influence our emotions but emotions that are informed with the godly theological direction as Paul teaches us in Colossians and Ephesians in a covenantal and theological context.

One of the primary goals of praise songs should be to stir up, instruct and edify one another towards love for Christ. We are to speak to each other, to admonish, to instruct and exhort each other in the context of congregational singing. According to the scriptures excellent praise is thankful, covenantal, and theologically powerful. Rob Smith summarizes,

> So to draw the obvious conclusion, singing and making music are vital means not only of addressing one another with the word of God (thereby edifying the church) and making melody to the Lord (thereby praising our Savior), but of being filled with or by the Spirit and so growing up into Christ. And that (as I have suggested) includes coming to emotional maturity in Christ. As Jeremy Begbie expresses it: "To grow up

---

14. Smith, "Music, Singing, and Emotions," 471.
15. Law, *Serious Call to Holy Life*, 164.

into Christ is to grow up emotionally as much as anything else, and carefully chosen music in worship may have a larger part to play than we have yet imagined."[16]

In some circles worship music is seen as a tool for emotional leverage. Music is used to whip people into a "spiritual" frenzy after forty verses of the same line, each verse has added guitar, then drums, then clapping, then dancing, then—well you get the picture. Everything gets louder and wilder with endless repetition. This is actually a common technique in pagan religions. In Africa many churches have taken traditional religious practices from traditional tribal dances and music, mixing this idea into Christian worship. The same thing happens in America where pop culture is blended with musical praise. Such practices basically transfer pagan techniques and ideas into worship music with minor changes in the lyrics to reflect a faintly Christian message about how God is great, good, awesome or some other vaguely theistic concept. This is not what Paul instructs us to do in praise music; in fact, it's contrary to Paul's teaching.

We should not be afraid of the emotions of music, but we should never use music as a merely emotionally manipulative tactic to "get people into the mood of worship." Though popular, this approach bears little resemblance to the rich teachings of Colossians, Ephesians, and the whole book of the Psalms. Musical manipulation without good theology is common in all kinds of pagan religions; this is not what the scriptures teach us about Christian praise.

Churches that emphasize congregational singing with excellent music and beautiful theology are following Paul's direction. In fact, for many years in American Church history this was assumed to be the case. Today the churches which take this seriously will need to reject the ditties and repetitive beebop of modern pop psychology songs that pass off as musical praise. These songs are vague, pop culturish, and full of moralistic lyrics; not theologically deep lessons as Paul requires us to use. Rather than incorporating the rich theology of the scriptures many modern "praise songs" repeat lines such as, oh Lord, you make me whole, complete, give me peace, blah, blah, blah.

When compared to the scriptures, the vague, shallow, and self-centered lyrics are embarrassing. This may affirm existing religious feelings, but it certainly does not "teach" or "instruct" us in theology as God demands in the previous passages. Where for instance, is the

---

16. Smith, "Music, Singing, and Emotions," 474.

cross in this kind of banal praise? This is a great question—where is the gospel in pop praise?

Modern "praise songs" feel more like the praise of self-absorbed, spoiled, first world Christians whose theological depths haven't grown beyond a hip, moral discussion about sharing brokenness while at Starbucks. This kind of bland, self-centered praise bears little resemblance to the Psalms or to the great hymns of the faith. Douglas Bond puts it well when reflecting on a "praise song" that speaks of God's love as "free from demands." Is God's love really free from demands?

> Not only was it nonsensical, singing this made a mockery of the persecuted church, then and now. Isaac Watts put it far better: "Love, so amazing, so divine/Demands my soul, my life, my all."[17]

Theologically solid praise music will not only "encourage" us, but it will also confront us and strengthen us. This is the kind of musical praise that Paul describes as admonishing: theologically compelling praise. It's also why I keep emphasizing that godly worship should disciple us—this means discipline, which means shaping and forming us after the image of our savior, Jesus Christ. Songs that are full of teaching and admonishing are theologically powerful songs, and we need them.

The lyrics of many "praise songs" today are shallow, self-centered and often portraying Jesus as a boyfriend rather than our King or as our Great High Priest, but also modern "praise songs" have led to the opposite of what God wants. God says he wants us to sing as a congregation so that we teach each other good theology when we praise him. In many contemporary praise bands, their songs and their delivery make this impossible. Ironically, the sound systems are blaring the music so loudly that the congregation's voice becomes weak and even passive—defeating the very purpose of congregational engagement in praise. It's ironic and most proponents of contemporary praise music would be aghast at the comparisons that their professional "worship leader" approach to praise music and the practices of the medieval western church are very similar. Looking at medieval worship, Tim Keller describes it saying,

> Lay people passively watched the actions of priests and musicians. There was very little common prayer. The congregants prayed silently, individually, as priests behind a screen prayed inaudibly in Latin.[18]

17. Bond, "How NOT to Sing," para. 7.
18. Carson, *Worship by the Book*, 207.

This happens in many large churches today with praise music. People tend to clap their hands softly and slightly bounce up and down (I call this the Evangelical bounce or hop) as they passively watch the "worship leaders" who are essentially performing for them. Douglas Bond continues this line of thinking arguing,

> Today, singing is now largely done for us by commercially popular, celebrity entertainers, or those who imitate them. The congregation has become avid listeners, but increasingly inept participants in full voice singing.[19]

Such practices run contrary to Paul's words in Col. 3:16.

> Let the word of Christ dwell in you richly, teaching and admonishing **one another** in all wisdom, singing psalms and hymns and spiritual songs, with thankfulness in your hearts to God.

Singing the Psalms

The best place to learn robust singing is found in the Psalms, and there was a time in American history when this was a basic assumption of praise in worship. In fact, the very first book published in America was the *Bay Psalm Book*. The colonists knew the value of the Psalms in worship and many of them used the Psalms exclusively. The scriptures never advocate an exclusive use of the Psalms, but there are so many benefits to singing the Psalms in worship that it's hard to know where to start.

First, they help us to observe the nature and structure of solid praise songs with superb theology like Paul is instructing us to sing. They contain so many vivid examples of what Paul refers to as teaching, instruction, and admonition. Singing the Psalms helps us not merely to admonish each other, but we even admonish ourselves. So, the psalmist can say, "Praise the Lord Oh my soul, oh my soul the Lord praise!"

It's most likely that the designation Paul uses in Ephesians and Colossians as "psalms, hymns and spiritual songs" is actually a common way of referring to the 150 Psalms of the Torah or Old Testament. Of course, this doesn't in any way require us to sing the Psalms exclusively because there are many other sections in the scriptures filled with inspired songs. Still, if a church expects to have healthy, robust, and

---

19. Bond, "How NOT to Sing," para. 26.

excellent praises in worship there is no doubt that this church must sing the Psalms as a staple part of their musical diet.

The last 5 of the 150 psalms are prayers of praise, and they are packed with references to massive sounds of musical praise, shouting, clapping, and dancing to the Lord in worship. Hallelujah or Alleluia is a transliterated word from Hebrew, which literally means "*Praise the Lord!*" In singing the Psalms we sing praise to the Lord in his own words. This means that we really can't get a theologically bad praise song from the Psalms since they come from God and there is no better place to receive excellent theological instruction in praise songs then from God himself. This should speak for itself. A healthy church regularly needs to sing the Psalms in worship.

Another great benefit to singing the Psalms is that it helps us to memorize vast sections of the Bible. Not only does the church benefit from theologically excellent songs but singing the Psalms consistently in worship helps God's people to hide his word in their hearts. Music has a profound way of helping us to experience and to remember the scriptures. John Frame says,

> Poetic and/or musical form enhance the word of God in various ways. In particular, poetic-musical forms impart vividness and memorability to God's words. That vividness and memorability, in turn, drives the word into our hearts, so that it becomes precious to us and motivates us to praise and obedience . . . God is not interested only in getting his word into our hands; he wants to get it into our hearts (Pss. 1; 119:11; 34, 36, 69, etc.,: Col. 3:16).[20]

In the Psalms we learn that praise comes in a variety of forms are variegated, covering the whole range of human experience. We can sing to the Lord about our sorrows, joys, and hope in the midst of great struggles. Often the Psalms will take the time to develop a theological theme that opens and closes having developed a powerful theological truth. If a church commits to singing these kinds of songs and not merely small praise ditties, then the church will be strengthened and blessed with a robust steadiness to face all of life with the fullness of God's own inspired songs/prayers—some of which speak to the painful realities of life—even death itself. Carl Trueman comments,

---

20. Frame, *Worship in Spirit and Truth*, 112–13.

In the psalms of lament, the Church has a poetic language for giving expression to the deepest longings of a humanity looking to find rest not in this world but the next. In the great liturgies of the Church, death casts a long, creative, cathartic shadow. Our worship should reflect the realities of a life that must face death before experiencing resurrection.[21]

Singing the Psalms in worship must be central to praising God in worship. In his book, *Faith, Hope and Love*, Mark Jones offers to help the church guard against false worship, and he argues that using the Psalms is a central means of doing so. He writes,

> How many churches today regularly sing the Psalms, which are the very words of God? Some complain that so much contemporary worship is too emotional. I would argue that, in some sense, it is not emotional enough. By this I mean that much contemporary worship needs to lay aside the superficial feel-good approach in exchange for the range of emotions expressed in the Psalms that characterize the Christian life (e.g., lament, joy, thanksgiving, duress). What better way to express our love for God than to use the words he has inspired through those who have loved him?[22]

Singing the Psalms provides us with a formidable deterrent against theologically weak praise songs and provides beautiful, poetic language for expressing the whole gamut of human emotions and experience. Such music makes us better people. Using the Psalms powerfully connects our lives with all of the saints who have walked before us to glory. We not only sing with Moses and David; we share their experiences in songs together in a powerfully mysterious way that gives texture to our shared experiences in the faith. What a great way to live in unity with Christians in the past and those all over the world today who also use the Psalms in worship.

We are not exclusively limited to the Psalms or to whether or not a song has seven verses per se. Our praise should be musically and theologically excellent per I Cor. 14:40. This means that some songs will be long and highly developed while others will be very short such as a doxology. The scriptures use doxologies in worship and as sayings from one Christian to another. The word "doxology" comes from two Greek words; *doxa*, meaning "praise, honor, glory" and *logos*, meaning

21. Trueman, "Tragic Worship," para. 12.
22. Jones, *Faith, Hope and Love*, 192.

"a word, saying, or a reasoned discourse." Basically, a doxology is speaking words of praise. The angels sang a doxology at Jesus' birth: "Glory to God in the highest heaven, and on earth peace among those whom he favors" (Luke 2:14)! Other doxologies include Rom. 11:36; 16:27; Eph. 3:21 and I Tim. 1:17. We can learn to love singing God's own words to him, to each other and to the watching world. At a certain stage or place in worship it would be appropriate to sing,

> To the King of the ages, immortal, invisible, the only God, be honor and glory forever and ever. Amen. (1 Tim. 1:17)

The actual songs from the scriptures teach us so much about praise music partly because they were forged in the experience of redemptive history. Our people experienced God's mighty hand in their lives and they sang about it. While we rely heavily on the songs in the scriptures, we should also be inspired to be continually creating new songs of praise to God.

Perhaps if we focused on the covenantal and theological quality of songs that we sing, then we might be able to avoid the over simplified debates about contemporary vs. traditional music. We might even have a deeper and more productive conversation about what constitutes excellent worship music.

Sing To the Lord a New Song

Crafting and singing new songs of praise to God is a healthy activity for the church that may be the natural result of or might even become impetus for reformation and revival. This is also a great way for local congregations to cultivate a joyful community together. Some churches have deliberately sought to create their own music together and they have found that creating and singing praise songs has a deeply moving effect. If Paul's admonition is true that there is a dynamic involved in singing praise, and it makes sense that praise plays a vital role in revivals and reformations. John Frame notes,

> Many references to music in Scriptures are found in connection with periods of revival in Israel (I Chr.16:2; 2 Chr. 15; 23; 29; 35). In church history, too, revival usually produces new waves of music for the church . . . Periods of revival, when great numbers of people profess Christ and believers are renewed in their faith, almost always produce new developments in hymnody. The Protestant Reformation produced new hymns on the

Lutheran side and new psalm arrangements on the Calvinists side. Both Lutherans and Calvinists borrowed musical styles and occasionally whole tunes from secular sources. They chose words in vernacular languages, rather than Latin.[23]

Producing music that is accessible and in the vernacular language is a deeply historical impulse of the church in reaching God's people in their heart language. Guided by scriptural theology, the church uses praise songs to educate the people of God. I mean educate in a historic sense—the word, educate, came from a Latin word that means "to draw out or to call forth." For classical culture, to educate someone was to call out in them the best of their humanity as they learned truth, beauty, and goodness. The educator didn't merely fill them with data or information, rather the teacher presented, challenged, provoked, etc. the learner with truth, beauty and goodness in a way that called the student to these ideas. Somehow the educator was to strike a chord in their student's souls so that the student was drawn to their purpose as a human being. In the same way good praise music calls out in the people of God their desire to love and to serve him as they should. Such praise reminds us who we are in Christ including all of the hopes, dreams, aspirations and longings of what it means to be a sinful human being saved by the grace of God in Christ and living faithfully unto our destiny in him.

Christians need to sing like this! We need to sing the powerful songs of our faith together as we walk as one people in our difficult and oftentimes painful road to glory. We need each other and singing with each other in worship gives glory to God and blesses us together and calls out in us who we are in Christ. Christian worship directs us to love God together as his people who share his love in the context of living with each other as God's covenant community—not alone. The Psalms and the scriptures and our contemporary experiences are a splendid source of these kinds of worship songs.

We should also include in our worship music a strong emphasis on old/great hymns. I said "old" because most great hymns are songs that have stood the test of time; thus, they tend to be older. This has become difficult because many people are convinced that "old" songs cannot be used in churches because "old" hymns represent a traditionalism that they believe will destroy the church—by which they really mean the

---

23. Frame, *Worship in Spirit and Truth*, 113–15.

popularity of the church. Old songs to them represent 'dead orthodoxy.' This is sad idea.

Actually, I'm not sure if some of these people really have any interest in the "church" per se. That is to say, their ecclesiology or lack thereof causes them to have a disdain for the church—especially as it has manifested itself historically. They, therefore, refuse to allow anything "old" or "traditional." This has not always been the prevailing notion in liturgical church history. According to T. David Gordon,

> For nineteenth centuries all previous generations of the church (Greek Orthodox, Catholic, Protestant or Revivalist) in every culture employed prayers and hymns that preceded them and encouraged their best artist to consider adding to the canon of good liturgical forms. That is none were traditional in the sense of discouraging the writing of new forms; and none were contemporary in the sense of excluding the use of older forms. So now why this insistence that many, most or all forms of worship be contemporary?[24]

Though Gordon may be overstating the case with which the church has transitioned at least smoothly through liturgical and musical styles throughout the past, his point is well made. Today there are many churches which have become virtually obsessed with popularity and relevance to the point that they appear to loathe historical liturgical practices that they perceive to be "traditional," and therefore not contemporary.

They seem to be almost "anti-church." Their ecclesiology (doctrine of the church) is not always clear, but they tend to despise all things historical or what they call traditional. Such things are referred to as "religious" and therefore somehow negative. They have replaced biblical ecclesiology and scriptural liturgy with the theology of pop culture. In adopting pop culture as their standard these "churches" have adopted an anti-church mentality. We might even say an anti-worship mentality.

In their incessant search for significance and recognition they have excluded the most historically powerful items that have always made Christianity a dominant though not "popular" force in any culture in which it exists. It has been God-centered worship and God-centered theology; not popularity or relevance that has made the church so influential throughout history. In a calculated but deadly decision many

---

24. Gordon, *Why Johnny Can't Sing*, 43.

leaders have chosen the self-destructive path of pop culture as the guide for praise music. It's self-destructive because as Ken Myers states,

> Popular culture's forms are not capable of sustaining the Christian conviction of a holy, judging God who demands repentance and promises the joy of obedience.[25]

Echoing Myer's sentiment Allen P. Ross makes a similar argument:

> churches are always trying to make worship more meaningful. But usually, these efforts focus on new methods and different styles designed to make worship livelier and more relevant rather than on how to inspire worshippers to see the true and holy God of glory. In an effort to simplify things and make them relevant, the meaning and the mystery has been lost.[26]

D. Martyn Lloyd-Jones speaks of the modern churches endless and incessant search for what they think will be "the" thing that propels the church to become popular. Lloyd-Jones says,

> And so one has seen fashions and vogues and stunts coming one after another in the Church. Each one creates great excitement and enthusiasm and is loudly advertised as *the* thing that is going to fill the churches, *the* thing that is going to solve the problem. They have said that about every single one of them. But in a few years, they have forgotten all about it, and another stunt comes along, or another new idea; somebody has hit upon the one thing needful . . . here is the thing, and everybody rushes after it; but soon it wanes and disappears and something else takes its place.[27]

This is a sound reason why returning to our rich history in hymnody is an important part of solid praise music in worship and keeping the church steady to its mission. These songs are not trying to fit themselves into a pop culture pattern, rather they communicate an excellent theology that teaches us timeless truths in all the best ways. They have more than a couple of verses of vague God-talk. Like scriptural psalms, excellent hymns develop theological themes that encourage us, teach us sound theology, and focus on God's glory. Our songs should not mimic pop culture, but our songs should cultivate in us the truth, beauty and

---

25. Myers, *All God's Children*, 182.
26. Ross, *Recalling Hope of Glory*, 37.
27. Lloyd-Jones, *Preaching and Preachers*, 35.

goodness that pop culture is constantly trying to diminish. We come back to James K.A. Smith's earlier point:

> Christian worship, we should recognize, is essentially a *counter*formation to those rival liturgies we are often immersed in, cultural practices that covertly capture our loves and longings, miscalibrating them, orienting us to rival versions of the good life. This is why worship is the heart of discipleship.[28]

If the church's music is a pale mimicry of pop culture, Christians will never experience what Smith means by a rival liturgy because worship will be essentially the same consumeristic, self-serving distraction as pop culture—continuing our dance down an endless, vacuous road of exhaustion. The church could actually become aware of the difference between a musical jingle that better fits an advertisement for soda and a sober song that praises the sovereign, triune God of creation. At present in many churches there is no discernible difference.

Excellent musical praise in worship might offer a beautiful contrast to the triteness and exhaustion of pop culture. Pop culture has an interest in the passing fades and the evanescence of the latest beat. Traditional hymnody, however, stands in stark contrast to this way of thinking and good songs can helps us see it. They can call us to it–or to Him. Good praise music may work in shaping God's people's tastes and interests towards eternity; not merely the here and now.

Worship is the church's most important place for discipleship so using hymns that are theologically healthy and musically beautiful will discipline and strengthen God's people. It may also provide a vital connection with our past and a metric for truth, beauty, and goodness for the future. Singing like this helps us to be better people!

Another benefit of great hymns is that they are written to be congregational songs. They are not designed for a praise band performance in front of the church, instead they inspire us to sing together as God's covenant community, as a congregation. In fact, some of them call us back to the days when our forefathers were brave, missionaries whose songs spoke of the power of Christ to sustain Christians and to convert once barbaric nations with the authority of the gospel. We can sing ancient Irish hymns which embolden us as God's people to gather together in worship and remember the great deeds that God has done and God's grace that our people have experienced. In this sense as noted earlier

---

28. Smith, *You Are What You Love*, 25.

excellent songs build our character and encourage us to unity with our past and to a sense of destiny for our future.

Since worship is a gathering of many individuals into the one body of Christ, excellent hymns have a natural liturgical quality to them that encourage the unity of the body with the past and the present. Likewise, great hymns provide us a superb connection between older and younger generations. To this day I become emotional when I sing certain hymns that remind me of my mother and grandmother. Whenever I sing "Great is Thy Faithfulness" I can hardly keep from weeping with joy and emotion that God used my mother and grandmother's songs to touch my own heart as a child and to provide me with an anchor for my soul. I'm even more moved when I sing these songs with my own children and grandchildren as we share in generations of joy in God's grace together. Good hymns whether old or "contemporary" can do the same. For instance, I find my heart moved also when I sing a contemporary song such as "In Christ Alone" with my children and grandchildren in worship: I imagine that one day in the future they will feel the same way as I described feeling when they sing In Christ Alone with their children's children.

Perhaps we might say that along with the Psalms, the backbone of praise music in worship should be the scriptures combined with new songs and old hymns. I think a simple but helpful litmus test for your church might be a humble look at whether your musical praise includes a healthy mixture of all three of these kinds of songs. If your church only approves of songs written before 1879, then your church is probably theologically unhealthy. If your church exclusively sings contemporary songs with two verses and a chorus that is repeated ten times, then your church is probably an unhealthy church as well. If your church's praise music reminds you of a rock concert complete with spotlights, guitar solos, and lead singers who raise their hands and softly speak into the spotlight so you know they are really having a great spiritual experience on the stage in front of you—your church is not only unhealthy but doubtless has the incurable theological disease that I call pop culturitis—you need to leave it and find a healthy church as soon as possible.

A healthy church will be singing the Psalms, composing new songs, and celebrating the ancient hymns of the faith. The young, the old, and those yet to come will be blessed in this kind of church. Calvin R. Stapert beautifully summarizes this idea when describing the value of early church history for learning about praise music. He notes,

Much of what we can learn from the early Christians we can learn from their example. We would do well to heed their praise of the psalms and follow their example of making them central to our music—not just snippets and a few favorites, but complete psalms, indeed, the whole Psalter with its full-orbed expression. We could also enrich our singing with the best of their hymns. Their value is enduring, and they can serve our hymn-writers as models of texts that address God communally in language that is simple yet dignified, poetically excellent, and redolent with scriptural vocabulary, stories, sentiments, and imagery. We would also do well to follow their example of making psalms and hymns a part of our daily life. We must teach them to our children and find ways and occasions to use them regularly.[29]

What's a "good" song?

What about new songs? How do you evaluate new praise songs for worship particularly for sound theology? This is a serious challenge for the church in every age, but especially in a time when "pop culturitis" is infecting churches. We can discover some good direction from Douglas Sean O'Donnell in his book, *God's Lyrics: Rediscovering Worship Through Old Testament Songs*. The first part of his work, which is worth the price of the whole book, contains five sermons preached by O'Donnell on the five great songs of the Old Testament:

1. The Song of Moses: *Te Deum* of Triumph (Ex. 15),
2. The Song of Yahweh: An Exodus from Israel's Apostasy (Deut. 32),
3. The Song of Deborah: A Punctured Temple, a Pouring Out of Joy (Judg. 5),
4. The Songs in Samuel: The Barren Woman and the Fertile King (I Sam. 2 & II Sam. 22),
5. The Song of Habakkuk: A Time to Wait—for Wrath (Hab. 3).

The second part of the book applies the key themes found within these songs. For a simplified approach, he excludes the Psalms and looks at smaller songs of praise in the Old Testament. From his observation of these Old Testament texts, he provides us with four characteristics of a biblical song that help us to judge "good" praise songs: (1) magnifying the

29. Stapert, *New Song for Old World*, 194.

Lord (2) recalling salvation history (3) rejoicing in God's just judgments (4) exhorting us to godliness. I love this approach because it's so obvious and so simple. If you want to know what constitutes a "good" praise song, look in the Bible. He reminds us of the elementary yet neglected theological truths that constitute good praise as exampled for us in the scriptures. This will be praise songs that according to O'Donnell,

> exhort us to be Lord centered in our singing. They remind us to remember and rejoice in God's mighty acts in history, including his just judgments. And they urge us to moral transformation- to grow in godliness or true wisdom.[30]

If you are writing a modern hymn, or selecting ones for your church, it helps to know how God himself composes a praise song. The songs you find in the scriptures are not judged by their length per se but by primarily by their theology. In the forward to Obrien's book T. David Gordon summarizes the basic theological characteristics of a "good" praise song:

- The Lord is the center of every song. In the text he is addressed, adored, and "enlarged."
- God's mighty acts in salvation history are recounted first (not merely or primarily or personal experience of redemption) are recounted.
- God's acts of judgments are rejoiced in. (*note: this one really feels strange*)
- God's ways of living (practical wisdom) are encouraged.[31]

This is amazingly basic, but profoundly powerful. Just take a simple look at popular praise songs and evaluate them from this modest standard. You will be sorely disappointed in many contemporary songs—especially some of the most popular ones. Gordon continues,

> Contemporary worship music centers more on our experience of religion than it does on God's saving acts in history, that in them we as worshippers are more prominent than he who is worshipped, that God's judgment is almost never mentioned in them . . . (they are) narcissistic, pietistic, sentimental and

---

30. O'Donnell, *God's Lyrics*, xxi.
31. O'Donnell, *God's Lyrics*, ix.

Pollyannish . . . He (God) is everyone's friend and no one's enemy; he may elicit our affection, but not our awe.[32]

With this in mind it's no wonder that today's "popular" approach to praise in worship is not only theologically weak, but it is producing weak people. If the church presents itself as an institution designed to feed your every "need," then discipleship is lost and the possibility of edifying, which means strengthening and building up is also lost. How could someone be physically healthy if they only ate cotton candy? The same is true spiritually.

Pop culture churches will not shape the kind stalwarts of the faith who could compose and sing "Oh Sacred Head Now Wounded," or "How Firm a Foundation," or "Be Thou My Vision." Or what of Martin Luther's great hymn, "A Mighty Fortress is Our God?" This is not a theoretical loss, we are losing a whole generation of Christians to weak and unsteady theology taught in our songs, which means weak and unsteady morality. If we are what we sing, then many in modern Christianity are frail, self-centered, consumers; and such frailty leaves them open to the false remedies and the unsteadiness of heretical winds of doctrine.

If we are challenged to sing and to produce great songs of praise, then we also must think about the need to educate our young people not only about musical quality, but also regarding poetic and literary quality and most of all to teach them theological quality. We need a whole group of believers who are ready to tackle the subject of musical praise in worship. There is much to consider and it's beyond the pale of this little book. John Frame sets forth some of the challenges regarding musical choice and quality:

> We must also consider the appropriateness of its text, the relation of text to tune, and the "musical languages" intelligible to the worshipers. Also, judgements regarding musical quality should not be made hastily. . . we must remind ourselves that just as human languages differ in the way they express common meanings, so there are differences in "musical languages."[33]

Choosing the appropriate musical composition and lyrical content for praise songs in worship is a duty, which requires careful attention to musical principles and close consideration to theological quality. This includes using appropriate musical instruments to accompany our

---

32. O'Donnell, *God's Lyrics*, xi.
33. Frame, *Worship in Spirit and Truth*, 119.

praise. This small book makes no pretense to scholarly endeavors into either musicality nor instrumentality, but I do wish to encourage us to more, and more study. There is much to do! Leithart encourages us to investigate the Old Testament's teachings on music,

> Because David's reign saw the inception of worship through song, the portions of the Bible that describe this period, especially Chronicles, provide more material on worship music than any other section of the Bible. Attention to these passages will help to address both long-standing and contemporary debates about church music.[34]

My own experience in American and now in African worship has reminded me that the musical, linguistic, and instrumental genres of praise songs will vary from place to place around the world. I recall fondly how one little boy in a village church in Africa used an old jerry can as a drum, and it was the only instrument the people had available. It was a beautiful time of praise and worship, and the little guy played his jerry can excellently. We can and should use a variety of instruments in worship and the scriptures place no limits on them. If the musical accompaniment is supporting congregational singing and enhancing our ability to praise God with great songs of praise then we have no limits other than the guidelines of beauty and excellence found the scriptures.

Praise as Warfare

We have already noted that worship is warfare. Likewise, praise is a kind of warfare! In Col. 3 Paul speaks of putting to death the old man; putting to death sin. Shortly after this he reminds us that singing to one another in songs, hymns and spiritual songs plays a role in the battle to put to death sin. He says something similar in Eph. 5 where we see that singing helps us to do combat against the forces of the wicked one. Believers who are singing are helping themselves and others to go to war with sin. Singing is a part of the battle!

In worship we sing as part of this ongoing combat against the forces of darkness. In worship we sing of the sovereignty of God over all of history and even the future. This is powerful. Ps. 8 teaches us something quite amazing about worship praise and warfare. The Psalmist says,

---

34. Leithart, *From Silence to Song*, 15.

> O LORD, our Lord, how majestic is your name in all the earth! You have set your glory above the heavens. Out of the mouth of babies and infants, you have established strength because of your foes, to still the enemy and the avenger. (Ps. 8:1–2)

Imagine how amazing it is to consider that our praise is something that silences the enemy and the avenger! God is pleased to use our praise to defeat his adversaries. One simple way this happens is that when we praise the Lord in worship, we proclaim his glory and victory over the forces of darkness. His work of salvation is declared loudly to the watching world and to the realm of angels and demons all around us as we praise the Lord. We are reminded of Miriam's song in Ex. 15 when the people of God sang and praised him saying out loud that the Lord is a warrior, and he saves his people.

In writing this chapter I am reminded of the powerful story of what some have called the singing revolution. The name singing revolution refers to the struggle of three small Baltic states, Latvia, Lithuania, and Estonia. These three tiny nations were fighting for freedom from the colossal power of the Soviet Union. At the end of the 1980's the Soviet Union was powerful but starting to crumble. The tiny Baltic states had no real hope of standing against the tanks and mighty armies of Russia, but they had songs. With no artillery, tanks, or armored vehicles the people determined to sing their way to freedom. For years these little states resolved that though they had no military weapons per se, they could sing—and sing they did. Through the power of singing, they awakened a genuine patriotic fervor that no Soviet soldier could suppress.

In their homes and in the public squares thousands of people gathered to sing the songs of their past that contained the dreams and aspirations of their ancestors. These songs awakened their souls to their respective histories and the deep longing that was roused in their hearts to be free of oppression. After years of subjugation and tyranny, their songs resuscitated an indomitable spirit of hope that could not be suppressed. When most people think of weapons for a revolution, they probably would not think that songs would be the weapon of choice. Yet, songs were a major force that unified and galvanized what would otherwise be a hopeless battle against overwhelming odds.

If this can be true of earthly, political, and national struggles, then how much more should be hope that God will use our songs to unify and galvanize his people! The great victory of our sovereign warrior God was manifested for us as he crushed one of the most powerful armies of this world order as he saved his people. Egypt represented slavery to evil forces and God defeated our foes and set us free. This overwhelming victory is one of many such conquests that our God will accomplish in history and so we sing of it. We sing of our God's conquests here on earth as he marches forward with us to the final consummation of all things. We sing about the past triumphs of our Great triune God, and we sing about the future victories he will also win for his people. The future belongs to the Lord, and we should proclaim this in our songs. In this sense praise in worship is a powerful act of spiritual warfare as we sing out loud of the salvation of Jesus Christ. We praise God and we remind ourselves and the whole created realm that one day every knee shall bow, and every tongue will confess that Jesus is the Lord.

We sing of the hope of the future as we shout to each other the same hope of the psalmist who sang that God "will judge the world in righteousness and the peoples in faithfulness; He will judge the world with righteousness and the peoples with equity." (Pss. 96:13; 98:9; etc.) We announce in our songs that the Lord reigns; let the peoples tremble! (Ps. 99:1) We shout to God, to each other, and to the watching realms around us that God is mighty, and he will defeat all his and all our enemies!

The scriptures indicate that this kind of militant praise and spiritual warfare stirs us to hope in God, but more importantly it stirs up God on behalf of his people. The scriptures tell us that God hears our prayers and praise and responds with great power. Listen to Ps. 18:6–14

> In my distress I called upon the LORD; to my God I cried for help. From his temple he heard my voice, and my cry to him reached his ears. Then the earth reeled and rocked; the foundations also of the mountains trembled and quaked, because he was angry. Smoke went up from his nostrils, and devouring fire from his mouth; glowing coals flamed forth from him. He bowed the heavens and came down; thick darkness was under his feet. He rode on a cherub and flew; he came swiftly on the wings of the wind. He made darkness his covering, his canopy around him, thick clouds dark with water. Out of the brightness before him hailstones and coals of fire broke through his clouds. The LORD also thundered in the heavens, and the Most High uttered his voice, hailstones and coals of fire. And he sent out his arrows and scattered them; he flashed forth lightnings and routed them.

There is an amazing story in 2 Chr. 20 that should inspire us to sing praise as a kind of proclamation of the victory of God over his enemies.

When Israel was being attacked by an overwhelming enemy, they worshipped God. Notice that the "tip of the spear" in King Jehoshaphat's attack against the enemies was praise!

> Then Jehoshaphat bowed his head with his face to the ground, and all Judah and the inhabitants of Jerusalem fell down before the Lord, worshiping the Lord. And the Levites, of the Kohathites and the Korahites, stood up to praise the Lord, the God of Israel, with a very loud voice. And they rose early in the morning and went out into the wilderness of Tekoa. And when they went out, Jehoshaphat stood and said, "Hear me, Judah and inhabitants of Jerusalem! Believe in the Lord your God, and you will be established; believe his prophets, and you will succeed." And when he had taken counsel with the people, he appointed those who were to sing to the Lord and praise him in holy attire, as they went before the army, and say, "Give thanks to the Lord, for his steadfast love endures forever." And when they began to sing and praise, the Lord set an ambush against the men of Ammon, Moab, and Mount Seir, who had come against Judah, so that they were routed. For the men of Ammon and Moab rose against the inhabitants of Mount Seir, devoting them to destruction, and when they had made an end of the inhabitants of Seir, they all helped to destroy one another. (II Chr. 20:18–23)

This story indicates that God was moved to fight Israel's enemies when God's people praised him. It is like the walls of Jericho falling down at the blasts of horns, like the confusion of the Midianites to Gideon's trumpets. Here the same confusion is coupled to the singing and praise of the people of God, which provoked God to crush the enemies of his people. This is something of a pattern in the scriptures that should encourage us to sing with our whole hearts that God would route his enemies and bring his kingdom. Our most powerful weapon against the forces of darkness is not lobbying legislative representatives but lobbying the hosts of heaven with heartfelt praise in the assembly of God's warrior saints.

This is so powerful for us to consider as we gather in corporate worship to praise God in songs and then to imagine that such singing may provoke heaven itself to mysterious movement. Such movement that we hope will shake heaven and earth with his power. Indeed, the scriptures indicate that even the angels are moved to action with the people of God as we praise him. We learn the mystery that sometimes the angels join us in our songs of praise. Rev. 5:11–12:

> Then I looked, and I heard around the throne and the living creatures and the elders the voice of many angels, numbering myriads of myriads and thousands of thousands, saying with a loud voice, "Worthy is the Lamb who was slain, to receive power and wealth and wisdom and might and honor and glory and blessing!"

This is how we should sing in worship. As the people of God, we should sing a new song to the Lord. Sing with all your heart and sing to the glory God. As we come together in worship, let us agree and let us sing the words of Ps. 100: 1–5.

> Make a joyful noise to the Lord, all the earth! Serve the Lord with gladness! Come into his presence with singing! Know that the Lord, he is God! It is he who made us, and we are his; we are his people, and the sheep of his pasture. Enter his gates with thanksgiving, and his courts with praise! Give thanks to him; bless his name! For the Lord is good; his steadfast love endures forever, and his faithfulness to all generations.

CHAPTER 4

Prayer in Worship

IN CORPORATE WORSHIP WE are meeting as God's people and prayer is central to this gathering. Like all the other elements of worship, prayer and posture are linked. If you recall the image of a courtroom as a good illustration of assembling for worship, then you can think of prayer in worship as the voice of God's people corporately speaking to their judge/king/savior. In Christ and by the Holy Spirit our prayers enable us to speak to God as having a standing in his court—the great court of heaven. Just as in an earthly courtroom, we will pay attention to our posture depending on the situation.

In New Testament worship God meets with his people similar to how God met with his people in the Old Testament temple. The temple was the place where God met with his people. It was there that he spoke to them through priests, received offerings and sacrifices, heard their praises, blessed them and their children and of course listened to their prayers. The temple was characterized as a house of prayer. Jesus himself affirms this when he quotes from Isaiah 56:7 saying that the temple was a house of prayer for the nations (Mark 11:17). What was prayer like at the temple where God met with his people?

In worship we are gathered not as a collection of individuals but as the corporate body of Christ. This means that following the pattern of prayer in the Old Testament, we sometimes pray in worship as one man leads us together in prayer. Solomon's prayer at the dedication of the temple is a great example of this kind of prayer (see I Kgs 8:23-53). At this point it may well be appropriate for the congregation to sit as the pastor prays. Sitting, however, is not a common posture for prayer.

Solomon's prayer is a beautiful and robust prayer—full of great theology, which prayers in worship should contain. He kneels down and lifts up his hands and prays! His posture is thus powerfully connected to his prayer, which prayers in worship should also display—posture matters! In this little book, we are attempting to look at not only the postures of worship but the substance as well. In fact, substance and style or prayers and postures are always interconnected.

Solomon's prayer is instructive in its posture and substance. As he prays at this great assembly, he provides what Hughes Oliphant Old argues is something of a picture of the ministry of prayer as it was carried out in the Temple.[1] Solomon opens his prayer recounting the great covenant faithfulness of God to his promises. This indicates that God's covenant faithfulness is one of the key foundations of prayer in worship. This also means that robust prayer will include some mention of the faithful character of God as a common feature of prayers in worship, particularly prayers that open worship services and those that lead the people in praising God. This is yet another reason to rely heavily on the Psalms because they do the same thing—they are packed with constant references to what God promised he would do and how God faithfully did what he promised. This should be common for prayers in worship. In fact, a simple loving trust in God and his faithfulness becomes for the basis of all our prayers. Because we love him and trust him, we pray to him.

God's faithfulness as a theme in prayer also helps us with simple things like asking for forgiveness in our prayers. The covenant faithfulness of God is the basis on which Solomon prayed reminding the people of God that if they sinned, they could come to God for forgiveness. It calls to mind the beautiful words of I John 1:9

> If we confess our sins, he is faithful and just to forgive us our sins and to cleanse us from all unrighteousness.

God's faithfulness is the foundation of prayer—particularly our prayers of confession. Such public penitential prayer was an expected feature of prayer in the temple, and it should also be a regular part of our worship in the New Testament as well.[2] In fact, this has come to an even more

---

1. Old, *Worship*, 91.
2. Old, *Worship*, 92.

powerful fulfillment in the New Testament through Jesus Christ. One writer states:

> Whenever the church assembles, wherever believing hearts are lifted to God in prayer, we ourselves enter with boldness into the holiest in the heavenly sanctuary, through the blood of Jesus which has consecrated for us a new and living way of access to God (Heb. 10:19–22; 12:18–24; 4:14–16; 6:19–20; 7:17–19, 25; Eph. 3:11–12).[3]

Therefore, one of the prayers that should be an ordinary part of any worship service is a prayer of confession of sins. At this point it is appropriate for the congregation to kneel down and pray together a corporate prayer of confession. Notice I said the congregation. A prayer of confession is for the congregation.

Using a prayer of confession in worship is foreign to many Evangelicals, but it is one of the more traditional and historical prayers in Christian worship. The loss of such prayers of confession is not an indication of their worth or worthiness, but rather of a degraded theology that belittles sin often replacing the concept of sin with vaguer notions of "brokenness" and "weariness," etc. It also reflects an unfortunate evangelical emphasis on the individual over the community.

This is where good theology is important. For instance, the scriptures teach us that the actual brokenness of our lives comes from sin—either our own sins or the sins of others, or life in a sin-filled world. Thus, prayers of confession are a vital part of Christian worship and Christian theology. When the congregation prays to confess their sins, it is a powerful and central feature of Christian worship and of who we are as forgiven sinners. We depend on the grace of God through Jesus Christ to forgive us our sins and provide us access to God. Without it, we would have no way to pray and no hope. Jesus is always making intercession for us—he is our great high priest who prays for us and because he is our priest, we are able to enter into the presence of God the Father. Therefore, prayers of confession are an important part of proclaiming the gospel in worship.

I have heard odd objections to kneeling for a prayer of confession. One such objection is that the posture of kneeling was forbidden at the Council of Nicea (325AD). The Council of Nicea did forbid kneeling for prayer, but it also forebad any other posture except standing for Sunday worship services. The council required standing as the only posture

3. Isbell, "Hear Ye Him," 67.

allowable in worship on Sunday and in celebration of Pentecost. They reasoned that since Sunday was a day of resurrection therefore the only appropriate posture on this day is standing, which was a posture of victory. Kneeling represented penance rather than resurrection and thus they argued that kneeling was not appropriate for Sunday worship.

Objecting to kneeling as an appropriate posture using the rules of canons issued at the Council of Nicea is a bit insincere. The Council also issued numerous canons regarding self-castration, the proper day to celebrate Easter, the ordination of bishops and other canons that few Protestants today would take seriously. Likewise, the canon prohibiting kneeling was later reversed especially in western churches. These Protestants also use the Nicene Creed adding the infamous phrase, and the son. Such addition has no ecumenical authority in any subsequent councils, but most Protestants who use the creed include the phrase. Consequently, it's hard to take such objections seriously.

More importantly is the question of whether there is scriptural warrant for such a posture in prayer. Bryan Chapell argues nicely that the church's worship service should communicate the gospel not merely in outward words, but in the whole structure of its liturgy—in forms and in patterns the gospel should be included as what Chapell describes as "embedded" into everything we do in worship.[4] Historically, traditional Christian worship included something in the liturgy about sins and forgiveness because the gospel is so central to worship. This means that sin is a central theological issue for Christians to think about in worship—most especially the grace, the love, and the forgiveness that we have in Jesus Christ.

Today the issue of sin in some praise meetings is deliberately avoided, which undermines the gospel. This may well be a strong argument for adding kneeling as a helpful antidote. Chapell is right to note that no matter what we do in our liturgies, we are communicating something—so it needs to be the gospel. He says,

> If one goes along with what is either historically accepted or currently preferred, an understanding of the gospel inevitably unfolds. If a leader sets aside time for Confession of Sin (whether by prayer or song, or by Scripture reading), then something about the gospel gets communicated—even though the message

---

4. Chapell, *Christ-centered Worship*, 17–18.

may not have been intended . . . Liturgy tells a story. We tell the gospel by the way we worship.[5]

The gospel is the good news that Jesus died on the cross and rose on the third day to save sinners. This means that prayers of confession act as an ongoing reminder of the gospel in worship that is proclaimed in our preaching, sung about in our praise, and heard in our prayers—and yes, included even in our postures. They are so important to a full worship service to God that John Calvin added the following:

> Besides the fact that ordinary confession has been commended by the Lord's mouth, no one of sound mind, who weighs its usefulness, can dare disapprove it. For since in every sacred assembly we stand before the sight of God and the angels, what other beginning of our action will there be than the recognition of our own unworthiness? But that, you say, is done through every prayer; for whenever we pray for pardon, we confess our sin. Granted. But if you consider how great is our complacency, our drowsiness, or our sluggishness, you will agree with me that it would be a salutary regulation if the Christian people were to practice humbling themselves through some public rite of confession. For even though the ceremony that the Lord laid down for the Israelites was a part of the tutelage of the law, still the reality underlying it in some manner pertains also to us. And indeed, we see this custom observed with good results in well-regulated churches: that every Lord's Day the minister frames the formula of confession in his own and the people's name, and by it he accuses all of wickedness and implores pardon from the Lord. In short, with this key a gate to prayer is opened both to individuals in private and to all in public.[6]

It appears from this that in Calvin's Geneva some of the ministers prayed the prayer of confession, which seemed to be the custom in a few places historically. I want to challenge this practice I have observed in many good churches. These churches include a prayer of confession, but they do so by having minister pray on behalf of the people. This seems a bit odd since a prayer of confession is not something someone else prayers for you. In fact, as adamant as many Protestants have been about criticizing "priestly" traditions because the priest does everything on behalf of people, this is something to reconsider. A prayer of confession should be

---

5. Chapell, *Christ-centered Worship*, 18–19.
6. Calvin, *Institutes of the Christian Religion*, 3.4.11 (p. 635).

a corporate prayer in which the people are all engaged in it. The most appropriate practice would be for the congregation to pray a prayer of confession corporately—and most appropriately—on their knees together as a posture of humility and contrition.

This is yet another example of how the church's worship service is the most important aspect of Christian discipleship. For instance, using excellent and beautifully formulated prayers of confession is a way to help us to articulate and to understand the gospel deeply and clearly. Great prayers form and shape our thoughts in exceptional ways. There are many great examples of these kinds of prayers. The following is a closing excerpt from John Calvin's *Form of Ecclesiastical Prayers and Songs*:

> May you, therefore, have mercy upon us, most gentle and merciful God and Father, in the name of your Son, Jesus Christ our Lord. And as you blot out our vices and blemishes, extend and increase the graces of your Holy Spirit to us day by day, so that as we acknowledge our unrighteousness with all our heart, we might feel the sorrow that gives birth to true penitence, which as we mortify our sins may produce fruits of righteousness and innocence pleasing to you, through Jesus Christ our Lord.[7]

Another beautiful gem comes from the seemingly timeless Anglican *Book of Common Prayer*, which is one of the English language's greatest liturgical sourcebooks for worship. In it, Thomas Cramner writes:

> Almighty and most merciful Father, We have erred and strayed from thy ways like lost sheep, We have followed too much the devices and desires of our own hearts, We have offended against thy holy laws, We have left undone those things which we ought to have done, And we have done those things which we ought not to have done; *And there is no health in us.* But thou, O Lord, have mercy upon us, miserable offenders. Spare thou them, O God, which confess their faults. Restore thou them that are penitent; According to thy promises declared unto mankind in Christ Jesu our Lord. And grant, O most merciful Father, for his sake, That we may hereafter live a godly, righteous, and sober life, To the glory of thy holy Name. Amen.[8]

These form prayers provoke a common question about prayers in worship: should prayers be spontaneous, or should they follow a set form? First, we should know that we are not on the horns of this dilemma. We

---

7. Calvin, *Form of Prayers and Songs*, 308.
8. Gibson and Earngey, *Reformation Worship*, 396.

can and should use both. In using form prayers, I hope you will easily note that the prayers previously quoted are magnificent examples of great prayers. Their grammar, syntax, vocabulary, and theology are so obviously superior to the ramblings of many contemporary worship leaders whose prayers are peppered with stuttering, bumblings such as "Daddy God we just want to come to you and just say, just that you are just so awesome." If you think I'm exaggerating, then you haven't recently attended a large Evangelical church in America.

Great prayers from historic liturgies certainly have more excellence and beauty than the spontaneous stuttering of sloppy, ill-prepared and theologically uneducated "worship leaders." Still, you might ask, do all our prayers in worship need to follow as set form? Of course, the answer is "no," we should not exclusively use form prayers, but we should certainly use them in worship.

Even many of the Puritans and Scottish Covenanters of the seventeenth century who rejected the form liturgies of the Anglican Church did not reject form prayers altogether as a matter of principle. They rejected the requirement of forms of prayers and the obligation for certain postures for communion, etc. In particular, they did not believe that the scriptures gave the civil government the authority to demand certain rites such as kneeling at communion, sign of the cross, etc. As such they rejected the idea of arbitrarily "requiring" specific forms or postures; not that forms and postures were somehow wrong per se.

The most significant Scottish Covenanter leader, Alexander Henderson, who led Scottish clerics in resistance to Charles I's liturgical changes, which actually developed into a civil war did not object to the use of such form prayers or prayer books in worship. Henderson resisted the King because he did not believe the church or the state had the divine authority to "require" or "force" the use of forms, prayer books or liturgies in worship. He was not opposing the use of form prayers per se, but he resisted the issue of authority or what Henderson called, "blind obedience" to required forms of liturgy.[9]

In fact, someone who would try to reject the use of form prayers altogether will have a bit of trouble because our savior himself gave us a form prayer commonly called the Lord's Prayer (Matt. 6:9-14; Luke 11:2-4), which is also useful in worship. Therefore, one cannot reject form prayers outright whether in private or in corporate worship. In

---

9. Jackson, *Riots, Revolutions, Scottish*, 52–58.

fact, one cannot formulate a scriptural argument for the sole use of either spontaneous or form prayers. Both have a proper place in worship, and both are blessings in worship.

I might add, however, that anyone who leads in a worship assembly and addresses God in prayer should not do so unprepared. It's one thing to pray without using a set form, but it's quite another to pray without some meaningful preparation. Remembering the courtroom illustration, we would never stand before the judge without first having reflected on the words and approach we would use in speaking to him. I recommend spending quality time preparing for any prayers in public worship. One beneficial habit is weaving portions of the Psalms into your prayers to provide exceptional form and content in theology. This helps us to be more excellent in our prayers and it helps people to hear God's own words prayed to him and therefore it helps us to hide God's words in our hearts. Whether in lament or in praise, the Psalms provide a variety of excellent prayers for us to use in our prayers. If you're honest you will note that rarely does your own small experience match the elevated quality and depth of the Psalms of David and Solomon.

Certainly, the minister or the elder praying in worship should be prepared and his prayers should be first-rate. At the same time, he should be careful not to pray so that he is impressing the church with his eloquence and rhetoric. This comes under Jesus' own warning not to be hypocritical in public prayers. He says in Matt. 6:5,

> And when you pray, you must not be like the hypocrites. For they love to stand and pray in the synagogues and at the street corners, that they may be seen by others. Truly, I say to you, they have received their reward.

Like the whole of worship, our audience in prayer is not merely the people around us, but our primary audience is God, himself. Prayer is communication with God, and it should be the best we can offer. Herman Hoeksema remarks,

> Prayer is a holy art; and if we would analyze it and expound some of its underlying principles, we will have to approach our task in an attitude of holy reverence. It is the highest possible expression of what lives in the believers' heart by grace. Not in our works, not in our sacrifices and offerings, but in our speech,

in the words of our mouth, and particularly in our prayers it is that God is glorified the most.[10]

We use a variety of styles in our prayers because prayer comes in a variety of shapes and forms. If you ask a child about prayer, they will most likely say that prayer is "talking to God." It's true that prayer allows us to speak to God and since communication is at the heart of every loving relationship, prayer is vital to our relationship with God. However, beyond merely "speaking to God," we could think of prayer using the Westminster Shorter Catechism Q/A 98,

> Prayer is an offering up of our desires to God with things agreeable to his will, in the name of Christ with confession of our sins and thankful acknowledgement of his mercies.

In principle this definition covers most everything though not in detail. For instance, there is not specific mention of praise, but it could be understood as a part of "thankful acknowledgement of his mercies." Our prayers should include praise not merely for God's mercies, but also for who God is in all his power and greatness, as creator, sustainer, etc. This is particularly true of prayer in an assembly for worship.

As already noted, scriptural worship is what we call "dialogical," and prayer is a central part of this dialogue. In worship we dialogue or communicate formally with our God, and he communicates back to us in word and sacraments. In one sense, we could call worship a corporate conversation with our God. Different parts of worship involve God speaking to us. In the greeting, the call to worship, the reading and preaching of the scriptures and benediction—God is communicating to his people through an ordained pastor/elder. In other parts of the worship service the worshipers communicate to God, through praise, and here we are thinking of particularly through our prayers.

In a worship service, prayers are an offering up to God our desires. It might, therefore, strike us as odd that many churches actually tell folks to bow their head and close their eyes. This is not a common scriptural posture for prayer, but it is a very common posture among Protestants. Instead, we look heavenward and lift our eyes and hands to God asking him to hear us because of Jesus Christ. The great puritan Matthew Henry wrote on prayers of praise saying,

---

10. Hoeksema, *In the Sanctuary*, 9.

> Let us now lift up our hearts along with our eyes and hands to God in the heavens. Let us stir ourselves up to take hold of God as we seek his face . . . We lift up our souls to you, O Lord. Help us to direct our full attention to you with undistracted devotion. Keep our hearts from being far from you as we draw near to you with our mouths and honor you with our lips. With humble boldness we enter the most holy of all places through the blood of Jesus.[11]

In prayer the voice of God's people ascends to him through Jesus Christ offering him praise, thanksgiving, intercessions, supplications, and a variety of expressions of communication. In this case, a posture of standing with eyes and hands raised to heaven would be most appropriate. As an essential element of public worship, prayer must be offered in faith, in the name of Jesus and by the help of the Holy Spirit.

Churches can benefit from praying what are sometimes called a collect prayer. The word comes from the idea that the prayer is a collection, gathering or summary of the ideas from the scripture reading used in worship for a particular day. A collect prayer is usually short prayer succinctly focused on a theme such as love, unity, or purity as found in the following written by Thomas Cramner:

> Almighty God, unto whom all hearts are open, all desires known, and from whom no secrets are hid; cleanse the thoughts of our hearts by the inspiration of thy Holy Ghost, that we may perfectly love thee, and worthily magnify thy Holy Name; through Christ our Lord. Amen.[12]

Such prayers are a useful and a beautiful blessing for crying out to God and in doing so they also reinforce the teachings of our savior in worship. This helps us to remember that worship is discipleship. So, while our liturgy should be centered on God, it is also the principal means of discipleship. These short, but powerful prayers can also have good benefit for those the congregation whose attention often fads after several minutes of a prolonged theological tome that comes in the form of a prayer.

After a greeting and call to worship the minister may offer a prayer of invocation: asking God to send his Spirit to be with them in worship. We already mentioned a prayer of confession of sins: asking God's mercy, forgiveness and restoration. It's appropriate for a minister to pray for

---

11. Henry, *Way to Pray*, 2.
12. Rice and Huffstutler, *Reformed Worship*, 113.

illumination before preaching God's word and when he finishes preaching to prayer for the Spirit to apply God's word to our hearts. In worship we pray at the reception of the offering, at baptisms, at the Lord's Supper, at moments of pastoral concern, and in all fitting occasions in which we speak to God. As we pray by faith according to the will of God, he is pleased to listen to us and to respond to us with love and blessings, and each of these various kinds of prayers should give attention to posture.

In worship our prayers ascend upwards to heaven like incense. The image of prayer as incense is common in the scriptures. This image teaches us that God is pleased when his people pray to him like someone who smells the sweet aroma of beautiful perfumes or incense. Ps. 141:2 says,

> Let my prayer be counted as incense before you, and the lifting
> up of my hands as the evening sacrifice!

As those gathered in the presence of our God and King we want to speak to God with our prayers and we want them to ascend to him as sweet-smelling aromas that please him.

There are so many references to God's reception of worship and sacrifice as someone who is soothed by a beautiful perfume. The image reminds me of coming home from work early in my marriage and smiling because I smelled the beautiful fragrance of my wife's perfume lingering in our house. I was comforted and moved when I smelled her perfume in our home, our pillows, our car and everywhere we shared life together. This is what we want in worship. We want God to hear our prayers and be pleased with them as if he were breathing in the aroma of a comforting fragrance of someone he loves. The scriptures tell us that God is pleased with the prayers of the righteous.

> The sacrifice of the wicked is an abomination to the LORD, but
> the prayer of the upright is acceptable to him. (Prov. 15:8)

We often think of prayer as "asking" for things. However, the scriptures provide a variety of prayers for us. This is certainly why God has not offered us a single "form" prayer, but as noted in our earlier definition of prayer God teaches his people about the underlying principles of prayer. Paul says in Phil. 4:5 that when we are anxious, we should approach God with prayer and supplications. We find prayers described as requests, intercessions, pleading, thanksgiving, praise, etc.; the natural activity of God's humble peopled—and God loves to receive them.

Postures accompany the various kinds of prayers. For instance, raising hands in prayer is part of the natural posture of someone humbly pleading with God in prayer. We raise our hands in prayer to God as we grapple with any of the things in our lives that are serious, painful, important, etc. The posture of raised hands in prayer is an image of someone who is pleading with God as if he were a poor beggar asking for something with his empty hands. The empty hands opened upwards are a symbol of both the need we have and the hope that our empty hands will be filled by God. This is also what we see in this posture in the scriptures.

To my fearful reformed friends, I should add that here we are not referring to merely to raising hands as is common in contemporary worship. The Bible rarely associates raising hands with "ecstatic praise," like people do at rock concerts or as many who wave their hands individually in contemporary worship services. Rather the raising of hands in prayer with palms upwards is more common in the scriptures. The scriptures speak of spreading out the palms or opening up the hands to God. See Ezra 9:5

> And at the evening sacrifice I rose from my fasting, with my garment and my cloak torn, and fell upon my knees and spread out my hands to the LORD my God.

Biblical scholar, Daniel I. Block comments that the practice of raising hands in worship for requests, entreaties and prayers is a common, natural gesture of worshippers. Worshippers, Block says,

> would spread out their palms to YHWH, to the temple, or to the sky/heavens (I Kgs. 8:22, 54; 2 Chr. 6:12-13). Contrary to pervasive practice today, the First Testament rarely associates "raising the hands" with praise.[13]

We see for example one great example of a lifting up our empty hands in prayer in Psalm 63:4-5 where the psalmist speaks of a serious problem that is answered when he raises his hands in prayer. It is as if God filled his empty hands with the answer he needed when he prayed as soon as he raised them to God.[14] In places like Ps. 63:4-5 the Psalmist actually equates the posture with the prayer. The New Testament does the same thing in I Tim. 2:8,

---

13. Block, *For the Glory of God*, 196.
14. Block, *For the Glory of God*, 196.

> I desire then that in every place the men should pray, lifting holy
> hands without anger or quarreling.

Lifting up our hands is a literary device called a metonym, which is when a related word or phrase is substituted for the actual thing to which it's referring. In this case raising hands can be substituted for prayer and vice-versa. So just as we would naturally kneel for our prayers of confession, we also would naturally raise our hands in prayer for our needs, intercessions and in thanksgiving for the answers to these prayers.

Raising hands in prayer is a very ancient and apparently common posture for prayer. The posture was so common that in the early Middle Ages people referred to it as the *orant*: praying with palms raised. The orant can be found on depictions as early as the catacombs of classical Rome, in very old carvings and ancient art throughout Christian history. These depictions are pervasive in the east and the west and throughout church history showing men and women with their hands raised in prayer.

Raising hands in prayer and praise is not only ancient it is scriptural. Ps. 134:2 commends this posture for public worship saying,

> Lift up your hands in the sanctuary and praise the LORD.

As noted earlier, this posture is so basic to prayer that Paul uses it as something that virtually stands in the place of prayer. I Tim. 2:8,

> I desire then that in every place the men should pray, lifting holy
> hands without anger or quarreling.

One major obstacle to raising hands in worship is fear. Because raising hands in worship is associated with charismatic or Pentecostal practices, some people fear it, thus defining their worship liturgies from fear rather than faith. To contrary, faith should guide us in worship, not fear. By faith as embodied beings we kneel to confess our sins and by faith we lift our hands as beggars to ask God for help and to praise him. It might be worth noting that one of the most common postures for prayer in many contemporary worship services is sitting down. Yet of all the postures that the scriptures refer to in prayer none indicates sitting down as a commended posture! This of course does not forbid such a posture, but it surely reminds us that sitting is not a scripturally recommended posture for prayer and it might need to be reconsidered as the primary posture in prayer in worship.

It also reminds us that it may be time to reconsider how we have structured the posture and liturgy in our worship services in general. If we are going to use the scriptures to look to what God thinks will bless us then standing, kneeling, and raising hands are some of God's suggestions worth considering. While you may feel free to reject my own personal suggestions, hopefully you won't feel the same liberty at rejecting God's suggested postures as anything other than good postures for prayer. Don't let fear define your worship—worship by faith.[15]

In prayer we come to our God by faith in Jesus Christ and we speak to him in especially in worship. Prayer is one of the most important activities we do in private and in public worship. Along with the study of the word of God one pastor argues that "prayer is one of the two ultimate tests of true spirituality."[16] Adding to this idea Martin Lloyd-Jones says,

> Prayer is beyond any question the highest activity of the human soul. Man is at his greatest and highest when, upon his knees, he comes face to face with God.[17]

Because prayer is such a vital and central part of who we are as Christians it must be a vital element of our public worship. Terry Johnson aptly notes,

> Prayer is primarily drawing near to God (e.g. Jas. 4:8-10; Heb. 4:15,16; 10:19-22). What am I doing in prayer? I am consciously moving into the presence of God. Prayer was evolving in my thinking from being primarily about requests (an experientially sterile idea) to being primarily about fellowship with God. Prayer is that time when I draw near to God to contemplate his greatness, search my soul, confess my sin, and plead for help.[18]

Notice that Johnson references Jas. 4 where there is a promise that if we draw near to God, he will draw near to us. May God give his church a renewed sense of the importance and centrality of prayer and thus a deep desire to draw near to God in prayer in worship—longing for the promise fulfilled in Christ that he will draw near to us. If this is true, and it is, then using appropriate postures in prayer will most certainly deepen our experience when praying in worship.

---

15. While Christians are at liberty to use many postures, we must also ask the reasonable question as to which postures are most appropriate for public, corporate worship. Since worship is a gathering of many people in one location it would stand to reason that falling on the floor prostrate would not be appropriate for public corporate worship. While it may be fitting for private prayers of a certain character there are natural and reasonable (by the light of nature) guidelines for certain postures in prayer.

16. MacArthur, *Jesus' Pattern of Prayer*, 13.

17. Lloyd-Jones, *Studies in the Sermon*, 2:45.

18. Johnson, *When Grace Comes Alive*, 18.

CHAPTER 5

Preaching in Worship

IF WORSHIP IS A formal dialogue between God and his people, then preaching should be thought of as the voice of Jesus at the center of this great conversation. According to John 10 Jesus tells us that his sheep hear his voice which is the primary source of direction for them. He says, my sheep hear my voice, and they follow me. Rom. 10:17 also reminds us,

> So faith comes from hearing, and hearing through the word of Christ.

Of all the elements of worship preaching is often treated either as a theological lecture or time for funny stories and moral exhortation. This also tends to reduce preaching to an entirely intellectual enterprise. However, preaching is no less an embodied experience than any other part of worship. As the voice of Christ in worship, preaching is one of the most substantial issues for any study of worship. In this element of worship, no less than in others we should be looking at substance (theology) and the style (posture). Pastors should never think of their sermons as theological lectures where they are filling up their parishioner's brains with theological factoids. Rather, they should think of themselves as engaging with God's people in every way. They should actively engage their hearers and they should interact with them speaking in such a way that those who hear them should look, listen, shake their head in agreement, yes perhaps even say amen—and yes out loud.

If you want to really disrupt an overly theological sermon, try saying amen to a portion that moves you deeply! Yet, this is how a preacher should preach—the preacher should be calling out a response in the hearts of his listeners. The pastor's eyes should be looking into the eyes of God's people to see how they are responding to the voice of Jesus and the people should be actively engaged in the same way. Who could be passive when confronted with the voice of Jesus in such a way?

Preaching like this has been central especially since the Reformation in the days of Martin Luther. In fact, the Protestant Reformation was in no small part a consequence of renewed awakening in preaching. One scholar notes that during the Reformation,

> The sermon was so fundamental a part of church life. It also played an important role in the wider information culture of premodern society. In a world where most information continued to be conveyed by word of mouth, few could doubt that preaching represented one of the primary means of communication with a wider public. . . (and pastors) All, without exception, regarded preaching as fundamental to their duty as pastors, and to their evangelical mission.[1]

The same was true for many Protestant nations more than a generation after the Reformation began. In Scotland, for instance, Margo Todd explains that "the sermon came to be the central event of feast and fast, of regular Sunday worship and sacramental seasons."[2] Andrew Pettegree argues that,

> The role of preaching also tells us much about the culture of the new Protestant churches. This was intensely biblical. Sermons assumed a high level of interest in, if not always knowledge of, the text and meaning of Scripture. The expository method led congregations patiently through the books of the Bible, familiar and unfamiliar. The long regular hours of the expository sermons thus played an important catechismal function, even outside the formal catechism sermons set by many churches for Sunday afternoons . . . It was the bedrock around which the churches harnessed other communication media.[3]

---

1 Pettegree, *Reformation and Culture of Persuasion*, 10.
2. Todd, *Culture of Protestantism*, 24.
3. Pettegree, *Reformation and Culture of Persuasion*, 39.

The powerful and crucial role of preaching in worship meant that the scriptures were also made central to Christian life and culture. "The Bible, the Bible only," wrote Henry Chillingworth in 1638, "is the religion of Protestants."[4] Patrick Collinson comments that "since for Protestants religion was not one compartment of a segmented life but all-enveloping, this must also mean that the Bible only is the culture of Protestants."[5]

Since preaching is so essential to worship, what is it? What is preaching? Perhaps it should be obvious, but many people are confused. In some traditions preaching has been reduced to tiny moral lessons (sometimes called homilies) that always have a cute point so that everyone leaves church feeling like they heard a religious and "uplifting" message; they feel good, and this seems to be the basic point. Other traditions seem to have made the sermon into a time for running around or sitting on a stool and alternating between screaming and laughing and telling stories. For them preaching is a kind of religious entertainment and the preacher is the great showman. Lamenting this problem Michael Green says,

> The standard of preaching in the modern world is deplorable. There are few great preachers. Many clergy do not seem to believe in it any more as a powerful way in which to proclaim the gospel and change the life. This is the age of the sermonette: and sermonettes make for Christianettes.[6]

Preaching is different if you focus on what the Bible says about it. The word, preach, as it is used in the scriptures means to proclaim (Matt.10:7). Preaching could even be translated as heralding. In ancient days when kings and queens wanted their subjects to hear a message, they sent out their words by means of royal heralds or messengers. These heralds stood in well-known public places and proclaimed the words of their masters. It was accepted that as these heralds unsealed the letters from their rulers in front of the people and then proclaimed it that the message coming from the herald's lips were the very words of the king, himself. The royal messengers were not allowed to make up their own messages; the herald was the voice of the king. As such preaching in worship should be the clear proclamation of the voice of Jesus in all its fullness.

If preaching is not the proclaiming of God's message, then you can be sure the church will wonder from her Lord's direction as lost sheep

---

4. Todd, *Reformation to Revolution*, 35.
5. Todd, *Reformation to Revolution*, 35.
6. Green, "Editor's Preface," 7.

without the voice of their shepherd. This is why Robert Lewis Dabney, a nineteenth century author, on the subject of preaching, once said,

> The pulpit may always be taken as an index of that of the church. Whenever the pulpit is evangelical, the piety of the people is in some degree healthy; a perversion of the pulpit is surely followed by spiritual apostasy in the Church.[7]

Preaching is the proclamation of the word of God. *The Directory of Public Worship for the Orthodox Presbyterian Church* (II.A.3.a) says the following:

> In the sermon, God addresses the congregation by the mouth of his servant, and through his Spirit opens the ears of his people.

When we think of genuine biblical preaching, we should think of the Holy Spirit acting through the power of speech. Genuine preaching is a mysterious display of divine power and it's an amazing work of God. Regarding the power of preaching, the great preacher Martyn Lloyd-Jones noted,

> If there is no power, it is not preaching. True preaching, after all, is God acting. It is not just a man uttering words; it is God using him. He is being used of God. He is under the influence of the Holy Spirit; it is what Paul calls in I Cor, 2 'preaching in demonstration of the Spirit of power.' Or as he puts it in I Thess. 1:5: 'Our gospel came not unto you in word only, but also in power, and in the Holy Ghost, and in much assurance . . .' There it is; and that is an essential element of true preaching.[8]

Preaching is the authoritative proclamation of the word of God, and this is worth thinking about. In fact, preaching is in and of itself an authoritative act of God. According to Oliver O'Donovan,

> It was a Christian insight that the capacity to give instruction was actually a kind of authority, parallel to, through different from, the capacity to give effective commands . . . Jesus' teaching-ministry, then is taken by the evangelists to be something more than instruction. It is a disclosure of the reign of God, through which the authority of God asserts itself. Jesus'

---

7. Dabney, *Evangelical Eloquence*, 27.
8. Lloyd-Jones, *Preaching and Preachers*, 95.

authority consists in his capacity to bring us directly into contact with God's authority.[9]

This is true of preaching. Preaching displays the power of words in general, but more importantly it exhibits the power of God's words. R.L. Dabney argued truly that eloquence is the "emission of the soul's energy through speech."[10] If we can imagine for a moment that Dabney is at least partially correct, then the parallel in preaching is astonishingly powerful. Imagine preaching as divine eloquence: the emission of God's celestial energy and essence through the speech of a minister of God! What a great image!

In fact, this image parallels the images provided in the scriptures in multiple ways. It's an image that takes us back to the very opening words of the Bible: "in the beginning God." Yes, God spoke and by the word of his power and in speaking, he created all things. In creation through the power of words, God said let there be light—and light was. God's speech communicates true divine power and literally brings things into existence that did not exist prior to the divine speech act. This is sometimes called creation *ex nihilo*: out of nothing (except from the power of God's words). This is most certainly why John's gospel refers to Jesus as the *logos*, the word.

Jesus is called many things, but this reference to him as the logos is powerful. He is the one who makes sense of everything as the word of God incarnate. God speaks personally in the world in the person and work of Jesus Christ, and it's Jesus' ongoing participation or what one might even say Jesus' ongoing speech that holds the universe in existence. Jesus' spoke and the world came into existence and Jesus continues to hold things together by the word of his power. Paul speaks about centrality of Jesus' power in Col. 1:15–17.

> He is the image of the invisible God, the firstborn of all creation. For by him all things were created, in heaven and on earth, visible and invisible, whether thrones or dominions or rulers or authorities—all things were created through him and for him. And he is before all things, and in him all things hold together.

Likewise, God speaks in preaching with the same kind of divine authority, and we should pay attention. This can be overwhelming to think about, and quite exciting. When a preacher preaches the word of

---

9. O'Donovan, *Desire of the Nations*, 89.
10. Dabney, *Evangelical Eloquence*, 32.

God faithfully and the Holy Spirit uses these words to awaken sinners, direct them, teach them, illuminate their hearts, awaken their conscience, soften their hearts, provoke them with sorrow towards repentance, and more, then this is the same power at work in us by which God also created the world. Paul captures our imagination regarding this power by referring to us to the work of resurrection in Eph. 1:16–20.

> I do not cease to give thanks for you, remembering you in my prayers, that the God of our Lord Jesus Christ, the Father of glory, may give you the Spirit of wisdom and of revelation in the knowledge of him, having the eyes of your hearts enlightened, that you may know what is the hope to which he has called you, what are the riches of his glorious inheritance in the saints, and what is the immeasurable greatness of his power toward us who believe, according to the working of his great might that he worked in Christ when he raised him from the dead and seated him at his right hand in the heavenly places.

By the word of his power, God created the world and raised Jesus from the dead, and this is the same immeasurably great power that is at work in us—especially in the ongoing work of preaching. In preaching like in the very creation of the world God speaks and by the word of his power the dead come to life, hearts of stone become hearts of flesh, and light dispels darkness. Yes, think of this, in preaching there is a sense in which God's words are spoken like we saw in Genesis. Through the preacher, God says "let there be light in the souls of men"—and light is! Preaching is the amazing power of God at work in us that comes to us from our risen savior in heaven who speaks through his ordained preacher here on earth with the power of God. What an amazing thing to experience in worship! One critical element of this way of thinking is to remember as already noted that the power and authority of preaching is not from the eloquence of words per se, but the persuasiveness, beauty, and power of God's word through the Holy Spirit. Speaking to God's command in II Tim. 4:2 to preach the word. Jay Adams is right to say,

> Preachers today have no authority for preaching their own notions and opinions; they must "preach the Word"—the apostolic Word recorded in the Scriptures. Whenever preachers depart from the purpose and the intent of a biblical portion, to that extent they lost their authority to preach. In short, the purpose of reading, explaining, and applying a portion of Scripture is to obey the command to "preach the Word." In no other

way may we expect to experience the presence and power of the Holy Spirit in our preaching.[11]

As God speaks, he creates. In preaching, God's speech is an inherently powerful act that divinely awakens the dead to new life in Christ and then directs them to follow Christ. Preaching is the most important part of the discipleship in worship. The Scottish preacher, James Stewart once said that the aim of all preaching was,

> to quicken the conscience by the holiness of God, to feed the mind with the truth of God, to purge the imagination by the beauty of God, to open the heart to the love of God, to devote the will to the purpose of God.[12]

The power of preaching is ironic because it's a medium that appears to be weak. Since preaching is ministerial and declarative and thus lacks the coercive power of things like the use of police force, etc., it is apparently weak. This is particularly true because genuine preaching includes the cross, which to the world is a glaring weakness and a colossal failure.

> And I, when I came to you, brothers, did not come proclaiming to you the testimony of God with lofty speech or wisdom. For I decided to know nothing among you except Jesus Christ and him crucified. And I was with you in weakness and in fear and much trembling, and my speech and my message were not in plausible words of wisdom, but in demonstration of the Spirit and of power, so that your faith might not rest in the wisdom of men but in the power of God. (1 Cor. 2:1–5)

Such preaching depends entirely on the persuasion of God's words that Paul says are not used inappropriately to trick, intimidate, or manipulate. These are words that form an apparently weak and even foolish message. Paul goes on to say,

> For Christ did not send me to baptize but to preach the gospel, and not with words of eloquent wisdom, lest the cross of Christ be emptied of its power. For the word of the cross is folly to those who are perishing, but to us who are being saved it is the power of God. For it is written, "I will destroy the wisdom of the wise, and the discernment of the discerning I will thwart." (1 Cor. 1:18–19)

---

11. Adams, *Preaching with Purpose*, 19.
12. Stewart, *Heralds of God*, 26.

Paul was not objecting to the traditional notion of eloquence as beautiful persuasion. Every preacher should want to be eloquent per se. Rather, he was simply objecting to those who spoke publicly like the ancient sophists as merely linguistic showmen. Men who used lofty words and semantic illusions to impress their hearers and to trick their listeners into a false conclusion. R. L. Dabney notes,

> The spurious and unworthy art, which is here rejected, was that of the Greek Sophists—a system of mere tricks of logic and diction, prompted by vanity and falsehood, and misguided by a depraved taste. It was this pretentious rhetoric so scathed by the sarcasm and reasoning of Socrates in *Gorgias*.[13]

If Paul refuses to use sophistic tricks and manipulation, then how does preaching ever accomplish anything? The clear answer is that the Holy Spirit uses the foolishness of preaching God's word to save and to sanctify sinners. The gospel Paul says is the power of God unto salvation and Paul spoke of the central means by which the gospel is promoted—in preaching! Gardiner Spring reminds us,

> The pulpit is powerless where the cross of Christ is not magnified. Christ must be the theme, the scope, the life, the soul of the pulpit. It may have the subtleties of philosophy, the attainments of accomplished literature, and the enticing words which man's wisdom teaches; but it has no powerful attraction of God's truth, where Christ is wanting. The preacher may not hope to see the strong cords of earth broken, the fetters of gold dissolved, or any of the fascinations of sin disturbed by which the spell-bound mind is held in bondage, until he throws around it the stronger attractions of the redeeming love. There is wondrous power in the pulpit where the cross is lifted up, and where instead of attracting men to himself the minister of God would fain attract them to his and their Savior.[14]

This means that preaching should involve careful preparation and extraordinary skill. Martin Luther believed that a preacher should study hard to know the word of God to communicate it clearly to the church. Speaking of Martin Luther, one author notes,

> Some preachers, he wrote in 1542 are lazy and no good. They do not pray, they do not study, they do not read; they do not search

---

13. Dabney, *Evangelical Eloquence*, 17.
14. Spring, *Power of the Pulpit*, 46.

the Scripture ... In truth, you cannot read too much Scripture, and what you read you cannot read too carefully. Luther's sermons were built around a careful exposition of the Scripture text. He followed the text form first to last, usually in a continuous sequence of sermons that dealt over a longer period with a whole book or Gospel. The method would become the leitmotif of the great reformers, many of whom left, as a principal legacy of their writings, great series of such expository sermons.[15]

For Luther, the pastor was fundamentally a preacher/prophet who proclaimed the words of God. This meant that the pastor/preacher needed to be well trained and attentive to the needs and frailties of his people. He is to study, understand and then communicate God's word to God's people with passion, love, and clarity. One pastor in the early days of the Protestant Reformation stated,

> The sermon ought to be held with great warmth and fervent love for the listeners, for their improvement and edification in God as takes place among the pious. Thus, the sheep of Christ hear the voice of their Lord, the true shepherd. They follow it because they recognize it.[16]

This approach creates a beautiful dynamic between the pastor and his people in weekly worship. As a pastor I can tell you that when my people looked up at me with hungry eyes from week to week, I was inspired to feed them well. Those longing eyes were often weary with struggles of personal sin and battles of weakness and frailty, and they longed to hear the good news of Jesus Christ for comfort and encouragement. Because of this experience, as a theological teacher now, I have often encouraged both preachers and their congregations to be good participants in the preaching and in the listening of God's word.

I have an illustration from my experience as a teacher too. When I taught high school, I oversaw many kinds of classes. I taught introductory classes where the students were required to be there but didn't want to be there; this was more of a struggle as a teacher. To the contrary, when I taught advanced level classes full of excellent, eager students, I was inspired and challenged to do my best for every class. They called me to it. Their excellence as students made it easier for me as a teacher. I never wanted to come to class unprepared because I knew my students would

---

15. Pettegree, *Reformation and Culture of Persuasion*, 18.
16. Pettegree, *Reformation and Culture of Persuasion*, 22.

be ready. This created a great dynamic for me as the teacher and for the students as well. They drew out of me something as a teacher that helped me to draw out of them their best as students. It was a mysterious and great experience that I have never forgotten. In fact, I remember looking forward to seeing the faces of those bright students who were also looking forward to hearing me teach. What an awesome dynamic for teacher and students! The same is true for preaching in worship.

An old fella in Mississippi once told me that when I preached, I should go to church prepared to look into the faces of my congregation and to watch for the Spirit of God "to be reflekin' off the faces of God's people." When their faces shine up to you and your face shines back to them, he said, it "refleks" the beautiful work of God in mysterious ways. It's something, he said, every preacher should want to be a part of—he was so right.

This means that in preaching there is a mutual obligation for preacher and listener. The Westminster Shorter Catechism speaks to this in two questions,

> Q. 89. *How is the word made effectual to salvation?*
>
> A. The Spirit of God makes the reading, but especially the preaching, of the word, an effectual means of convincing and converting sinners, and of building them up in holiness and comfort, through faith, unto salvation.
>
> Q. 90. *How is the word to be read and heard, that it may become effectual to salvation?*
>
> A. That the word may become effectual to salvation, we must attend thereunto with diligence, preparation, and prayer; receive it with faith and love, lay it up in our hearts, and practice it in our lives.

I love this simple admonition to attend to the preaching of the word of God with diligence preparation and prayer, receive it with faith and love and lay I up in our hearts, practicing it in our lives. This makes it clear that preaching involves activity for the preacher and the listener. When we hear the proclamation of the word of God, we should respond and receive it. Can you imagine your own life and the life or an entire congregation where this tiny, little phrase is genuinely practiced? I'm telling you that this would be a church on fire for God!

In many ways it's not too hard to imagine doing this. It would mean making sure that you got a decent night's sleep the day before worship.

It would mean that you would make whatever kinds of adjustments in your life and the life of your family to get ready for worship with care. Every father and mother knows the frustration of crying children who can't find their shoes when it's time to get into the car and go to church. It happens from time to time. We all have those days. However, we should try to do whatever we need to do to attend to the preaching with "diligence, preparation, and prayer."

Imagine an overall disciplined approach to worship where you tried to get ready for church beyond just putting on the right clothes. Your whole life would begin to be organized around and unto worship. You would certainly try to organize your thoughts, and your home around the word of God and worship. You would be praying and looking forward to hearing from God. As the Psalmist describes a deer that pants for water, so my soul longs for God. We could observe an apt description of our hope as we prepared to worship; particularly as we prepare to hear the preaching of God's word. An old puritan preacher was said to remind his listeners that they may sometimes not be able to attend worship because their donkey fell into a ditch. However, he reminded them, that if your donkey is in the ditch every Sunday, it's time to either get a new donkey or fill the ditch!

This idea includes our children. Everyone, including our little ones, should prepare for worship. We should do what we need to do to "let the little children come unto me." Many churches today send out their children from worship to a "children's church" for skits, plays and silliness; it's hard to imagine the teaching and enormous discipline we have lost in today's churches when we dismiss our children from worship.

It was quite common for churches who take preaching seriously not only to include their children in the preaching of God's word, but to require their young people to take an active role as listeners in worship. They ought to be required to listen to the voice of Jesus and remember it. Margo Todd reminds us that at one time in Scotland the inclusion of children in the preaching process was quite serious,

> For an illiterate population, the requirement of repeating the main points of the sermon later to one's master or parent provided an incentive for learning the doctrine by listening very carefully in church.[17]

---

17. Todd, *Culture of Protestantism*, 42.

Excluding children from worship can erode the discipline of mind as well as the mere ability to sit quietly learning and listening to God with self-control that they otherwise would learn in worship. This is also one of the many blessings of making preaching a central part of godly worship even for our children.

Preaching is not a forum for jokesters and storytellers. While a preacher may well use wit and likewise, he may tell a story, such rhetoric should not be for merely clowning around or making people laugh. Preaching should be as beautiful and as eloquent as possible, and the preacher will need illustrations. Jesus himself taught primarily using illustrations that made sense of his teachings for his listeners.

Though not guided by jokes and silly stories the greatest preachers always sought to preach so that the everyone could understand them and thus they directed the voice of Jesus from the highest to the lowest of all listeners. Christopher Ash outlines this in the following:

> The learned Calvin used to preach in Geneva in ordinary French so that any Genevan could understand it, without drawing attention to the great scholarship that lay behind his sermons . . . J.C. Ryle was a highly educated man with a cultured and learned style. But when he ministered in rural parishes, he realized they would not understand him; and so, he 'crucified' his style . . . Luther, like so many whose ministries have been greatly used for the transformation of the church, was a distinguished scholar. But he was very insistent on the need for clarity and simplicity in his preaching: Cursed are all preachers that in the church aim at height and hard things, and, neglecting the saving health of the poor unlearned people, seek their own honor and praise . . . Spurgeon says of some preachers that they 'think in smoke and preach in a cloud. But there is nothing spiritual about preaching in a fog of learning. We must strive for clarity, clarity, clarity.[18]

A serious approach to preaching in worship has positive consequences in many areas of life. In the past, preaching as a central element of worship has both demanded and generated a culture of the word—a literate culture! As an implication this meant that the church needed to train/disciple it's people to read, to write, and to think, which also encouraged serious demands for education, a common feature of Christianity. The sermon of the preached word of God has meant that

---

18. Ash, *Priority of Preaching*, 62–63.

Christianity creates a logocentric or word-centered community. According to James Davidson Hunter,

> The church is, first and foremost, a worshipping community whose life centers on the word of God.[19]

Our lives are centered on the word (*logos*) Jesus Christ. The consequences are brilliant including producing a culture of literacy and reading in serious Christian communities where preaching is central.

Such a focus also carried attendant consequences that are largely lost today. For instance, if the reading and especially the preaching of the word of God was central to a worship service, then as already noted, the church had an associated responsibility to teach its members to be a literate, thinking community. Studies reveal that America has been steadily losing its capacity for advanced reading, and literary skills, and thus I would add the ability to think deeply.[20] T. David Gordon in his skillful little book, *Why Johnny Can't Preach* notes,

> As more Americans lose this capability, our nation becomes less informed, active, and independent-minded. These are not qualities that a free, innovative, or productive society can afford to lose.[21]

I personally believe that this is linked at least in part to the decline of excellent preaching in worship. This has been a source of serious concern for me personally as I have watched American culture slide towards Gomorrah and as previously agreed upon moral norms are destroyed and now openly mocked. I lament the loss that sound preaching could be providing the people of God in this great moment! This is especially painful because the attacks upon traditional family life, traditional moral norms and basic assumptions about humanity and culture are largely connected to linguistic trickery, which a more intelligent culture might easily detect.

Revolutionary thinkers have always targeted language as an important part of their effort to undermine whatever traditional ways of living they are attempting to dismantle. This is very true today. For instance, questions of gender and sexuality are confused by referring to things like homosexuality and/or transgender activity as issues of

---

19. Hunter, *To Change the World*, 184.
20. "Reading at Risk," 21.
21. Gordon, *Why Johnny Can't Preach*, 36.

"equity." Racial questions are wrapped in words like "privilege," which are laced with underlying meanings that require one to think clearly about not merely vocabular meaning and etymology of the words per se, but also on the deeply important nature of assumptions about history, culture, human nature, morality, ethics, etc. T. David Gordon reminds us of the shocking loss here,

> Those human sensibilities (one's capacities to know, understand experience or appreciate certain realities) essential to expository preaching have largely disappeared.[22]

By expository preaching Gordon refers to a virtually lost practice of preaching through large texts of scripture. Let's say a minister decides to preach through the book of Genesis. This means that he and his listeners would be taken through a large work of primarily historical narrative, but they would also be taught through a book that includes history, law, and theology. The preacher and listener would be taken through the whole process of thinking about ancient history, literary devices, literary structures, logical arguments, moral sentiments, and much, much more. Again, Gordon laments,

> Our culture's sensibility of composed, thoughtfully organized communication has disappeared as a common trait.[23]

We are in this sense more exposed and more vulnerable to the attacks of the wicked one who uses craftily designed lies and deadly, but beautifully presented false doctrines to destroy us. It is hard to say how much is a cause and how much is an effect in our cultural/moral decline, but we surely should recognize that God's provided remedy in preaching has lost its clarity and centrality in worship. Preaching has been replaced by any number of items deemed more "relevant." Almost thirty years ago Martyn Lloyd-Jones lamented that films, songs, and testimonies have filled the vacuum left as preaching has declined.

> This is said to attract people to the gospel and to persuade them to listen to it. If you can find an admiral or a general or anyone who has some special title, or a baseball player, or an actor or actress or film-star, or pop-singer or somebody well-known to the public, get them to give their testimony. This is deemed to be much greater value than the preaching and the exposition of the

---

22. Gordon, *Why Johnny Can't Preach*, 36.
23. Gordon, *Why Johnny Can't Preach*, 38.

gospel. Have you noticed that I have put all this under the term *'entertainment?'* . . . This is what the church has been turning to as she has turned her back upon preaching (italics mine).[24]

Serious preaching involves much more. It encompasses a whole array of items described following from part of an old ordination sermon:

> With all possible seriousness preach to your people the Christ whom St. Paul ador'd, the Grace which he taught, the Faith, the Life, the Spirit, the Hope, the Love, and the Sacraments and other services which he recommended. Open to those that sit under your ministry, the foundation of all Religion the Divinity of the Scriptures, and their sufficiency, the Covenant of Grace, the Terms of acceptance with God and the suitableness of the Mediator provided for lapsed creatures, the Riches and Fulness of the Divine Promises, the odiousness and malignity of Sin, the Nature, Necessity and Excellence of Holiness, and the certainty and importance of things eternal.[25]

When preaching devolves into something silly and trivial, the people hearing it are not receiving the kind of sound ethical discipline and direction necessary to live holy lives. Many people in the pews, for instance, would have trouble citing the ten commandments from memory. Furthermore, if trivial preaching follows the culture rather than leading it with the ethical instruction of a God, then the people lose a sense of direction in multiple ways. The result is confusion.

One such concern is the loss of a basic sense of guilt or shame that people ought to feel when they do something that God considers wrong. Here I'm not talking about false guilt or false shame, but a genuine godly sorrow that when something is wrong, we ought to feel shame for it and this sense of shame and guilt leads us to repent and come to Christ for him to remake us in his image. Today we don't have this kind of moral guidance and as such the culture has lost direction. One thinker, James B. Twitchell, notes the loss of shame in American culture saying,

> When I was growing up in the 1950's, public drunkenness, filing for bankruptcy, having an abortion or child out of wedlock, drug addiction, hitting a woman, looting stores, using vulgar language in public, being on the dole (what there was of it), or getting a divorce was enough to make you hang your head . . . Want to feel shame today? Wear a fur coat, smoke in public,

---

24. Lloyd-Jones, *Preaching and Preachers*, 17.
25. Davies, "Puritan Preaching," in *Worship of English Puritans*, 184.

grow fat, have breasts too small or a nose too big, don't recycle, eat meat ... Where did shame go? Or, better yet, how did it get redirected to such often trivial concerns?[26]

One source could well be the trivialization of preaching in worship. Of course, the full answer is more complex and complicated than assigning it to a single cause. Yet, assuming that worship should be a place of intellectual, cultural, and moral direction for millions of Christians then preaching should at least blip the radar screen as one of the usual suspects.

As we think just a bit more on preaching, *The Directory for Public Worship of the Orthodox Presbyterian Church* (III.A.3.b.) provides us with a helpful outline:

> The preacher is to instruct his hearers in the whole counsel of God, exhort the congregation to more perfect obedience to Christ, and warn them of the sins and dangers that are around them and within them. A preacher fails to perform his task as a God-appointed watchman on Zion's walls who neglects to warn the congregation of prevalent soul-destroying teachings by enemies of the gospel.

Preachers are called to proclaim the word of God in all its fullness—not to entertain, but to be the voice of Jesus. This can be serious and at times it includes the watchman's warning of judgment such as we find Ezek. 33:1–6.

> The word of the LORD came to me: "Son of man, speak to your people and say to them, If I bring the sword upon a land, and the people of the land take a man from among them, and make him their watchman, and if he sees the sword coming upon the land and blows the trumpet and warns the people, then if anyone who hears the sound of the trumpet does not take warning, and the sword comes and takes him away, his blood shall be upon his own head. He heard the sound of the trumpet and did not take warning; his blood shall be upon himself. But if he had taken warning, he would have saved his life. But if the watchman sees the sword coming and does not blow the trumpet, so that the people are not warned, and the sword comes and takes any one of them, that person is taken away in his iniquity, but his blood I will require at the watchman's hand.

---

26. Twitchell, *For Shame*, 1.

In summary, we could say that preaching should be focused on Christ and his work as well as all the implications related to what this means to be in Christ. In this sense preaching should be Christological. "Christological preaching," says, T. David Gordon, "feeds the soul and builds faith."[27] He continues,

> Faith is not built by preaching introspectively (constantly challenging people to question whether they have faith); faith is not built by preaching moralistically (which has exactly the opposite effect of focusing attention on the self rather than on Christ, in whom our faith is placed); faith is not built by joining the culture wars and taking potshots at what is wrong with our culture. Faith is built by careful, thorough exposition of the person, character, and work of Christ.[28]

Many people point to the miracles in Acts as the primary means of power in the church. However, even miracles that accompanied Jesus' teachings were not done as individual or disconnected displays of divine authority. They were connected to teaching the word of God. In the book of Acts miracles were part of the apostolic ministry, but never as events disconnected from the word of God. Oliver O'Donovan notes,

> Jesus' power was deployed as a demonstration of God's rule, and their function was to draw attention not to themselves but to the *preaching* of the Kingdom (italics mine).[29]

Preaching like this is how the people of God individually and corporately grow in Christ. In fact, preaching is the primary means of spiritual and numerical growth in the church. From the beginning of the church, preaching was the primary means by which the astonishing growth of the church occurred as Luke records it in the book of Acts. According to David Eby,

> Luke's purpose is obvious. He is teaching how the Word of God is to be preached. He is showing what kind of preaching brings church growth. . . Acts is a manual that God has provided for preachers on preaching. The logic is simple. Here's God's textbook on church growth. *Church growth is preaching growth* (italics mine).[30]

27. Gordon, *Why Johnny Can't Preach*, 75.
28. Gordon, *Why Johnny Can't Preach*, 75–76.
29. O'Donovan, *Desire of the Nations*, 96.
30. Eby, *Power Preaching*, 29.

CHAPTER 6

The Sacraments in Worship

MORE THAN MOST PARTS of Christian liturgy, sacramental worship promotes embodied worship as a whole person. As embodied beings we need the sacraments as a regular part of worship. The sacraments provide us with an embodied mystery necessary to a healthy spiritual life. Some have said that the sacraments use physical matter and physical movements that in the natural order would do for our bodies, what in the supernatural order, they do to our souls. We need the sacraments!

Speaking of the sacraments as a necessary part of worship presents a challenge since we are working in a context where too many Christians describe worship as if it were solely a "spiritual" experience which for some means primarily listening to a great sermon or for others it means having an emotional "religious" experience. As a virtual theme in this book, I will keep noting that this tends to promote either an overly cerebral or an overly emotional approach to worship while belittling our physical existence and our need for a fully human experience in worship that connects to our "spiritual." The sacraments are God's clear reminder that worship includes our physical needs as human beings with real bodies. The sacraments are a beautiful mystery because they are physical, tangible objects that teach us of metaphysical, spiritual realities.

A sacrament is a tangible, physical sign, and seal of the saving grace of God that Jesus Christ has given to the church. It should be obvious since worship involves kneeling, raising, and clapping hands, singing, shouting, and much more that we are to worship God as embodied beings. We need the sacraments. Regarding the sacraments Calvin says,

> because we are of flesh, they are shown us under things of flesh, to instruct us according to our dull capacity and to lead us by the hand as tutors lead children.[1]

I love the illustration of God holding our hands by means of the sacraments. I remember when one of my young sons wanted to follow his older brothers in jumping off a high rock into a swimming area below. His brothers were already in the water yelling for him to jump and he almost went, but he was seriously afraid. I told him to jump too, but he was too frightened for words alone and he said, "daddy hold my hand and we'll jump together." I already told him that he could do it, but there was something so emboldening for him when I took hold of his hand and said I'm jumping with you. God speaks his gospel to us in his word and then he holds our hands in the sacraments adding a personal and beautiful confirmation that says I am with you, and you can trust me. Like a worried child who needs the touch of his father's hands, we need the sacraments.

The sacraments are powerful and necessary parts of true worship that require us to live and to experience the world as embodied beings. One author notes beautifully,

> The sacraments forbid us from escaping the world and the other in order to explain the world and the other. They forbid us from escaping relationships, escaping history, escaping the body, and finding refuge in the realm of "pure" ideas. They commit us to discovering truth in and through the other, in and through relationship, in and through the body, in and through love. They commit us to this world even as they call us to the next. They show us the next world, in order to allow us to become in *this* world living presences of love, living beacons of joy and hope, living icons of God's own love, through and within the experience of love.[2]

The sacraments make it abundantly clear that God wants to hold our hands in worship and thus not only to forbid us from escaping our physical lives in the here and now, but to encourage us to became as

---

1. Calvin, *Institutes of the Christian Religion*, 4.14.6 (p. 1281).
2. Sweeney, *Abiding the Long Defeat*, xxii.

Sweeney noted, "living presences of love."[3] Using physical things such as water, wine and bread God does not merely remind us, but requires us to acknowledge our embodied nature in worship. Worship openly and practically encourages us to glorify and enjoy our God as physical creatures in a physical world. We will see this more pointedly when looking at the Lord's Supper—after all, what could be more physical than eating! The sacraments, oddly, are not warmly received in all circles—and this seems to be motivated less by faith and almost entirely by fear.

The New Testament reference to these rites or rituals use the word, mysteries, which the early church applied to the administration of baptism and the Lord's Supper (see Rom. 16:25-26, Eph.3:3-13, Col. 1:24-27). When the Scriptures were translated into Latin, the word, mystery was replaced with the Latin word, sacrament, which has fallen into disfavor among many Protestants.

I remember once coming home from university and speaking to a family member who was a Baptist pastor. When I mentioned that I was excited because we were learning about the sacraments in my church history class, he literally took hold of my arm as he moved seriously closer to me saying, "please don't ever use that word, the word, sacrament. You sound like a Roman Catholic." I was struck by this because the people from church history that I was studying at the time were all Protestants! The word, sacrament, struck a chord of fear in my uncles' heart that surprised me.

For the record the word sacrament is not Roman Catholic. It derives from the Latin, *sacramentum*, which has a history that is related to the ancient Roman practice of soldiers pledging faithfulness and loyalty using the physical exchange of items connected to the oaths of allegiance that were being mutually pledged. The church father, Tertullian, as early as the second century was one of the first to refer to baptism as a sacrament making the connection to the ancient Roman rites. The idea of sacraments, however, is older than classical culture—sacraments are part of what it means to worship God as an embodied human being.

It was actually quite common before the classical world of Rome that ancient peoples from biblical days participated in sacramental kinds of rituals as part of a normal relationship especially relationships that involved covenants or serious commitments that each party shared in the relationship. There was a basic assumption that the words of a

---

3. Sweeney, *Abiding the Long Defeat*, xxii.

covenant and/or relationship were properly felt and more personally received with the exchange of physical signs of the covenant. This is why we see our father Abraham doing things like eating meals and cutting up animals as part of his ritual, covenantal relationship with God. The ancient world, having never experienced the Enlightenment (which highlights the rational over everything), seems to have been comfortable with the spiritual and physical living in harmony—especially when it relates to religious matters.

In the New Testament God continues using physical items in his relationship with us to encourage us in his love. A biblical sacrament according to John Calvin stated,

> It is an outward sign by which the Lords seals on our consciences the promises of his good will towards us in order to sustain the weakness of our faith; and we in turn attest our piety towards him in the presence of the Lord and of his angels and before men. . . one may call it a testimony of divine grace towards us, confirmed by an outward sign, with mutual attestation of our piety towards him. Whichever of these definitions you may choose, it does not differ in meaning from that of Augustine, who teaches that a sacrament is "a visible sign of a sacred thing," or "a visible form of an invisible grace."[4]

We don't need to push our minds back into the ancient world to understand the value of such physical, tangibles expressions of love. For me personally, at weddings I love to hear the words, "with this ring I thee wed." In our culture we exchange rings as we exchange vows of love and commitment in a wedding ceremony. The future husband and future wife literally take hold of each other's hands and slip on a wedding band as a token of their fidelity and love while they are exchanging marriage vows. It's always amusing to see the new couple coming into the reception hall after the wedding holding up their new wedding rings and later fidgeting with the new symbol on their fingers as they marvel at what this new image means to their lives. They are married and the rings are physical symbols of their vows and of their new life together.

Sacraments are like wedding rings, but better. God employs the sacraments to hold our hands, to provide physical confirmation of his love and to encourage us in this love. The sacraments move us into a world of mystery that pushes us to recognize that our faith in Jesus

---

4. Calvin, *Institutes of the Christian Religion*, 4.14.1 (p. 1277).

Christ is not merely a doctrinal, cerebral commitment to dogmas, but rather our faith also involves a trust in Jesus Christ and the mysteries of what it means for the incomprehensible God of creation to love sinners such as we are. Certainly, the sacraments should never be removed from the context of faith that involves intellectual assent to the orthodox doctrines of our faith. Yet, the sacraments move us to the mystery of our embodied existence which involves holding God's hand even though he has no "hand" to hold.

It may be a good time for Protestants to rediscover the centrality and beauty of rituals in worship. Yes, rituals. For many Protestants with whom I speak the word, ritual is naughty word. It implies mindless religious repetition that has no place in a sincere, personal religious experience. In fact, for these Protestants rituals imply an impersonal and therefore improper act in worship. These ideas are laced with all kinds of bad ideas that separate the body from religious liturgy, which is never what God does.

In the sacraments God reaches down from heaven in the mystery of the physical objects so that our faith moves beyond a mere doctrinal assent to include a personal trust in the one who has died for us and loves us. God knows that we need more than mere dogma—we need to hold his hand. We do not, for instance, believe in a doctrine of Jesus Christ; we believe in the person of Jesus Christ and the sacraments require us to keep the ideas of assent and trust together as they capture our imaginations when we eat and drink the body and blood of our savior or when he washes us with the waters of baptism.

Here I do not mean the imagination by which we conjure up novel images in our minds, but the ability as those who bear the image of God to perceive and to receive images that point beyond the actual items to a spiritual reality at work in us. This is inherently mysterious, and this is what we need; aspects of worship that many Evangelical worship services are sorely missing: mystery. Chesterton, in his great work *Orthodoxy*, said "as long as you have mystery you have health; when you destroy mystery you create morbidity [death]."[5]

The sacraments are God's way of helping to stimulate in our souls the trust we need to follow him. This is not always a purely doctrinal thing. Many times, we face uncertainty and fears that are not answered simply by a doctrinal discussion; they are answered in holding God's

---

5. Chesterton, *Orthodoxy*, 9.

hand and knowing that you can trust him and follow him into an unknown and sometimes hostile future. In remember my grandmother feeling annoyed at my grandpa's funeral when well-meaning Christians quoted scripture verses about all things working together for the good. She said she was most comforted with the quiet physical presence of those who loved her and simply stood with her in her time of grief. The physical presence of her loved ones gave her deep, mysterious comfort that no words could provide.

In the sacraments God's presence is real and tangible. He washes us and feeds us in mysterious ways that inspire us to trust in him. The sacraments help us in times of fear, uncertainty, and doubt to look outside of ourselves and to look solely to Jesus. This helps us to move away from a dangerous kind of obsessive introspection in times of doubt to a healthy and hopeful looking outwardly to Jesus who can be trusted. He holds our hands, and physically stands with us to help us know that we can trust him. The sacraments are a necessary curative to the flood of doubts that flow into our lives and without the sacraments we might be paralyzed by fear and doubt. The sacraments turn us outside of ourselves as they turn our eyes to Jesus. What a blessing!

For Christians the sacraments are even more important than mere encouragement—sacraments are a divinely appointed means of grace. It is important to notice that a sacrament is not something the church created, which so many Protestants associate with Roman Catholicism, but a sacrament is something God instituted for us through the ministry of Jesus Christ. Sacraments are something he wants us to have, and they are not optional. The Westminster Shorter Catechism in Q. 92 summarizes it nicely it in the following way:

> A sacrament is an holy ordinance instituted by Christ, wherein, by sensible signs, Christ, and the benefits of the new covenant, are represented, sealed, and applied to believers.

Jesus provides us with these sacraments as tangible, physical signs, and seals of God's love that he promises to us in the Gospel. God works through the sacraments to give us grace. They are God's means of grace to confirm and strengthen us in the faith that he has already given us. What God promises to us in the Gospel (the forgiveness of sins) is confirmed in baptism and the Lord's Supper. The Gospel proclaims his promises in words and the sacraments by the power of Holy Spirit provides grace in confirming and encouraging us in the promises of our new life in Christ.

Like the Westminster Shorter Catechism, the Heidelberg Catechism in Q. 65 defines the two sacraments of baptism and the Lord's Supper as "holy signs and seals for us to see." Sacraments help us to appreciate the gospel and they assist us in trusting more firmly in the promises of the gospel. They are not additional extras or optional trimmings—they are central to what God wants us to have as blessings to us as we follow him. In the sacraments of the Lord's Supper and baptism, we are encouraged to remember God's covenant words, "I will be your God and you will be my people." I would remind the reader that the sacraments confirm God's work in us—not our work for God. The sacraments emphasize what God does for sinners through Jesus Christ. To review again Calvin says,

> The sacraments, therefore, are exercises which make us more certain of the trustworthiness of God's Word. And because we are of flesh, they are shown us under things of flesh, to instruct us according to our dull capacity and to lead us by the hand as tutors lead children. Augustine calls a sacrament a "visible word" for the reason that it represents God's promises as painted in a picture and sets them before our sight, portrayed graphically and in a manner of images.[6]

I will spend an entire chapter on the Lord's Supper or Eucharist but this chapter we will finish looking primarily to the New Testament sacrament of baptism. Baptism is one of the most central symbols of our faith. It is so central to Christianity that Jesus himself commands it in the Great Commission found in Matt. 28:19,

> Go therefore and make disciples of all nations, baptizing them in the name of the Father and of the Son and of the Holy Spirit.

Baptism is the tip of the spear in our kingdom warfare as Jesus announces the Great Commission. It marks out disciples as belonging to Jesus, and it simultaneously calls them to follow after the one by whom and for whom they have been marked out.

I had a friend from Syria who told me how important baptism was to Muslims where he lived. He said to my surprise that as a young man he was free to interact in many ways with Christians. He was free to be friends with Christians. He could attend Bible studies with Christians,

---

6. Calvin, *Institutes of the Christian Religion*, 4.14.6 (p. 1281).

worship services and he was even allowed to date a Christian woman. However, the one line he and others were never allowed to cross was baptism because baptism marks the one baptizes as belonging heart and soul to Jesus Christ. The Muslims he described understood that baptism calls one to a complete renunciation of all other gods and a whole-hearted pledge to Jesus alone. This has such radical implications that the Muslims take it seriously. After hearing my friends' stories, I wondered why Christians don't take baptism as seriously as Muslims?

In Rom. 6 Paul argues that our baptisms mark us out as those who are united to the resurrection work of Jesus Christ. Paul uses baptism to remind us, or as it were, to call us to our new life in Christ. He says,

> Do you not know that all of us who have been baptized into Christ Jesus were baptized into his death? We were buried therefore with him by baptism into death, in order that, just as Christ was raised from the dead by the glory of the Father, we too might walk in newness of life. Rom. 6:3–4

Oddly enough some people use these verses to argue that the mode of baptism must be immersion because of the death, burial, and resurrection imagery here. However, this passage has nothing to do with mode (for anyone) and everything to do with associating baptism with our union with Christ—most importantly in his resurrection power, which enables us to be holy as he is holy. Our baptism has a powerful connection to Paul's call that "we too must walk in newness of life." Baptism provides us with a mighty symbol that calls us to follow after Jesus Christ. In fact, every time each of us witnesses a baptism we are called to consider our own baptisms, and, in this experience, God urges us to continue to walk in newness of life. Connor Sweeney speaks nicely of this call on our lives as the gift baptism stating,

> Baptism is the first gift of the kingdom of heaven to the person, the in-breaking of that kingdom into the experience of the person as a fundamental call, summons . . . It is the gift that will allow a completely and utterly transformed relation to reality and to God for the person.[7]

According to *The Directory of Public Worship the Orthodox Presbyterian Church* (III.B.2)

---

7. Sweeney, *Abiding the Long Defeat*, 116.

The Lord Jesus Christ instituted baptism as a covenant sign and seal for his church. He uses it not only for the solemn admission of the person who is baptized into the visible church, but also to depict and to confirm his ingrafting of that person into himself and his including that person in the covenant of grace. The Lord uses baptism to portray to us that we and our children are conceived and born in sin and need to be cleansed.[8]

Baptism is a sacrament with water in the name of the Father, the Son, and the Holy Spirit. Biblically and historically the water should be sprinkled or poured on the person being baptized. This is true because the word baptize means simply to wash, and the only scripturally prescribed washings were all done by pouring or sprinkling. This is why throughout church history and even up to the present-day most Christians have baptized by sprinkling or pouring water on the person who is being baptized.

Wait a minute, all the pictures of the red-headed, blue-eyed Jesus that hang in basements of too many of our churches shows him getting dunked? Yes, says the Baptist that's because the Greek word for baptize means to dip or to immerse. They choose to stick with one of the many dictionary definitions and say it can only mean to immerse is an assertion even though it has no biblical warrant. Yet forward they go as if the dictionary settles it. It's true that if you look at a Greek dictionary one of the possible definitions of the word baptize is to dip or to immerse, but there are multiple other definitions as well. One of the options is to wash, another is to associate, etc. Which one do we choose? This is a much better question.

The answer is to this question is found in the Bible. Whenever we wonder about the nature of a word used in the Bible, we should look to the scriptures in order to see how the Bible itself uses the word and then choose the definition that the Bible uses. This makes it easy—the scriptures refer to baptism as washing. The one place we have the word baptism used with specific reference to its mode is in Heb. 9:10. Here almost all translators render the word baptisms as washings. This is obviously true because a baptism was a washing and furthermore there were no official Old Testament baptisms that involved immersions. (Heb. 9:10). Quite simply, to baptize in the Bible means to wash. To translate baptism as a washing, actually still doesn't settle the question of mode.

If looking at a dictionary does not settle the question of mode of baptism, then we are still left with the question: what is the mode of washing?

---

8. The Orthodox Presbyterian Church, *Book of Church Order*, III.B.2.

What does the Bible mean when it uses the word to wash? This too is found in the Bible. I really marvel at how so many people struggle with this one. If you look at all the "various washings" or baptisms to which Heb. 9:10 is referring, the mode in every single one of them is pouring or sprinkling. For instance, Heb. 9:10 was referring to Exod. 12:22

> Take a bunch of hyssop and dip it in the blood that is in the basin, and touch the lintel and the two doorposts with the blood that is in the basin. None of you shall go out of the door of his house until the morning.

Here the doorposts are to be sprinkled, washed, or baptized with the blood of the lamb. In Exod. 24:6–8 we can see one of the baptisms to which Heb. 9:10 is specifically pointing.

> And Moses took half of the blood and put it in basins, and half of the blood he threw against the altar. Then he took the Book of the Covenant and read it in the hearing of the people. And they said, "All that the LORD has spoken we will do, and we will be obedient." And Moses took the blood and threw it on the people and said, "Behold the blood of the covenant that the LORD has made with you in accordance with all these words."

What is quite amazing is that the one specific New Testament reference to baptisms as it relates to its biblical origin and meaning is so abundantly clear that almost everyone in almost every place in the history of the church baptized by sprinkling or pouring. It was not primarily until groups of radical anabaptists pushed for rebaptism and as radicals they began using immersion as a mode that a significant number of Christians used immersion as their mode. Of course, there were a few small outlying groups before the Anabaptists that baptized by dipping, but the history of the church is more than clear that baptism as it has its mode rooted in the Bible was pouring or sprinkling. (For more scriptural references to help with Heb. 9:10, see also, Lev. 4:6, Lev. 14:6-7, Num. 19:18-21.)

Even though church history testifies to sprinkling or pouring the scriptures are the final authority. The modes of sprinkling or pouring were the only methods or modes of baptisms in the Old Testament and thus when the New Testament uses the word, we already know the meaning of the word, baptize or wash. It means sprinkling or pouring. This makes sense because even when you move to blood that is sprinkled or oil that is sprinkled or any other the various baptisms of the Old Testament the image was that of God coming down from above and setting this baptized or washed person apart by God's sovereign action from heaven.

Yes, and here is another catch here, John the Baptizer baptized Jesus as a kind of Old Testament priest. As someone who grew up in a Baptist church this really rocked my world. When a friend challenged me to describe how John the baptizer baptized Jesus, I instinctively said that Jesus was immersed. My friend laughed and challenged me to find a single reference to baptism in the Old Testament where someone was dipped. I rushed to Naham the Syrian and he laughed again saying that this is an odd example of someone getting healed from leprosy and is not the same as pointing to all the normal baptisms in the Old Testament that John would have followed in baptizing Jesus, and to which Heb. 9:10. Even with the example of Naham, the mode is not entirely clear. A better way to discover the answer is by looking to the normal modes of washings. Think about it, when John baptized Jesus, he was acting like an Old Testament priest. He used a washing or baptism of repentance, and he followed the universally prescribed method of sprinkling or pouring which was used for all Old Testament baptisms or washings.

The previous discussion is primarily one you only need to have in America and in small segments of the west where Baptist have pushed the argument that baptize means to dip or to immerse. This is not a discussion that one needs to have with almost all Christian traditions across the world except of course where Baptists have sent missionaries who have also taught it to their unknowing followers. Otherwise, most of the rest of the Christian world baptizes by sprinkling or pouring and they have done so throughout history. Baptism means to wash, and the prescribed washings as conclusively shown in the scriptures are pourings or sprinklings.

Another novel position that Baptists have also pushed is the notion that only new mature converts are to be baptized. This is another historically and scripturally innovative idea that is unique to Baptists or baptistic traditions, which unfortunately is most of the Evangelical world in America. Having grown up a Baptist I am happy to push back at this novelty. It should really carry some serious weight that almost the whole Christian world through almost the whole of Christian history baptized by pouring or sprinkling and they baptized the children of believers.

The New Testament pattern for converts is to believe and to be baptized—they and their household. Yes, mature men and women who become new believers are baptized after they profess Jesus Christ. But the New Testament evidence is equally clear that when this new believer is the head of a household their household is also baptized. The Philippian jailer and Lydia are a few clear examples. This is nothing more than following the normal biblical pattern that comes from the Old Testament which constantly reminds us that the promises are for us and for our posterity. When God gave Abraham circumcision as the sign of the covenant the sign went to Abraham and his household.

If one looks at the New Testament as if it were entirely new and having no roots or connection in the previous scriptures that we call the Old Testament, then one could possibly take the novel position that children are excluded from the covenant signs. If, however, you are willing to see the Old and New Testaments as connected then you move naturally form the Old into the New. This requires a person to have a proper understanding of the whole of the scriptures. You are not allowed to make up things from scratch. Instead, you start in the Old Testament and the moving to the New Testament you think about the scriptures as a one book.

Acts 16 reveals the normal biblical pattern for conversion that God had been using for thousands of years. It's not difficult to see, but many find it difficult to accept. When God entered into relationships with his people in history, he always interacted with them in terms of covenants that included their families. This is why when God gave Abraham a sign of his covenant with him the covenant sign belonged to him and to his household. In the Old Testament it was circumcision and in the New Testament it is now baptism. It's really this simple.

Likewise, baptism of our children proclaims to the world and all the devils that beset them that our children belong to the Lord. Children of believers are to be set apart for Christ and they are called to live solely unto him. Is this not what every Christian parent believes already? Is this not what every Christian parent desires for their children? I have seen so many attempts to replace infant baptism with other ceremonies that struggle to fulfill the basic, natural, and genuine instincts of Christian parents. Dedication ceremonies have become essentially dry baptisms. These dry baptisms fulfill the parent's authentic and godly instincts to proclaim publicly that their children belong to God and that the parents want the whole world to know that they promise to rear their children in the fear and nurture of the Lord.

Why do parents have such genuine and sincere desires—because they are parents! They do so because this is the nature of Christian parenting. We belong to Jesus and all that we have been given also belongs to Jesus. Thus, the most precious gifts that God has given to us are the souls of our children. These desires are not only right and proper, but they stand at the heart of why we should baptize our babies. They are disciples of Christ, and they should be baptized. We do so in obedience to God's command to baptize disciples.

If your children are not disciples, then what are they? Parents have a command to train their children in the fear of the Lord. But why? It's because all children born to Christian parents are by their birth made disciples of Christ. Otherwise, why has God commanded us to bring them up in the faith? Children of Christian parents are disciples of Christ.

I have been to services where babies are brought to the front of the church for dedications, prayers, and even strange oil anointing ceremonies. Why do churches do all these practices that are not even found in the scriptures when the command to baptize disciples is at the heart of the Great Commission and the commands to parents already prove that our children are our most important disciples.

Baptism contains in it all of the aforementioned actions what God has commanded—baptize disciples. In baptism we have a public dedication ceremony, which calls the parents and the children to follow the Lord. In baptism we have a God-given symbol of the hopes and aspirations we have for our children. In baptism we pray for our children to renounce the world and the devil and to serve Jesus Christ all the days of their lives. In baptism the children are given a sign and mark of their membership in the covenant community of God. Parents, your instincts to dedicate your children are genuine and they flow from biblical commands. Rather than creating your own ceremony, you should dedicate your children with Christ's commanded ceremony or rite of baptism and pray for the power of the Holy Spirit to call them to their baptism's purpose in Christ. This combines your divinely created instincts and desires as parents with the Holy Spirit's sign and seal to call our children to Jesus—what a blessing!

The Holy Spirit works in and through baptism to call our children to God in a way that only God himself can do. We all need the powerful work of the Holy Spirit to fulfill the calling we have in life in Christ. When God's Spirit works in the sacrament of baptism, we witness amazing things. John Calvin says,

> The sacraments properly fulfill their office only when the Spirit that inward teacher, comes to them by whose power alone hearts are penetrated and affections moved, and our souls opened for the sacraments to enter in. If the Spirit be lacking the sacrament can accomplish nothing more in our minds than

the splendor of the sun shining upon blind eyes, or the voice sounding in deaf ears... but charged with great effect when the Spirit works within and manifests his power.[9]

We often miss what Calvin is emphasizing. When the Holy Spirit charges baptism with the great effect of God's grace it manifests his power. Baptism makes a difference! I once heard a guy ask me if baptism really matters. After all, he said, it's not necessary to salvation. When I said that of course all Christians should be baptized and of course it makes a difference, he asked what would happen on a desert island. His example went something like the following:

> Suppose a man was stranded on a desert island and a bottle containing the scriptures washed upon the beach. The man read the Bible and believed in Jesus. Since he became a believer but there was no minister and no church, he couldn't be baptized yet he would still go to heaven.

Admittedly, the desert island illustration is an exception. But this is precisely why it does not matter to ordinary life. We do not make exceptions the rule. In fact, exceptions prove the rule. Ordinarily, baptism is both necessary by Christ's command and a blessing by the work of the Holy Spirit.

In Matthew 28:19 Jesus instructs His disciples to "go and make disciples of all nations, baptizing them in the name of the Father and of the Son and of the Holy Spirit." To be baptized means that we have been buried with Christ (Rom. 6:4), clothed with Christ (Gal. 3:27), and circumcised with Christ (Col. 2:11-12). Baptism is the sign and seal that our sins are forgiven (Acts 22:16 & I Pet. 3:21) it is a sign of the presence of regeneration (Titus 3:5). Baptism marks us out from the world and calls us to everything promised to us and to our children in the Gospel (Acts 2:38-39). Baptism may be one of the most powerful and yet neglected means of grace that Christ has given to us.

In Baptism we are sealed with the promises of adoption. We and our children are adopted into the family of God with all the rights and privileges of our new family. What a blessing we have in baptism! In closing, Conor Sweeney says,

> By baptism, your reality becomes the reality of participation in the Father's gift of Himself to the Church in Christ and the Spirit

---

9. Calvin, *Institutes of the Christian Religion*, 4.14.9 (p. 1149).

a gift which immerses you in the definitive relation of Christ's relation to the Father as son . . . So you are no longer a slave but a child, and if a child then also an heir, through God. (Gal. 4:4-7) . . . You are an heir. You are no longer bound deterministically to the law of sin. Your reality is now structured completely by the perspective of your adoption in Christ as a child of God the Father himself. . . . You have become a theological person, with a new theological history and genealogy. This is your new fundamental reference point, the place from which you now measure and assess your relation to reality.[10]

---

10. Sweeney, *Abiding the Long Defeat*, 119.

CHAPTER 7

Holy Communion

THERE MAY BE NO better example of modern worship practices rejecting embodied worship than the neglect of Holy Communion. Likewise, if the practice of infrequent Holy Communion is any indicator of the rejection of its centrality in worship, then modern Evangelical and Reformed Protestant churches have basically abandoned the use of the Lord's supper as a meaningful source of blessing and grace. The infrequent practice and the loss of importance seems to indicate that for many Evangelical and Reformed churches the Lord's supper is virtually worthless as a normal part of worship, and for serious students of church history, this is an alarming sign of weakness. According to John Williamson Nevin,

> The question of the Eucharist is one of the most important belonging to the history of religion. It may be regarded indeed as in some sense central to the whole Christian system. For Christianity is rounded in the living union of the believer with the person of Christ; and this great fact is emphatically concentrated in the mystery of the Lord's Supper; which has always been clothed on this very account, to the consciousness of the Church, with a character of sanctity and solemnity, surpassing that of any other Christian institution.[1]

Nevin was writing these words in 1846, but the problem has grown steadily worse. The well-known twenty-first century teacher, R.C. Sproul, echoes Nevin's concerns saying,

1. Nevin, *Mystical Presence*, 53.

I am convinced that where the sacrament of the Lord's Supper is taken lightly the people of God are sorely impoverished. Without both Word and sacrament, we face a spiritual famine . . . The light of the sacrament of the Lord's Supper is in eclipse. The shadows of postmodern relativism have covered the table. For the Lord's Supper to be restored to the spiritual life of the church there must be an awakening to its meaning, significance and power.[2]

I agree with Sproul and I hope this little book on embodied worship spurs many Christians to re-think that value of the Lord's supper in worship. It's also worth noting that one of the most significant debates among the newly forming Protestant leaders of the Reformation was a debate about the nature and meaning of the Lord's supper, Holy Communion or what is sometimes called the Eucharist. But why; why should a simple practice of eating bread and drinking wine maintain such a place of central import for worship? Before we tackle this question, let's first glance at a brief summary of the subject.

Jesus instituted the Lord's Supper, Holy Communion or Eucharist on the night in which he was betrayed. The synoptic gospels all record this great event (Matt. 26:20-30, Mark 14:17-26, and Luke 22:14-23).

> Now as they were eating, Jesus took bread, and after blessing it broke it and gave it to the disciples, and said, "Take, eat; this is my body." And he took a cup, and when he had given thanks he gave it to them, saying, "Drink of it, all of you, for this is my blood of the covenant, which is poured out for many for the forgiveness of sins. I tell you I will not drink again of this fruit of the vine until that day when I drink it new with you in my Father's kingdom." (Matt. 26:26-29)

Paul also records this in I Cor. 11:23-26,

> For I received from the Lord what I also delivered to you, that the Lord Jesus on the night when he was betrayed took bread, and when he had given thanks, he broke it, and said, "This is my body which is for you. Do this in remembrance of me." In the same way also he took the cup, after supper, saying, "This cup is the new covenant in my blood. Do this, as often as you drink it, in remembrance of me." For as often as you eat this bread and drink the cup, you proclaim the Lord's death until he comes.

---

2. Mathison, *Given for You*, ii.

While John 18:28 may refer generally to the days of the Passover feast (days sometimes called the Feast of Unleavened Bread) the synoptic gospels make explicit connection with the Passover meal and the Lord's Supper. For instance, Matt. 26:19 says,

> And the disciples did as Jesus had directed them, and they prepared the Passover.

The Passover meal remembers/commemorates the day when the people of God were liberated from the final plague in Egypt. That night the angel of death "passed over" those who were covered by the blood of the lamb were saved. They sprinkled the blood over the threshold, which represented their household, and they were protected from the judgment they otherwise deserved to receive (Exod. 12).

If the Passover meal had been a time of merely remembering an event, then perhaps a discussion about what happened in the old days, may have satisfactorily accomplished remembering God's act of salvation. However, in the original meal and those that followed it, the Lord also required the lamb to be eaten. John W. Nevin explains an obvious but amazing point related to how the Passover event of placing the blood as an outward exhibition was related to the eating of the Passover meal:

> It was not enough that this outward exhibition of the blood should take place, the ordinance made it necessary also that the sacrifice should be eaten. In this case at least, more was intended by this than an act of general communion with God. It represented the necessity of a true, living conjunction with the sacrifice itself. The lamb whose life was poured out as an offering for sin, must be itself incorporated as it were with the life of the worshipper, to give him a fuller claim on the value of its vicarious death. It became to him an atonement, by entering really into his person.[3]

What an amazing point! In the Passover meal and much more so in the Lord's supper, the lamb whose life was poured out as an offering for sin is eaten and incorporated with the worshipper providing him/her with real union with the sacrificial lamb of God and as such union with the life that comes from the lamb. This helps awaken us to a fuller appreciation of John 1:29 where he introduces to Jesus, saying, "behold, the Lamb of God who takes away the sins of the world." In the Lord's Supper we have explicit connection to the Passover meal, which illuminates Paul's great

---

3. Nevin, *Mystical Presence*, 306.

announcement in I Cor. 5:7 that Christ, our Passover lamb, has been sacrificed. Certainly, when we are told to do this in remembrance of him, we are flooded with all the incredible links to the blood of the lamb and how this lamb is given for us—for the life of the world.

There is also an amazing sense in which the Lord's Supper acts as not merely the last meal of the Old Testament but also as the inaugural meal of the New Testament in powerful fulfillment not solely of the Passover, but of all the great meals that God gave us in the Old Testament and of the theological implications of eating. For instance, there is very strong connection with the Old Testament covenant meal that God gave Moses, the priests and the seventy elders of Israel on Mt. Sinai (Exod. 24:1–11). At this meal Moses sprinkled the blood of the covenant on the people saying, "This is the blood of the covenant."

Jesus connects our fellowship meal, the Eucharist, between God and his people in his own words saying, "This is my blood of the covenant." In these words, Jesus is taking upon himself the fulfillment of Moses' words. In the Lord's Supper we appreciate the entirety of the New Testament's teachings that Jesus is the one to whom the whole of the scriptures has been pointing; summarized in Luke 24:27.

> And beginning with Moses and all the Prophets, he interpreted to them in all the Scriptures the things concerning himself.

We also see an astonishing connection to Heb. 9:11–14.

> But when Christ appeared as a high priest of the good things that have come, then through the greater and more perfect tent (not made with hands, that is, not of this creation) he entered once for all into the holy places, not by means of the blood of goats and calves but by means of his own blood, thus securing an eternal redemption. For if the blood of goats and bulls, and the sprinkling of defiled persons with the ashes of a heifer, sanctify for the purification of the flesh, how much more will the blood of Christ, who through the eternal Spirit offered himself without blemish to God, purify our conscience from dead works to serve the living God.

The Lord's Supper signifies and seals in us the fullness of Jesus' sacrificial work as our Passover lamb. As we receive this meal by faith the Spirit of God brings us into holy communion with our Lord and with all that it means to be united with Christ. The Lord's Supper is a rich and powerful meal that symbolizes so much more than many Protestants (especially Evangelical and Reformed traditions) usually imagine. A low view of the importance of the body in spiritual things, may partially explain this lack of appreciation and why so many Protestants neglect communion as a normal part of their worship.

In celebrating the Lord's Supper, we are obligated actively to recall his work and the grace, healing, hope and love that comes to us from Jesus Christ. Paul reminds us that we are required to remember the work of Jesus with active faith and the Lord's supper is something we are commanded to do. In I Cor. 11:24–25 Paul says,

> and when he had given thanks, he broke it, and said, "This is my body which is for you. *Do this in remembrance of me.*" In the same way also he took the cup, after supper, saying, "This cup is the new covenant in my blood. Do this, as often as you drink it, in remembrance of me (emphasis mine)."

The Lord's Supper or Eucharist is a means of grace by which God is helping us to remember and to experience his covenant faithfulness in the work of Jesus Christ. The meal also proclaims or preaches the work of Jesus in physical forms that we experience as embodied beings. For instance, in I Cor. 11:26, Paul teaches us the following:

> For as often as you eat this bread and drink the cup, you proclaim the Lord's death until he comes.

How does a meal "proclaim" the death of Christ? First, this indicates that there is much more to this meal than simply consuming bread and wine, which needs to be developed.

Robert Letham describes how various references in the New Testament do not capture the fullness of the meal by themselves, but rather each of them adds an insightful dimension to the meal, constructing a fuller meaning than is often appreciated.[4] For instance, in Acts 2:42; 20:7 we find it referred to as *the breaking of bread*. In I Cor. 10:21 Paul refers to it as the *Lord's table*. In I Corinthians 11:20 Paul calls it the *Lord's Supper* and in I Cor. 10:16-17 he speaks of the cup and bread as a participation or *communion* in the body and blood of Christ—this is why many refer to this meal simply as communion. Lastly, a very popular term arises from the account of Jesus' institution when it says he "took bread, *gave thanks*, broke it and said." (Matt. 26:26-27, Mark 14:22-23, Luke 22:17-19, I Cor. 11:23-24) The word of thanks is that is

---

4. Letham, *Lord's Supper*, 5.

used is the Greek word, eucaristeo. This is where we derive our English word *eucharist*—meaning a meal of thanksgiving (emphasis mine).

Here the potent theology of the eucharist is presented as more than a simple time to remember the death of Christ, at least equal if not more focus should be given to the awareness of life-giving power that comes from the body and blood of Jesus Christ. This demands us to see the "remembrance" as more than a mere intellectual or theological time of reflection. It means we remember by eating we feed on Christ. Breaking bread at the Lord's table as feeding on Christ was a common notion throughout history. The puritan Edmund Calmuny describes this, saying,

> God spreads a table before us and provides us with food so that, eating and drinking and feasting together, we may receive nourishment for our spiritual life and supports for our spiritual welfare.[5]

God loves his people and he invites them to eat a covenant meal with him, which is a rich expression of warmth and fellowship. In this meal we are reminded that God loves us so much that he gave himself for us and that he wants to have intimate union with us in this great thanksgiving meal.

According to John Calvin, in the Lord's Supper Jesus Christ "attests himself to be the life-giving bread, upon which our souls feed unto true and blessed immortality [John 6:51]."[6] Calvin teaches about the Lord's supper explaining that the mystery of our union and communion with Christ is shown through visible signs because the reality itself is by its very nature, incomprehensible.[7] Our union with Christ is so rich and so deep that mere words cannot capture its meaning. God connects his words with an embodied experience of union with him in this meal.

Think about this! God's love is so rich and so deep that mere words cannot capture it—it's a mystery. Eating and drinking go beyond the mere rational to the mysterious love of God who gives us life. Mystery then is central to embodied worship and most pointedly in the Lord's Supper. Please do not think that the supper is irrational. It most certainly is not irrational. Rather, it's what we might call suprarational in

---

5. Calamy, *Puritans on the Lord's Supper*, 27.

6. Calvin, *Institutes of the Christian Religion*, 4.17.1 (p. 1284).

7. Calvin, *Institutes of the Christian Religion*, 4.17.1 (p. 1284). See also, Mathison, *Given for You*, 17.

so far as it points us to the incomprehensible love of God in Christ. The Eucharist points us to the immeasurable greatness of his power as outlined in Paul's prayer in Eph. 1:18–19.

> having the eyes of your hearts enlightened, that you may know what is the hope to which he has called you, what are the riches of his glorious inheritance in the saints, and what is the immeasurable greatness of his power toward us who believe, according to the working of his great might.

Indeed, since this union is knit together with Jesus' incarnation and the mystery of how God became flesh, the meal is extraordinary. This is certainly why we can't restrict the Lord's supper to a mere act of remembering Jesus' death as if it were simply a memorial service. The supper is far more powerful than simply a different way to "remember." John W. Nevin helps us again saying,

> (the holy communion/Lord's supper) It is not *simply* an occasion, by which the souls of the believer may be excited to pious feelings and desires; but it embodies the actual presence of the grace it represents in its own constitution; and this grace is not *simply* the promise of God on which we are encouraged to rely, but the very life of the Lord Jesus Christ himself. We communicate, in the Lord's supper, not with the divine promise *merely*, not with the thought of Christ *only*, not with the recollection *simply* of what he has done and suffered for us, not with the lively present sense *alone* of this all-sufficient, all glorious salvation; but with the living Savior himself, in the fulness of his glorified person, made present to us for this purpose by the power of the Holy Ghost (emphasis mine).[8]

Notice that I highlighted the words that Nevin used to emphasize that the Lord's supper was certainly a time to remember, to recall and to reflect, but none of these activities represent the fullness or comprehensive character of what we are doing. Sometimes many Protestants consider "remembering" as the completeness of Holy Communion, but it is actually only one part of a much fuller experience of the mystery of God's grace in feeding us on Christ. In short, the supper is not merely about our reflection on Jesus or on how we feel about him, but rather its Christ offering his objective work and what he does to feed and to bless us in the experience of this sacrament. While it should be obvious, the

---

8. Nevin, *Mystical Presence*, 60–61.

supper is as much more about Christ and his work in sustaining us by his grace as it is about us per se.

Nevin's qualifications using the words, merely, and/or simply help us to note that certainly faith and remembering are required for the right receiving of the supper. Yet just as importantly it's not a mere act of faith that feeds us, but centrally it's the mysterious, objective work of Christ in feeding us on him as a means of confirming in us the faith that he has already given to us. We are nourished as Christ himself feeds us in this mysterious supper.

We must maintain that the believer of course receives the supper by faith, and Nevin properly outlines scripture's teaching which pushes us into the realm of mystery. So, he reminds us saying,

> The participation is not *simply* in his Spirit, but in his flesh also and blood. It is not figuratively *merely* and *moral*, but real, substantial and essential (emphasis mine).[9]

Here he is not arguing for a Roman Catholic teaching that the priest "transforms" the bread and wine into the actual, physical body of Christ, which is then automatically infused into the one who receives it.[10] There is nothing automatic about the transfer of the grace of God through the authority of the church in Nevin nor in the scriptures. Yet the sacrament cannot be reduced (as in so many Protestant traditions) to a mere remembrance of Jesus. This reduction has surely contributed to the neglect of the Eucharist. Perhaps people think of that the Lord's Supper is like adding a testimony time or a skit to worship rather than an essential means of grace. If it's a mere time to "remember" then it is not an essential means of grace—it's just an optional activity. Remember that Jesus did not say take and think but take and eat.

We can't reduce communion to a bare memorial of Christ's death as if it were the work of the person receiving it rather than the mysterious work of Christ through the Holy Spirit. For instance, if our experience of Christ depends on the keenness and ability by which we think

---

9. Nevin, *Mystical Presence*, 63.

10. This doctrine if often called transubstantiation, which teaches that the priest has the power through formulaic rituals to miraculously transform the bread and wine into the actual body and blood of Christ as part of a priestly sacrificial offering that once transformed has a kind of automatic grace and power that comes directly into the person receiving it. On the note of being a re-sacrifice of Christ and on the issue of automatic grace that comes through the authority of the church, this position has long been denied as scripturally untenable and even a false teaching.

about or remember Jesus then it tends to make the supper something of a rationalistic and individualistic effort/work. If we do this, then the mysterious supernatural work of the Holy Spirit through Holy Communion is eroded, and it tends to be replaced with a theological, moral exercise that depends more on the individual's ability to "remember" than on the Spirit of God to feed him.

This may well account for why so many churches deny their young children access to the table that would otherwise seem to belong to them naturally as young disciples who are in need of spiritual nourishment. In some traditions, before a young person can come to the table, the elders require an extensive theological examination fit more for an adult seminary student than for a child who has simple but credible faith in Christ that our Lord himself encourages.

Perhaps Jesus' instruction to let the little children come to me is overused in some ways, but it's instructive for the Lord's Supper. He did not say, let the theologians come to me, but let the children come to me. In our context this indicates that one's level of theological or even moral maturity should not be raised too high in order to determine if one is prepared to receive the Lord's Supper. One must be able humbly to "do this in remembrance of me" and "examine himself." While this does require a basic prerequisite of faith it does not demand a highly developed theological acumen as if the supper were a doctrinal exam for graduate students.[11]

Furthermore, it is not our intellectual or theological insight that gives the supper its power. This idea creates an overly rationalistic approach to something that is in fact what I call suprarational: something that though not irrational is beyond the ability of the mind to comprehend completely. God's power in the supper doesn't appear merely because we have theological facts in our minds. This would undermine the very nature of God's use of an image, and it tends to reduce the supper to a theological and moral contemplation on the work of Jesus—whatever this contemplation actually means. This overly theological or overly rational approach strips the supper of its mysterious and transformative supernatural power that resides in Christ and not in us.

---

11. Please note that this author is not arguing for what is sometimes called paedocommunion, which admits infants to the supper who are not able to remember the death of Christ. Still, the ability to examine oneself (I Cor. 11:28) as a prerequisite for coming to the table does not create a theologically high hurdle but rather a measure of simple faith and an ability to follow Jesus that even a very young child can possess.

It can't be emphasized enough—it's an image! The meal is a sign and seal of the covenant of grace using the image of eating and drinking, which is itself inherently mysterious.

Let me note again that the supper is not irrational. It can be understood to a certain degree as a physical preaching of the gospel, and the gospel must be heard and understood. This understanding needs to come from the actual preaching and/or teaching of the gospel from God's word so as to provide the image with a basic meaning. The mystery of the supper should always be accompanied by the direction of God's words, but it can't be reduced to merely or simply to a memorial time to remember what Jesus did for us.

The mystery of the meal continues as we maintain that there is an objective though not automatic grace that is present in the Lord's supper. Christ is present in the communion meal and it's his powerful presence communicated to us by grace through the Holy Spirit that feeds us on him. Likewise, we need to insist that in the supper we truly receive Jesus Christ by the work of his Spirit. Of course, we feed on him by faith as we receive this grace, but the grace we receive comes to us from the truly present person of Jesus Christ in this holy meal. Yes, this is a profound mystery: what John W. Nevin referred to as mystical. Nevin summarizes it saying,

> In the old Reformed view, the eucharist is regarded as carrying in it a peculiar specific grace; as having a truly mystical character; as possessing an objective force; as including a real participation in Christ's person; as reaching this through the medium especially of his flesh and blood, that is his true human life.[12]

This is not in concert with the Roman Catholic view that the priest miraculously transforms (sometimes called transubstantiation) the bread and wine into the actual body and blood of Christ. Neither do the scriptures teach Martin Luther's attempted compromise where Luther argued that the physical presence of Christ though not miraculously becoming the bread and wine themselves are yet physically present "in, with, and under" the elements. (sometimes called consubstantiation)[13] The earliest Protestant debates hinged on the insistence of both Roman and Lutheran traditions of the "physical" presence. This poses a problem since the actual physical presence of Christ is in heaven.

---

12. Nevin, "Doctrine of Reformed Church," 432.
13. Letham, *The Lord's Supper*, 23–24.

Nevin argued that the resolution came from John Calvin who using the scriptures and ancient Christian sources navigated away from the idea of a "physical" presence to the idea of true and real presence spiritually. Ronald Wallace offers a helpful summary of Calvin's view in the following four points:

1. The body of Christ, in which he wrought our redemption and apart from which we cannot be saved, in being communicated to us in the sacrament remains, throughout the participation, in heaven, beyond this world and retains all its human properties...

2. Communion with the body of Christ is effected through the descent of the Holy Spirit, by whom our souls are lifted up to heaven, there to partake of the life transfused into us from the flesh of Christ...

3. Partaking of the flesh of Christ in the supper is thus a heavenly action, in which the flesh is eaten in a spiritual manner...

4. The presence of the body of Christ in the Supper, though it may be called a real presence and a descent of Christ by the Spirit, is nevertheless also a "celestial mode of presence" and leads to no localization of the body of Christ on earth, no inclusion of it in the elements, no attachment of it to the elements.[14]

Perhaps when we speak of the real objective presence of Christ in the supper some people are confused. It may help to think about this with regard to God's presence everywhere in the world. He holds creation together by the power of his presence. According to Colossians 1:16–17, Christ is present in creation. He is also present in the preaching of the word of God, and in many other things. His presence does not depend on the intelligent and willful acceptance of this presence by anyone.[15] In a similar way, God's presence in this sacrament is objectively real regardless of what we happen to believe about it.

In Romans 1 we see that rebellious people reject God's powerful omnipresence in creation and instead they worship the created rather than the creator. Their rejection has massive consequences for their own lives, but their rejection of God's presence has no objective bearing on

---

14. Mathison, *Given for You*, 29.

15. This stands in contrast with Charles Hodge's argument against Nevin that spiritual things are present "when they are presented to the intelligence so as to be apprehended and enjoyed." Hodge argued that Christ's presence in the Lord's supper is "a presence of virtue and efficacy not of propinquity." Littlejohn, *Mercerburg Theology*, 53.

it. In fact, the reality of God's presence becomes the grounds for which they are ultimately condemned. So, the objective presence of Christ in the Lord's supper does not depend on the intelligent apprehension of it by any individual.[16] At the same time Paul's warning of the misuse of the supper in I Corinthians indicates something quite like Rom. 1 except with a more potent context that reminds us Christ's special presence is something of a divine ordeal. It's the objective reality of God's presence that condemns those who take the supper, but who live in rebellion against it. This relates to why Paul can warn,

> Whoever, therefore, eats the bread or drinks the cup of the Lord in an unworthy manner will be guilty concerning the body and blood of the Lord. (1 Cor. 11:27)

Certainly, the application of the blessings of the supper depends on the Spirit's awakening of the individual to it, but the actual, objective presence must be distinguished from its' reception and/or rejection. This helps us to speak of the Lord's supper in the same objective way the scriptures do when Jesus says, "this is my body." Jesus Christ is present in the Lord's supper in a real, spiritual way. This is why John Calvin could rightly note,

> What I have said [regarding the need of faith to properly receive it] is not to be understood as if the force and truth of the sacrament depended upon the condition or choice of him who receives it. For what God has ordained remains firm and keeps its own nature, however, men may vary. For since it is one thing to offer, another to receive, nothing prevents the symbol consecrated by the Lord's word from being actually what it is called, and from keeping its own force. Yet this does not benefit a wicked or impious man. But Augustine has well solved this question in a few words, "If you receive carnally, it does not cease to be spiritual, but it is not so for you."[17]

There is a deep mystery to the Lord's Supper that is very profound and should not be diminished by reducing it to a simple memorial. God wants us to seek him as our ultimate hope and satisfaction—he teaches

---

16. I mention this in regard to an argument made by the nineteenth century American theologian, Charles Hodge who said that spiritual things are present "when they are presented to the intelligence so as to be apprehended and enjoyed." This essentially transforms the supper into an individual/subjective event with the individual fundamentally at the center of its efficacy rather than Christ. Littlejohn, *Mercerburg Theology*, 53.

17. Calvin, *Institutes of the Christian Religion*, 4.14.16 (p. 1291).

this telling us to eat and drink what he calls his flesh and blood and if we do so by faith we are fed, nourished, and satisfied. Jesus is our life, and the supper pushes us to the profound passage in John 6 teaching us that Jesus is the bread of life.

Though not in the immediate context of the Lord's supper nor speaking directly to its institution per se, John 6:47–58 does in fact teach a truth connected to Holy Communion. According to Robert Letham,

> From John's perspective . . . looking back on the life, ministry, death, and resurrection of Jesus as a whole, he saw Jesus' speech as directly connected to the later introduction of the sacrament. From this later authorial standpoint the two were in effect part of the same reality.[18]

It is no small matter that many scholars who argue that Jesus was not referring directly to the sacrament of the Lord's supper in John 6, "nevertheless end up recognizing that what Jesus taught here finds its fullest expression precisely in the eucharist.[19] This is why for most churches until about the nineteenth century the Lord's Supper or Holy Communion was an ordinary part of a Christian worship service.

This seems to be the case from the earliest accounts in church history. The *Dicache* for instance, written about AD 100 provides the most primitive written record of worship in which the worshippers gave thanks for the bread and wine. This account of the Lord's Supper referred to it as the Eucharist. The writings of the famous Justin Martyr (circa AD 155) also refer to the church giving thanks for the Lord's Supper.

Hippolytus of Rome writing his well-known work, *Apostolic Tradition*, around AD 215 uses similar language to Justin Martyr and the *Didache* establishing that the Lord's Supper or Eucharist was a regular part of Christian worship and was something received with great praise and thanksgiving. This position stands resolutely at odds with contemporary Protestant practices.

Evangelical Protestants in general and Reformed Presbyterians in particular have a problem when it comes to the practice of the Lord's Supper. They tend to treat it as if it were something unnecessary and optional or worse as something that may need to be avoided rather than a central means of feeding and providing grace to the people of God. Presbyterians, for instance, have this nagging thing called the Westminster Confession of

---

18. Letham, *The Lord's Supper*, 8–9.
19. Letham, *The Lord's Supper*, 10.

Faith, which teaches clearly that the Lord's Supper is a positive "means of grace." The Lord's Supper is a means or instrument whereby the people of God are fed and blessed. Westminster Confession of Faith 29.1 says,

> Our Lord Jesus, in the night wherein he was betrayed, instituted the sacrament of his body and blood, called the Lord's Supper, to be observed in his church, unto the end of the world, for the perpetual remembrance of the sacrifice of himself in his death; the sealing all benefits thereof unto true believers, their spiritual nourishment and growth in him, their further engagement in and to all duties which they owe unto him; and, to be a bond and pledge of their communion with him, and with each other, as members of his mystical body.

According to the Confession, the Lord's Supper is essentially a positive and blessed means of grace that nourishes us and helps us grow in Christ. Because the Lord's Supper feeds the people of God, it is fundamentally helpful and effective in blessing God's people. If this is true, then why not feed the sheep?

Yes, why not feed the sheep weekly? Those unaware of its central position in the history of Christian liturgy have sometimes turned the question upside down. I have actually heard some people ask me to show in the New Testament grounds for weekly supper. This might be a legitimate question for Christians who don't know the earliest records and whose traditions don't include a confession that affirms the positive and blessed character of the Lord's Supper as a means of grace. However, for Protestants whose confessions and traditional practices already affirm that the Supper as a means of grace, then the actual burden of withholding the Supper from the people of God is on them. Why not feed the sheep? This is the question. If the Lord's Supper is essentially positive and beneficial, (as Jesus has said) why not feed them at every opportunity?

Of course, what this *may* mean is that many within Reformed, Presbyterian and Evangelical Protestant circles don't believe in the essentially positive and blessed character of the Lord's Supper. They don't practice what their confessions (which are supposed to represent the Scriptures) are preaching. To the contrary, they almost seem to fear the Lord's Supper as a potential danger or a potential harm to the church rather than a blessing. Personally, I have met many who take this position out of an ever-present and looming fear of becoming "Roman Catholic." After all, they say, couldn't people take it for granted? Wouldn't weekly communion become rote or mechanical? Doesn't Paul warn of sickness and even death for those who take in an unworthy manner?

These are fearful and weak arguments (if arguments at all) because they attempt to disprove something positive and good by pointing to "potential" abuses. I remember a professor in my university once reminding us of a maxim as if everyone should have already known it: "the abuse of something is never a good argument against it." Please let this sink in! The abuse of something is never a good argument against it.

A simple example may suffice. We all know, for instance, that cars are routinely abused, and many people are killed in them. In fact, they are one of the most dangerous and deadly things we use every day. Does this keep us from properly using our cars to drive to work or to travel for holiday? Of course not! If you want me to stop using my car, then you would need to prove that there is something inherently wrong in the proper use of it or that its positive benefits are outweighed by the dangers.

Nobody would be dissuaded from driving a car because there is a potential to have a wreck. For most of us the benefits far outweigh the potential hazards. The best approach would be to teach people how to drive safely. We should try to be responsible in the way we use our vehicles. As my old professor reminded us, we should all know that the abuse of something is never a good argument against it—not for cars and certainly not for the Lord's Supper.

The abuse of something is also not used for other legitimate practices in weekly worship. Arguably, collecting an offering is one of the least necessary for personal encouragement in worship. Do any of the same churches who argue for quarterly or monthly communion practice this kind of infrequency in tithing? Do they practice the same principle when taking up an offering? What could be more potentially rote or mechanical than passing a plate and dropping some money in it? What if someone just dropped in their tithe check without properly reflecting and/or properly worshiping? Has this potential abuse ever stopped a church from collecting the offering weekly?

I'm not trying to be grumpy about this just to make people angry, but people may pass the plate without thinking, and this potential abuse has not kept these same church leaders from limiting the opportunity of worshipping God by giving tithes and offerings. Should they limit the opportunities to praise God through the giving of tithes and offerings in such an odd way as infrequent tithing? They do not seem to be as concerned about passing the plate as they are about offering Holy Communion—why?

Many Reformed and Evangelical Christians practice what I call an anti-tradition traditionalism. Without serious scriptural investigation they have taken an odd position that because they think the original Protestants were against Roman Catholic traditionalism, they therefore have established a new and very inflexible tradition of infrequent Holy Communion. In fear of "proto-Catholicism, they establish a peculiar anti-tradition traditionalism.

For my own Presbyterian tradition, the infrequent pattern of the Lord's supper in some ways originates from a series of odd and unique circumstances that were carried from Scotland thoughtlessly into American Presbyterian practice. In 1560 the newly formed Scottish reformed church adopted the *Book of Common Order*, a suggested though not authoritative directory for worship, which recommended monthly celebration of Holy Communion. The first *First Scots Book of Discipline* asserted that four celebrations a year was sufficient. However, this was rarely practiced because of the lack of qualified ministers. According to George B. Burnett,

> The primary case of infrequent or irregular Communions was the acute shortage of ordained ministers in the first generation of the Reformation.[20]

There was, however, more than a mere dirth of minsters. In the seventeenth century another dimension was added that changed the Presbyterian practice even more (and not in a positive direction). From 1626–1630 the Covenanter movement developed a pattern of meetings as frightened exiles from Ireland and Scotland gathered with groups of nonconformists from all over Scotland in "conventicles." The "godly" from all over the nation gathered in special camp style meetings "forming close relationships with each other as they shared in the mutual sufferings and longings for the reformation of Scotland."[21] These meetings were in response to Charles I's attempts to force certain communion practices (primarily kneeling) on the Scottish church. The nonconformists deliberately avoided communion in the conforming churches and fled to the countryside to have communion with each other. This practice though an encouragement to the future covenanter movement was also

---

20. Burnet, *Holy Communion in Reformed Church*, 14.
21. Jackson, *Riots, Revolutions, Scottish Covenanter*, 44.

imperceptibly changing the nature of the Lord's supper from an ordinary part of worship to an extraordinary and infrequent activity related to the hope for piety and revival that was part of sometimes a week-long preparation for the hoped-for movement of the Holy Spirit.

It appears that this transformed celebrating the Eucharist into an uncommon (maybe even unnatural) element of worship. This was developed and complicated even more by the Scottish covenanter ministers and sessions (elders) desire to use the supper as a test of extraordinary piety among their people. Rather than viewing communion as an ordinary means of assisting the weak and needy, they put obstacles and hurdles over which those who were already weak had to struggle to overcome.[22] One minister, Andrew Cant, for example, in Aberdeen suspended Holy Communion altogether for two years until the people "were weill catechist, because he alledgit they war ignorant."[23] The Covenanter's persistent connection with extraordinary piety and theological knowledge as a prerequisite for the Lord's Supper entrenched and developed a common practice of requiring communion tokens. These tokens were given to those who were interviewed by the local elders prior to administering communion in order to verify their genuine piety and knowledge so as to "fence" the table from those not properly reconciled with God and their neighbor.[24]

If you did not have a token, you could not take communion. Consequently, it was not unusual for a church to administer communion only one time in a year. The historical circumstances warrant a more thorough examination, but this should suffice to offer an adequate outline of Scottish reformed Presbyterian practices that were unfortunately imported into American Presbyterian practices oftentimes without serious thought.

The Scottish theologian, John Erskine, wrote in 1781 and argued that if Calvin had succeeded in establishing his desire for weekly communion, which for Erskine was the apostolic tradition handed to us from the New Testament, then the Scots would most certainly have followed this. Since Calvin lost, the Scots like so many other Protestant traditions

---

22. Oddly this reflects some strange practices in the Middle Ages when the Eucharist was withheld from laymen leading in some cases from denying people the wine altogether.

23. Burnet, *Holy Communion Reformed*, 170.

24. Burnet, *Holy Communion Reformed*, 170–75.

departed from more than a thousand years of common practices and moved into patterns of irregular and capricious practices.[25]

My own experience growing up in a fundamentalists Baptist church in Indiana confirms that our communion practices like those of the Scottish Presbyterians were connected to pietistic, individualistic, and erratic approaches to Holy Communion rather than to the idea that the Lord's supper was an ordinary means of grace that should be accessible as a normal and fundamental part of Christian blessing and discipleship in weekly worship. Every time the supper was given, the pastor placed an enormous emphasis on Paul's warning in I Cor. 11:27–32.

My little Baptist church had communion at best quarterly and I recall being quite terrified that if I did not eat and drink in a worthy manner (which for most of my adolescent years would have been rare) that something bad would happen, and I imagined that I might even die a horrible death because of eating and drinking in an unworthy manner. The thought that Holy Communion might have been a blessing to feed me in times when I was weak never occurred to me and apparently neither did such an approach occur to the leaders of my church. We were told explicitly that weekly communion was something Roman Catholics did, and we should avoid such things if we took our holiness seriously.

Anti-tradition traditionalism is just as damaging to scriptural practice as the original traditions against which anti-tradition traditionalism had been established. The good news is that many students of church history who are younger Protestants are happily questioning the anti-tradition traditionalism; and they are quite perplexed at the odd reasoning that says basically, to appreciate or deeply experience something one must do it as infrequently as possible. While this idea is patently absurd, it's used repeatedly as if it were a meaningful argument.

This is at odds with everything else that the church prescribes in worship. Most of these anti-tradition traditionalists still take up the offering every single Sunday. Honestly, this exposes the odd position as at the very least inconsistent and it makes no sense as an argument. Doing something less frequently has nothing to do with its depth or meaning.

Many recite the Ten Commandments, they recite the Lord's Prayer, they sing, they preach, and they do it every Sunday repeatedly. I have also heard some folks assert that if we had the Lord's Supper less frequently, we would appreciate it more. This one is actually harder to take seriously

---

25. Erskine, *Duty of Celebration of Lord's Supper*, 30–34. See also Burnet, *Holy Communion Reformed Church*, 18.

than other arguments. If something is a blessing, is less really better? If we assume that our confessions are a correct summary of the scriptures, then why would we want less of a blessing? Is this true in any other loving relationship?

If we have an opportunity for a genuine expression of love for someone, why wouldn't we try to show it as often as possible rather than as seldom as possible? Surely, we would say that these beautiful expressions of love should happen at every appropriate opportunity. Try telling your wife that you love her so much that you are going to start talking to her about this love, but only once a month. Ha, try telling your wife that you love her so much that you will start showing this love as infrequently as necessary, so it won't become routine. How ridiculous! I don't intend to be disrespectful to people, but honestly, it's time to start exposing these kinds of arguments for the flimsy and embarrassing opinions that they are. At almost any level, less is not better in a loving relationship. Why then would less be better regarding the Lord's Supper? If the analogy is a good one, then many of the common Protestant objections to weekly communion appear to be superficial if not silly.

What did Jesus mean when he said, "do this in remembrance of me?" Is remembering him once a month a seriously better practice than remembering him every week when you worship him? This is why preachers try to remind us every single week that God loves sinners in giving his only son, which is good news or the gospel, and since the Lord's Supper is a proclamation of the gospel why not repeat it in the same way. Repetition is not always bad, but it is as the saying goes, the mother of leaning.

This good news is preached in some form every single week, and nobody should object to hearing it too much. I recall as a boy that we used to sing a song about telling the old, old story. "I love to hear the story," the song said, "twill be my theme in glory, to tell the old, old story of Jesus and his love." Why do we think this way about almost everything except the Lord's Supper?

Our Protestant heritage is in great jeopardy. The first generation of the Reformation including Calvin determined that communion should be administered weekly. Believing that the Lord's Supper is a summary of the Gospel, Calvin understood there was an appropriateness that every sermon should conclude gospel preaching by partaking of the Lord's Supper as a seal to the gospel. His position was just a continuation of the ancient Christian practice from the earliest recorded history of the church.

True saving faith comes primarily by the preaching of the Gospel, and this Gospel is confirmed and sealed in us by the Sacraments. As noted already regarding the sacraments in general Calvin reminds us that in the Lord's Supper, "God leads us by the hand as tutors lead children."[26] Pastors and church leaders need to reawaken this idea and I am urging anyone who reads this book to go to your church leaders and respectfully request for more frequent opportunities to hold God's hand in this way!

As we look back to the question we posited at the beginning of this chapter "why is this issue so central." We see now something of what Bradford Littlejohn argues,

> Since this sacrament is the most intimate point of communion between Christ and the believer, Eucharistic theology is intertwined with one's view of union with Christ, and indeed soteriology as a whole. Also, what sort of nature man has (anthropology) and what sort of nature Christ had (Christology) are an unavoidable part of the picture as well. Since the sacrament is an ordinance of the Church, the account one gives of sacramental grace must include an account of the grace offered in the church more generally, thus involving ecclesiology as well.[27]

In John 6:51 Jesus teaches us that the bread is his flesh given for the life of the world. We can't miss the mystery and wonder of eating the body and blood of Jesus. In fact, it's worth noting that one of the major criticisms of early Christians that the classical Romans leveled against the new Christians was that they were cannibals because their common practice in worship was eating flesh and drinking blood.[28] This would not be a meaningful criticism of most of today's Protestants.

The apostolic and ancient church knew the importance of eating. This should help us to pause as we oftentimes eat without thinking. We rush into the kitchen and "grab a bite" and food becomes something like a body fuel that we use to keep us going or help us enjoy a movie or some other form of entertainment. Of course, it also needs to taste good and be quickly accessible. Alexander Schmemann notes with insight that "centuries of secularism have failed to transform eating into something strictly utilitarian."[29] This should be particularly true for the Christian.

---

26. Calvin, *Institutes of the Christian Religion*, 4.14.6 (p. 1281).
27. Littlejohn, *Mercerburg Theology*, 42.
28. Needham, *2000 Years of Christ's Power*, 85.
29. Schmemann, *Life of the World*, 16.

Eating is actually something worth thinking about. In his book on *Food and Faith*, Norman Wirzba notes,

> we can look at a meal and see only a random assortment of nutrients, oblivious to the grace of God made manifest in it. We can forget that food is one of God's basic and abiding means of expressing divine provision and care. To partake of a meal is to participate in a divine communication . . . It is to participate in forms of life and frameworks of meaning that have their root and orientation in God's caring ways of creation.[30]

If this is true, then it's no surprise that at the center of our relationship with Jesus Christ is a meal we call the Lord's Supper, Holy Communion, or Eucharist. This also means that such a meal should be a central and normal part of formal worship with our God. As noted already in this study, eating was at the center of the test in the Garden of Eden. God required Adam and Eve to think carefully about eating and what it meant for them to live; to have true life. When they sinned against God it had terrible consequences. Continuing the metaphor of eating, Alexander Schmemann says,

> For the wages of sin is death. The life man chose was only the appearance of life. God showed him that he himself had decided to eat bread in a way that would simply return him to the ground from which both he and the bread had been taken: For dust thou art and into dust shalt thou return. Man lost the eucharistic life, he lost the life of life itself, the power to transform it into Life. He ceased to be the priest of the world and become its slave.[31]

In the Scriptures, eating represents more than merely getting some nutrients. Though we may not think about it carefully, physical eating that sustains physical existence is filled with mystery. Alexander Schmemann mentions the following enlightening words:

> Man must eat in order to live he must take the world into his body and transform it into himself, into flesh and blood . . . the whole world is presented as one all-embracing banquet table for man. And this image of the banquet remains, throughout the whole Bible, the central image of life. It is the image at its

---

30. Wirzba, *Food and Faith*, xii-xiii.
31. Schmemann, *Life of the World*, 17.

creation and also the image of life at its end and fulfillment:" . . . that you eat and drink at my table in my kingdom.³²

Such implications are presented most powerfully and pointedly in the Lord's supper. This also helps to answer the earlier question at the beginning of this chapter—why this so important.

If I may, I would also like to suggest that focusing the attention of the Lord's Supper on the mysterious grace of God and moving it away from some kind of intense, personal emotional or theological reflection has had detrimental effects. Perhaps we could call this a memorialist view. That is to say that Holy Communion is basically a time for individual Christians to reflect in a deeply pietistic manner on their salvation. This view diminishes the power of the Eucharist as primarily a work that Christ accomplishes in us through/in the sacrament. Holy Communion is actually not so much about our reflection on Christ as Christ's love and commitment to us. This is critical!

The sacrament is not merely about our pledge to Christ but astonishingly it's about Christ's pledge to us. It is Christ who gives us his body and blood. It is Christ who reminds us that he loves us so much that he gave himself for us. It is Christ who through the mysterious power of the Holy Spirit fills us with grace to be renewed and to be confirmed in this grace. Ironically those who wish to see this sacrament as most importantly our pledge to Christ shift the focus more to ourselves and to our own personal reflection either emotionally or in some ill-defined theological reflection that may well create a unintended man-centered character to what should be a Christ-centered experience. In the Lord's Supper Christ staggeringly, incomprehensibly, and mysteriously holds our hands and tells us—I love you and I am with you.

It is this beautiful expression of grace and love from Christ that confirms and strengthens us in Christ and not our own prayers, intense preparation or concentrated spiritual activity that feeds us in his grace. Thus, no communion tokens are necessary. Thus, no week-long preparation is necessary. Thus, no two-week series on the Lord's Supper is necessary at all for receiving grace, because it is not our work, but Christ's work in us.

When we get saved, we don't merely get our sins forgiven—we get God! In eating the lamb of God our souls are nourished and fed in wondrous, mysterious ways that far exceed a mere remembrance that Jesus died on the cross. In the Eucharist we give thanks because all our

---

32. Schmemann, *Life of the World*, 11.

deepest needs and desires are met in Christ and through his work. Our deepest hunger for meaning, purpose and existence is filled in Christ and sealed for us in Holy Communion.

Arguing that this great meal can be summarized as a simple "remembrance" undeniably falls short of its place and power in our lives and in particular as a central part of our worship. It denies or at least diminishes our embodied existence and needs as human beings. All the things that tempt us to live for them such as money, friends, popularity, influence, power, sexual fulfillment, and any other temporary idol that would seek to supplant God as our only hope of meaning—they are all displaced and mocked as meaningless in the Lord's Supper. True meaning and ultimate satisfaction are signed and sealed for us in the Lord's Supper. What an amazing sacrament!

We desperately need to reassert the centrality of Holy Communion as an ordinary part of worship. Without the Eucharist as a regular part of worship we lose more than we have imagined. In closing Peter Leithart offers a challenging statement,

> Foodless worship is unthinkable in the Bible and has been unthinkable through most of Christian history. That didn't change at the Reformation. Most Reformers wanted to increase participation in and frequency of communion. Only recently have Christians become accustomed to seeing an empty table, or no table, at the front of the church. Ironically, the Christians who claim to be biblical are the ones who ignore the most consistent element of biblical worship. Christians in liturgical churches wonder if these un-festal gatherings, as joyous and edifying as they may be, qualify as Christian worship at all. They are as anomalous as a temple without a sacrifice.[33]

---

33. Leithart, "At the Table," para. 4.

CHAPTER 8

Grape Juice Christianity

THIS LITTLE CHAPTER IS tangentially related to embodied worship and it's a bit sarcastic, but also stands as a genuine challenge to Christians who say they believe the Bible, but who refuse to obey it in worship. The question hinges on whether you will obey Jesus' simple words, "all of you drink it." A reverent submissive believer would do what God says to do simply because he says to do it. Such a believer would not feel the need to exchange God's ideas with his own ideas—an extraordinarily presumptuous and man-centered position. This is exactly what grape juice Christians do: they exchange Jesus' teachings about wine in communion with their own ideas. Even worse they cloak their presumption in the traditional Christian language of humility. As such Grape Juice Christianity particularly in America has undermined orthodox Christianity and replaced it with a generic American moralism that no longer teaches the gospel.[1]

Grape juice Christianity is my own moniker that derives primarily from the practice of Christians who have replaced God's choice of wine with grape juice and who have also simultaneously replaced the ancient and central practice of the Eucharist or Holy Supper with religious entertainment in worship. Most grape juice Christians are those who we would probably designate as Evangelicals and those who claim to believe the Bible but refuse to do what it says because pop culture has replaced God's word

---

1. Unfortunately, these strange practices have been transported internationally all over the world through the missionaries who took it with them wherever they went.

as their final authority in worship. Jesus gave a simple command: do this in remembrance of me. Yet, they refuse to do it. In so doing, grape juice Christians have weakened and transformed Christianity into an almost historically unrecognizable religion most importantly in worship.

Yes, I'm arguing that for many Evangelical and Reformed traditions, the grape juice used (infrequently) in the Lord's Supper in worship is a symbol not as much of the blood of Jesus, but of deep weakness and amazing arrogance in Protestant Christianity particularly in America. As I already remarked such weakness is not limited to Evangelical Protestants alone, but also to a host of other traditions including my own doctrinally proud tradition of Reformed Christianity, which so often boasts of its robust theological commitment to the authority of the Bible.

Reformed Protestants are not immune from these ideas. Reformed thinkers are the "theological tough guys"—just ask us! Yet even the Reformed tradition, which sometimes presents itself as if it were a kind of theological special forces like the US Navy Seals—you may know them as Calvinists. Even these "reformers" retreat like cowards at the approach of Alcoholics Anonymous or at the apparently magical phrase, "once an alcoholic always an alcoholic." Better set aside the words and the theology of Jesus so we can be sensitive to the weaker brother. Better to be easy on a sensitive conscience and ignore God—really? These are the ethical preferences of grape juice Christians who pride themselves ironically on following the Bible, but because of strong cultural forces to the contrary, they refuse to follow it! If you take this approach combined with a view that worship is basically religious entertainment, then you may be a grape juice Christian yourself! If so, please pay attention to this little chapter.

Grape juice Christians are moralists who say they follow the Bible, but who have defied God's teachings that wine is a divine gift if for nothing else but as an element in the mystery of the Lord's Supper. Instead, these individualistic, moralists have substituted God's ethics for a false morality. They have positioned this false morality at the center of their worship practices. In so doing, they have plunged especially Evangelical traditions into a struggle for their very existence because they no longer take the Bible seriously at even the most basic practices of worship, for which grape juice provides an apt symbol. Consequently, they are also not taken seriously by others. Maybe their most serious problem is that God may have stopped taking them seriously in worship as well. This would be something to fear, and good reason for repentance.

The most dramatic rejection of historic Christian worship is found in grape juice Christianity's rejecting Holy Communion as a meaningful part of worship and worse yet, when the eucharist is infrequently practiced, grape juice Christians follow a silly kind of grape juice theology that has replaced Jesus' own testimony about wine. Jesus taught that wine is good. In fact, he made strong fermented wine at Cana and encouraged people to drink it. Let this sink in; Jesus encouraged people to drink wine. But alas, grape juice Christians know better than Jesus himself—they discourage using wine as if it were bad or at least something inherently flawed and dangerous. The painful irony for grape juice Christians is that they not only think they know more than Jesus, but they also contradict him.

I already mentioned that reverent submission is what God wants in life and most centrally it's what he wants in worship. It's something grape juice Christians refuse to give. In many ways the Christian life and particularly Christian worship is as simple as faithful, reverent submission to God. We should do what God says to do because he is God, and we are not. In essence, we do what he says because he says to do it. It's the most central challenge to grape juice Christianity wherever grape juice Christians are found in the world—this is a fundamental challenge especially in the subject of worship—do this in remembrance of me!

Instead of simple, faithful obedience, grape juice Christianity has reduced historic Christian worship into a kind of individualistic, subjective religious experience saturated with all the common elements of pop culture. To say that grape juice worship is man-centered is an understatement. Adding insult to injury, grape juice Christians' arrogance is cloaked in the language of biblical humility. If you are familiar with Christian history and then you compare the present grape juice Christianity's worship practices with this history, it's possible to wonder if you are really dealing with historic Christianity at all at least when it comes to worship. In 1923 J. Gresham Machen's dramatic and prescient warnings about the dangers of liberalism strikes me as appropriate to the popular worship practices when he noted,

> Christianity is battling against a totally diverse type of religious belief, which is only the more destructive of the Christian faith because it makes use of traditional Christian terminology.[2]

---

2. Machen, *Christianity and Liberalism*, 5.

Perhaps one reason that many evangelicals in general are not taken seriously is because they are not serious. There is no place more central to this flippancy in evangelical theology than in worship. Such thoughtlessness and flippancy in worship is related to an overall lack of interest in thinking deeply and earnestly about the scriptures. This is well known, and several books have documented the anti-intellectual character of Evangelical Christianity. For instance, Mark Noll's 1994 book, *The Scandal of the Evangelical Mind*, is a devastating critique of Evangelical Christianity's rejection of thinking much about theology. Noll says,

> The scandal of the evangelical mind is that there is not much of an evangelical mind . . . Despite dynamic success at a popular level, modern American evangelicals have failed notably in sustaining seriously intellectual life.[3]

I would highlight Noll's comment that evangelicals have had enormous popular success, and no place more dramatically and sadly than in worship. This may be the root of the problem—evangelicals are obsessed with popularity and pop culture. Evangelicals in many ways have abandoned the scriptures as their final authority and have turned to culture as their guiding authority.

This chapter is admittedly slightly caustic and a bit grumpy though it's a serious challenge to plead with Christians in general and Evangelicals in particular to return to the vigorous principles of the Reformation that some have called sola scriptura, the scriptures alone. This author would also add that these same commitments belonged to the early church as well making this issue not merely a "Protestant" thing but a Christian thing. It is long past the time for the church to take worship seriously; to begin practicing the Lord's Supper on a frequent basis and as a symbol of this submission to start using the elements that Jesus gave us in the Holy Supper simply because he gave it. I hope you are hearing this: just do what God says to do because he says to do it. This may be the simplest yet most profound challenge that all Christians face in worship and in life. This is the challenge that worship presents to grape juice Christians.

Submission to God represents so much of everything that one needs in order to worship him. We need a humility that recognizes who we are and who God is, which is exactly what the scriptures teach us. Ironically, this simple commitment to the Bible used to be a hallmark of what it meant to be called an Evangelical. I grew up in such a church.

3. Noll, *Scandal of the Evangelical Mind*, 3.

Some of you may know the song that I learned in Sunday school when I was a little boy.

> the B-I-B-L-E yes that's the book for me. I stand alone on the word of God the B-I-B-L-E—then we all yelled "the Bible!"

Furthermore, when I teach theology at seminaries, I want my students genuinely to believe this little song. My students have asked me many times if I have a single doctrine that is the most important doctrine in the scriptures. While I resist positioning one doctrine above another, I do think that when it comes to fundamental or basic doctrines one's doctrine of the authority of the scriptures is the standard from which all other doctrines are developed. If this doctrine is not solid, everything else is on dangerous ground. Such simple reasoning should strike those who claim to be Evangelicals as extremely important and quite fundamental for what an Evangelical used to believe.

The historian, David Bebbington, in his groundbreaking book, *Evangelicalism in Modern Britain: A History from the 1730s to the 1980s*, outlined and identified four major qualities which historians commonly use when defining what it meant and means to be "Evangelical." Ironically, the first of the four qualities were what Bebbington called, biblicism. By this he argued that for Evangelicals all essential truth was to be found in and based on the Bible. He added crucicentrism, conversionism, and activism. Yet, biblicism acted as something rather basic or foundational for Evangelicals. Biblicism was something of a lynchpin that held the other three together. This is no longer the case today, which means that one may well wonder if what we have called Evangelicalism really exists anymore.

Some contend that the decline in the Evangelical and mainline Protestant churches happened when liberal ideas from Europe took root in America which undermined the authority of the scriptures, and this is true. However, I submit that as powerful as the liberal movement became in undermining the authority of the scriptures, the weakening of scriptural authority in Protestant churches in America actually started long before liberal German ideas invaded seminaries. Rather, it came from within these churches themselves prior to liberalisms march through the mainline churches. This is a seldom told story and it is related to the origins of grape juice Christianity.

A major part of this story relates to the origins of using grape juice in Holy Communion. Evangelicals quite simply changed what Jesus taught about wine. One of the most powerful influences that moved the church in this direction was the novel idea that alcohol was a poison and therefore it should be avoided as a matter of good morality. Relying on "science," many "Evangelicals" taught that using alcohol was one of the most dangerous activities in human behavior. This along with many other cultural ideas changed the American Protestant churches in powerful ways not least of which were worship practices. Evangelicals began rejecting what God accepted and accepting what God rejected—particularly in worship.

It actually drove the church to diverge from God on the heart of the matter in worship, which is the gospel, and many "Evangelicals" began rejecting the basic teachings of the Bible in many ways but particularly in worship practices. I recall a preacher once saying that in worship the heart of the matter is the matter of the heart. This is true because sin is the most fundamental problem for humanity and God centered worship addresses sin as an essential aspect of approaching God through Jesus Christ. Evangelicals changed this basic direction in worship.

When the church rejected wine in communion, she did so in defiance of the basic idea that sin was the heart of humanity's problem—not food, not alcohol, nor any other external substance. When the church rejected the goodness and blessedness of wine as a gift from God, she did so based on a false morality that is foreign to the scriptures and alien to historic Christian ethics. This has undermined Christianity in America in ways that very few have considered seriously. Driven by moralism and pop culture, grape juice Christians created a false morality condemning wine, and then they brought this alien moral standard to God in worship expecting him to accept it as Cain did in one of the earliest stories in the scriptures.

Where did this come from? Where did anyone imagine the idea that God's good gift of wine was suddenly to be condemned as immoral? We can find part of the answer in an excellent work, *The Poisoned Chalice*. Here the author, Jennifer L. Woodruff Tait, outlines the history of the introduction of grape juice into the celebration of the Lord's Supper in the nineteenth century. As noted on the cover of her work, she reveals how "a 1,800-year-old practice of using fermented communion wine became theologically incomprehensible in a mere forty years." Woodruff also reminds us of the powerful connection between what it began to mean to be Evangelical and the historically novel position that alcohol was inherently evil.

Grape juice sympathizers triumphed and became identified first with Methodism and ultimately with the whole spectrum of evangelical and fundamentalist thought.[4]

Unfortunately, from 1846 to the early twentieth century rejecting wine as a good gift from God became an ironic symbol or badge of godliness and Christian virtue. Never mind that such a position is in direct contradiction to Jesus' encouraging the moderate use of wine for celebrating at the wedding of Cana and his command to drink wine in the Lord's Supper. According to such a view, Jesus' teachings were OK for his time, (probably they say because the water was bad back in those days). However, because we now know so much more about science today than Jesus did and he obviously didn't foresee the dangerous abuses of wine in more modern times, blah, blah, blah. Pause for a moment and consider the arrogance of demoting Jesus' teachings on wine as a relic of bad thinking from the past?? Of course, their rejection of Jesus' teachings was not presented as an overt rejection. Instead, they concocted a theory to justify their defiance: the "two wine" theory.

We should take serious note that a full-fledged theory of rejecting Jesus' teaching developed rapidly. It was a classic example of moralists who already had their minds decided against wine, then they began looking desperately for something to justify their views. For instance, Moses Stuart published an 1835 article arguing for dilution of communion wine with water and then in 1849 he argued for what would popularly be known as the "two-wine theory."[5] In spite of its theologically and historically novel character it became fabulously popular throughout American Evangelicalism. The "two wine" theory is the idea that whenever the Bible refers to wine positively it was referring to "unfermented" wine (grape juice). On the other hand, all the warnings about the abuse of wine in the Bible were referring to fermented wine with alcohol. This absurd but convenient notion though having no basis in church history in general or in theological history or for this matter it had no foundation in the scriptures became the substructure for changing communion practices in vast numbers of churches in America, and eventually all over the world.

The innovative "two-wine" theory argued that when Jesus mentioned wine in communion, he must have been referring to unfermented

4. Tait, *Poisoned Chalice*, 11.
5. Tait, *Poisoned Chalice*, 15.

wine or grape juice—the fruit of the vine. This had to be true because according to this new idea, alcohol was understood as a poisonous drug that must be avoided in order to be holy. Eventually, Thomas Welch created a method of pasteurizing freshly squeezed grapes which stopped the fermentation process and created what we today would call grape juice. This replacement of wine provided the novel "two-wine" theory with a practical option, and it also made the Welch family among the richest in the country. Thus, grape juice rapidly replaced wine in Evangelical church worship services. What Jesus accepted; Welch rejected. Typical of their love and obsession for novelty, American Evangelicals choose Welch over Jesus!

In choosing Welch over Jesus, they also turned the gospel on its head. Assuming that humanity's most fundamental problems were associated with our environment—the food we eat, the things we drink, etc. American moralistic Christians began to push for political and legal solutions to humanity's moral problems and saw the gospel not as the sole or even primary solution to the problem of sin, but as one solution among many—and a weak one too. The virtual obsession of grape juice Christians with what became known as the temperance movement motivated them to aim so high that some even argued that if temperance prevailed, the prisons in America would be mostly empty and a kind of heaven would come down to earth. This was presented as the nation's greatest moral battle—the crusade to rid the world of alcohol. The gospel was slowly and imperceptibly lost in this grape juice crusade for a moral America.

Conversion through preaching the gospel alone is one thing, but it depends on persuasion, which for a moralist is too weak. Likewise, it tends to belittle the idea that somehow our basic problem is sin; instead pointing to our problem as originating in food or drink. The apparent weakness of persuasion (the gospel) is something a strong moralist cannot abide. Thus, pushing the moralists to move from the central emphasis of converting a sinner's heart through the apparent weakness of persuasion such as preaching, to passing a law so people would be forced to be moral; this immediately appealed to temperance warriors as a stronger remedy to humanity's problems. Therefore, these virtue mongers were not content with the supposed power of preaching; they needed coercion, they needed laws.

American Evangelicals became obsessed with what was called the temperance movement. According to one author, Joseph Gusfield,

The movement sought to make America into a clean sober godly and decorous people whose aspirations and style of living would reflect the moral leadership of New England Federalism.[6]

For them the fickleness and weakness of depending on the Holy Spirit to convert people through the sole means of preaching had to be replaced with something more powerful: laws. Not just any laws, but the highest possible kind of law, a constitutional amendment. Imagine the colossal moral influence that Christians had in America that was so utterly wasted on the temperance movement, which was historically novel, scripturally unsustainable, and ultimately a cultural/political disaster! This should cause American Evangelicals to cringe with embarrassment at the momentous political and moral influence that could have been used for an authentic scriptural cause! The moralistic temperance movement not only failed miserably to provide genuine ethical direction to the nation, but it also essentially misdirected the nation away from the gospel and gutted Christian worship of a central, God-given symbol of the blood of Jesus to conquer sin: wine.

When you combine these ideas with an already man-centered approach to the gospel, you have a disastrous result. For instance, the Evangelical church had made it so incredibly easy to "follow Jesus" that all one needed to do is "accept Jesus into your heart as your personal savior." Whatever this phrase was supposed to have meant, it wasn't from the Bible, and it had little to do with serious discipleship or following after Jesus with one's whole life. The idea of lordship and thoughtful discipleship was entirely lost to what could be called easy-believism. The context was a period when waves of "revival" had swept through America in the 1820s in what is sometimes called the Second Great Awakening.

The famous Charles Finney had helped to pioneer an approach to "worship" that was essentially a massive psychological technique to "get people saved," which meant "persuading" them to come forward to what John W. Nevin called the anxious bench: a place at the front of the church to which people were psychologically bullied into "coming forward" to accept Jesus into their hearts. The altar call at the conclusion of a service replaced the Lord's Supper. The "worship" service principally focused on the subjective work of "getting people saved," rather than on celebrating the objective work of Christ and the cross to save us from sins. Heretofore worship services were generally concluded with a call to come to

---

6. Gusfield, *Symbolic Crusade*, 4.

Christ in the Holy Supper—to taste and see that the Lord is good. After the revivalist movement swept through Evangelical America, traditional Christian worship was replaced with gatherings to get people saved using the revivalist techniques and gimmicks.

Some referred to the novelty of the revival meetings and altar calls as the new measures. These new measures seemed to be fabulously successful in urging people to make decisions for Jesus, but they also had derogatory effects on historic worship. A few nineteenth century thinkers such as John W. Nevin saw these new measures as part of a whole system that degraded worship into something that would lead Christianity down a path towards excess, and fanaticism in worship. As were many of his writings Nevin said presciently,

> No satisfactory line can be drawn between this and the more advanced forms of extravagance, for which it prepares the way.[7]

Nevin warned that the church should never use the popularity of something as a true measure for the basis of changing the structure and nature of worship.[8] If so, then the church will move worship away from a reverent, God-centered activity into a man-centered endeavor which God had never intended worship to be. As early as 1844 Nevin was rightly warning the church that using such unsound and unscriptural techniques and methods merely because they appeared to produce popular results was a road to the certain destruction of worship. It transformed worship away from a powerful form of God-centered discipleship into a kind of spiritual theater. Nevin noted,

> The pulpit is transformed, more or less, into a stage. Divine things are so popularized, as to be at last shorn of their dignity as well as their mystery.[9]

Nevin's prescient warnings from the nineteenth century are virtually prophetic. D.G. Hart adds to Nevin's insightful critique saying,

> the problem is that evangelicals replaced the Lord's supper, the very means God gave his church to call believers to repentance and commitment with the altar call, a manipulative practice designed to generate a quick decision for Christ. Revivalism was just as destructive in reconfiguring the purpose of worship.

---

7. Nevin, *Anxious Bench*, 15.
8. Nevin, *Anxious Bench*, 33.
9. Nevin, *Anxious Bench*, 108.

Worship in evangelical circles is oriented primarily to reaching the lost rather than to ascribing power and glory to God. Once the gathering of the saints and the proclamation of the Word become chiefly a way to reach the lost, worship moves from its properly God-centered orientation to one in which pleasing men and women, preferably the lost (or in today's lingo, "seekers"), becomes the overarching goal.[10]

If the overarching goal is pleasing men and women, then that which authenticates truth and religious reality among Evangelicals was primarily their personal religious experience. Thus, worship had moved away from a solid commitment to the authority of the scriptures moving the center to people and their experience. Testimonies could replace preaching as a central part of worship and thus subjective human experience replaced God as the objective center of worship. The individual and his or her religious experience had become the driving force in Evangelical worship—not God.

The course of this trend has continued to grow in today's Evangelical world. Instead of serious preaching in worship directed to discipleship, Evangelicals have transformed preaching into entertainment-filled "conversations" where the hip pastor runs around on a large stage using props, skits, and a gigantic PowerPoint show that flashes behind him and around the stage on well-positioned screens. Everything is carefully crafted to entertain. Today the "worship leader" has the requisite haircut, cool skinny jeans and even better if you can see a few tattoos offering the audience a little "street cred." He then tells jokes, stories, and squeezes in a very "serious" lesson while the gospel is basically lost to the show.

If there is a presentation of the "gospel" in worship, it comes at the end of the show when the "preacher" calls people to accept Jesus as their personal savior. This trivialized and individualized "gospel" is just a small part of the show. Lesslie Newbigin reminds us of the dangers of such an approach:

> Evangelism is not some kind of technique by means of which people are persuaded to change their minds and think like us. Evangelism is the telling of good news, but what changes people's minds and converts their wills is always a mysterious work of the sovereign Holy Spirit, and we are not permitted to know more than a little of his secret working.[11]

10. Hart, *Recovering Mother Kirk*, 212.
11. Newbigin, *Lesslie Newbigin*, 144.

As noted earlier, Evangelicals turned away from serious thinking about worship. To be honest they rarely think seriously about any theology. Not surprisingly, this appears to have paved the way for the bland and meaningless theology that has become what one group of sociologists have called moralistic therapeutic deism. Moralistic therapeutic deism is a term that was introduced in the 2005 book *Soul Searching: The Religious and Spiritual Lives of American Teenagers* by sociologists Christian Smith and Melinda Lundquist Denton.

Smith's book is the result of the research project the "National Study of Youth and Religion". The term moralistic therapeutic deism is what Smith uses to describe the common beliefs among American youths. In summary moralistic therapeutic deism argues that there is a God up there somewhere and while he cares generally about right and wrong, he is mostly a distant ruler. Given the pathetic theology of worship in so many popular churches it's no wonder the basic theological ideas of moralistic therapeutic deism are so prevalent. One might wish to think that churches who are outwardly committed to the authority of the scriptures are immune from this theological trend. However, sadly even the most treasured area of resistance to this seemingly overwhelming power, worship, is no longer a place of resistance. Bland, moralistic theology flows naturally from a thoughtless approach to theology and a basic rejection of the guiding authority of the scriptures in worship.

Once "Evangelicals" subtly but genuinely rejected the authority of the scriptures, which had historically been a hallmark of what it meant to be Evangelical, all bets were off—even the ancient and beautiful mystery of the Holy Communion could be thrown aside for what is popular. Furthermore, one could arbitrarily replace wine with grape juice even though the idea that alcohol is poison can't be found anywhere in the scriptures. Nevertheless, this novelty—found nowhere in the Bible—replaced the Bible's teachings on wine. Then in order to follow a poisonous unbiblical theory about wine, worship itself had to be altered. To make matters worse by the beginning of the twentieth century a simultaneous and alien moral theory from popular groups was gaining ground. The polluted moralism which teaches those external things like wine constituted the basic moral impurity that had to be eliminated for good moral behavior. Moralism not only found a comfortable place in the church—it became central.

Eventually groups like AA latched onto the poisonous juice theory supplanting sin as the central interest of the gospel. Turning to AA as if it were a meaningful answer to the problem of drunkenness is like the church turning to a cheap moralistic fix for a much deeper problem. In speaking and reading about AA you will hear them saying something like the following: AA's concept revolves around that premise that alcoholism is an illness that can be managed, but not controlled. The scriptural language of drunkenness as a sin is lost to moralism. The language of sin is replaced with the language of psychology arguing that drunkenness is now an "addiction" rather than a sin problem.

Based on this scripturally foreign moralism God's originally ordained way of worship needed to be changed because everyone knows that when someone is an alcoholic you need to show him deference as the weaker brother. In order for everyone else to show they are strong they need to become weak? Yes, it even has a kind of biblical ring to it. The weak become strong or something like this. This is a little weird to be honest. Why doesn't it apply to using drugs like the Baptists drug of choice, caffeine in coffee?[12] It doesn't apply because it's counterfeit, and it always has been.

Unfortunately, this position is unscriptural as well as unsustainable. Isn't using drugs a poisonous pollution of the temple of the Lord? I love the cartoon I once saw of an overweight woman drinking diet coke and shoving a doughnut in her mouth as crumbles fell off her face began answering another woman with moral outrage who had asked her if she minded her smoking. The offended corpulent woman while struggling to swallow her doughnut said that she objected to smoking because her body was the temple of the Holy Spirit. There you have it; smoking is out, but caffeine and sugar are in. (Coffee, cokes, and doughnuts are after all the drugs of choice at almost all "fellowship" activities in churches.) Such are the arbitrary and frivolous rules of the moralistic Evangelicals—utterly convinced that by quoting the whole, temple of the Holy Spirit thing that their position is completely biblical.

American moralism has dug its way into the hearts and souls of moralistic Protestants for so long they don't even know how to tell the difference between a false morality and the Scriptural teachings on self-control and moderation. Some of the "arguments" that you hear attempting to forbid the use of wine are embarrassing and make you wonder if the proponents are so poor in their exegesis of the scriptures

---

12. No offense to Baptist. I grew up Baptist and it always amused me that the preacher would rave against the use of alcohol and other drugs then move us directly downstairs for a time of coffee and doughnuts between Sunday school and worship.

on this point—are they really at all trustworthy at other points. One is the silly notion that in Matt. 26:29 when Jesus institutes the Lord's Supper he refers to the wine as the fruit of the vine, which for these innovative exegetes could have meant grape juice.

Let me just dispense with the preposterous notion that somehow the phrase fruit of the vine could have meant grape juice. First, and rather significantly there was no such thing as grape juice as we know it in Jesus' day. It was not until the 1869 and the work of Thomas Welch that what we today know as grape juice was invented. Certainly, there would have been freshly squeezed wine with lower levels of alcohol, but this is not what Jesus was meaning. He was referring to the wine used at the Passover meal.

It is really as basic as understanding that the phrase fruit of the vine simply means wine. Nothing about this is difficult to comprehend unless you already have a prejudice against wine. The only reason you would think otherwise would be that you would want to try to import or introduce the idea of grape juice almost two thousand years before it was actually invented by the Welches. For the record, this is called *isegesis* (imposing an outside meaning into the text) rather than exegesis (drawing the meaning out of the text).

It is very simple and should not be controversial. Fruit of the vine was just a well-known phrase that meant wine. Let me provide an example of how well-known phrases work. What if my son wanted to go to a party on a university campus that he said was called a brew party and he said that the entry fee was to bring a six pack of brew. If he wanted to convince me he should be allowed to go, he might try a silly approach and say, "but Dad brew is a generic term that could include iced tea or coffee." The response to such a statement would of course be laughter—he shouldn't be taken seriously.

This isn't convincing because in the context, everyone knows that "brew" is not referring to tea or to coffee and it's especially silly because the common phrase "six pack" is without any doubt in this context referring to beer. Can brew refer to coffee—yes. Can a six pack refer to tea or soda—yes. But nobody would possibly be serious or could be expected to be taken seriously if he or she showed up at the beer party with tea, coffee, or sodas. Hopefully, no parent would take such a silly approach seriously either. Why then are so many grape juice Christians taken seriously? Why would pastors who teach such tripe also be taken seriously?

Again, to pick up on my own proud Reformed tradition, I hear the same thing in my churches. Fruit of the vine, we are told, is a phrase that could include grape juice since grape juice could also be considered the fruit of the vine. This is so odd and there is not even a remote possibility that since Welch's grape juice was invented in the nineteenth century that Jesus could possibly have referred to grape juice, which wasn't yet invented.

Furthermore, we don't have any historical doubt that Jesus was talking about wine because he was using an already known wine that the Jews had been using for Passover meals for more than a thousand years—there is no serious historical or theological doubt that Jesus is referring to wine commonly used at Passover. The only reason to doubt this is if someone wanted to introduce something from outside the text and insert it into our understanding of it. The only way to change communion wine into grape juice is by backing into this passage with an assumption that Jesus got it wrong because he must somehow have not yet known that wine was poison. If you simply look at the Bible and draw out its meaning, then you can't honestly come to the position that Jesus didn't know what he was doing in using wine.

Remember that this is intimately related to the gospel. Because the gospel teaches that humanity's greatest problem is sin, not the environment. The Bible never teaches that food or drink is inherently bad or that such things are at the heart of our problems. How could Jesus use wine, which is supposedly an inherently sinful object to symbolize his blood? Of course, food and wine are not bad things, and it is very simply because the Scriptures never teach such false morality. To the contrary, food and drinks are gifts from God to make our hearts glad as we try to live well in this world as embodied creatures. Moralism, on the other hand, is connected to exactly the kind of teachers against whom Paul warns the church in I Tim. 4:3–4 they are moralists.

> who forbid marriage and require abstinence from foods that God created to be received with thanksgiving by those who believe and know the truth. 4 For everything created by God is good, and nothing is to be rejected if it is received with thanksgiving, 5 for it is made holy by the word of God and prayer.

Of course, the abuse of either food or drink is a sin, but the food and drink themselves are good gifts from God and they are to be received as such. Abusing food is called gluttony and abusing wine is called drunkenness. This is fairly simple. To say that food or drink is bad when God has created them as good is a perversion of reality. Such an approach is no less a perversion of their good use than gluttony or drunkenness!

We should also have a simple respect for Jesus. If Jesus chose wine, then we should use wine. Likewise, Jesus chose wine as a symbol of his blood and there are many scriptural reasons why he did so. It's amazing that one would need to do this, but a quick look in the scriptures reveals that throughout the whole Bible wine is good and acts as a sign of God's blessings. Psalm 104:15 says that God gives "wine to gladden the heart of man." In Ps. 23:5, David speaks of God's great blessings using the symbol of a cup of wine overflowing. Ps. 116:13 speaks of praise and thanksgiving saying he will "lift up the cup" of salvation. Prov. 3:9-10 states that when we honor the Lord with our wealth and with the firstfruits of our land, "then your barns will be filled with plenty, and your vats will be bursting with wine." Repeatedly wine is listed among the abundant blessings God promises to Israel if they keep His covenant (Deut. 7:13; 11:14; 33:28).

A deep irony for grape juice Christians and the temperance movement is that in the scriptures the loss of wine was commonly seen as a curse—please let this sink in. (Deut. 28:39, 51; Hos. 9:2; Joel 1:10; Amos 5:11; Mic. 6:15; Zeph. 1:13; Hag. 1:11; Isa. 16:10; Jer. 48:33). This was due not only to the loss of the enjoyment of wine, but because wine was an important part of worship. Wine was central to the religious life of all believers in which it was used as a feature of their sacrificial offerings and liturgical practices—as a symbol of blessings (Exod.29:40; Lev. 23:13; Num. 15:5,7,10 18:12; 28:7,14; Deut.18:4; 1 Sam. 1:24; 2 Chr. 31:5; Ezra 6:9; 7:22; Neh. 5:11; 10:37, 39; 13:12).

Far from being a poisonous danger, wine was fundamentally a good thing and a kind gift from God—essential to worship. The holy leaders of Israel, the Levites, received wine for themselves from the tithes given by the worshipers (Num. 18:30). Average believers were also supposed to enjoy wine. As if the earlier verses were not enough, Deut. 14:26 urges God's people to enjoy alcohol as a natural part of their religious love and celebration before the Lord. This is shocking to grape juice Christians. Here God encourages faithful believers to enjoy feasting and drinking after they had made a long journey to Jerusalem to worship for a time where they should learn to fear the Lord. (Deut. 14:23). It's worth quoting in full, and spend the money for whatever you desire—oxen or sheep or wine or strong drink, whatever your appetite craves. And you shall eat there before the LORD your God and rejoice, you and your household.

In the sacrificial system, in meals, feasts and celebrations of all kinds, and in general living, God wanted his people to appreciate wine as a good gift from his loving hand. This doesn't mean that all Christians must drink wine every day (although some say that there are health benefits to the daily moderate use of wine). However, it most certainly means that we are not allowed to say that using wine in a religious celebration such as the Eucharist is something negative when God has said it is positive. We are also not allowed to replace what Jesus commanded with something that we prefer, especially when we do so using a false grape juice theology as a guide rather than the scriptures, which I hope we have seen is weak and alien to scriptural thinking.

Using wine in Holy Communion is not neutral or irrelevant. One of the many reasons that Jesus choose to use fermented wine in the Lord's supper is that wine represents not only the present blessings of God but perhaps most powerfully wine represents the future blessings of God. The fancy theological word for this is eschatological. Eschatology usually refers to the study end times or future prophetic blessings. In this sense wine is a symbol of eschatological or future blessings in Christ. This is why the prophets could refer to the eschatological blessings of the covenant using wine imagery. Listen to Isa. 25:6,

> On this mountain the LORD of hosts will make for all peoples a feast of rich food, a feast of well-aged wine, of rich food full of marrow, of aged wine well refined.

This is also why Amos could speak of the future covenant blessings of God as restoring the fortunes, planting vineyards and drinking wine (Amos 9:14). Eating good food and drinking good wine was a pervasive and beautiful image of eschatological blessings. The idea of reducing wine to a poison instead of a blessing is certainly not from God! Jeremiah speaks of future blessings in terms of wine (Jer. 31:12). Like David in Ps. 23:5 the prophet Joel speaks of the future blessings of God's covenant as vats overflowing with wine (Joel 2:24-25).

All of the biblical imagery of wine as a divine blessing is confirmed in Jesus' own ministry. It's no small thing that his first recorded miracle was changing the water into wine at the wedding of Cana. Transforming water into wine was Jesus' inaugural miracle as recorded in redemptive history. Wine became the opening symbol of the ministry of Jesus as messiah. Here Jesus created six twenty- or thirty-gallon jars of water into well-aged, highly fermented wine. He then encouraged the wedding party to enjoy it—and yes, he most certainly drank some himself. The eschatological imagery of wine comes into play in this inaugural miracle so powerfully.

The opening of Jesus' ministry provokes images of Isa. 25:6 where we are told that messiah will bring a new day of celebrating with a feast of rich foods and well-aged wine. In John 2 the story of the wedding at Cana the guests marvel that the wine Jesus created was "good wine," the "best" wine, which was well-aged wine. This enhances the character of his miracle in immediately changing water to wine, but it also highlights the emphasis on wine as marking the celebratory entry of our Lord. Jesus' wine would have been the kind of wine reserved primarily for kings, queens, and aristocrats who appreciated the aging and crafting process that such wines would need in order to be considered well-aged wines. This would have been the kind of wine that one author says would have been "too powerful and majestic to be cut with water."[13] Well-aged wines were the stuff of kings and queens—Jesus now gives such wine to us. What a marvelous way to open the ministry of our savior and to point to the great eschatological blessings we have in Jesus Christ. Likewise, what a marvelous way to celebrate his ministry in the Lord's Supper.

Wine unites God's people with the ultimate eschatological hope we have in Jesus' blood to forgive our sins and cleanse us of all unrighteousness. The blood of Jesus represents the remission of sins that we can only receive through Jesus Christ. It is our only hope in this life and in the life to come. What a fitting symbol that wine is used to represent the blood of Jesus Christ. Indeed, what better way for a drunkard to remember that the blood of Jesus conquers drunkenness than to drink wine in celebration of salvation. What a powerful, mysterious and ironic image—what a blessing!

Wine points us to all of the greatest blessings we have in Christ. It directs us to the great future hope we have as we are pointed to the wedding feasts we will eat with our savior when he makes all things right. Jesus drank wine at the last supper, and he promises to drink wine with us

---

13. Lukacs, *Inventing Wine*, 21.

in that future great wedding feast in heaven. Yes, even grape juice Christian will be drinking wine in heaven!

With all of the scriptural and also beautiful imagery of wine as a blessing, what a weird, weak, and neutered symbol that grape juice Christians have chosen to replace God's choice of wine with grape juice! But why? Why would the powerful, celebratory symbol of wine be replaced by grape juice? It certainly is not driven by scripture. This brings us back to something of a theme in this little study of worship. Worship should be driven by faith and not fear. Faith and obedience to the divinely appointed ordinances of God should be the directing and driving factors in worship. We should do what God says to do, simply because he says to do it.

When we simply receive by faith that Jesus gave us wine—not grape juice. Then we use wine by faith—God responds with blessings to us. We should never be driven by fear of the false theology of moralists or Alcoholics Anonymous. Faith and not fear moves us to receive what Jesus has given without question, worry or doubt. Fear might cause us to ask—what if people won't come to our church if we use wine? What if someone is convinced that they should not touch a single drop of alcohol and so they won't come to the Eucharist at our church? What if, what if, what if! Such fear should never drive worship practices. Faith and not fear should motivate all worship practices.

Behind these ideas is a basic challenge—are you humble and brave enough to say what God says? I have actually been surprised at the courage needed for many Christians simply to say what God says. I can provide you some examples that will probably send some of you into a bit of a frenzy. The scriptures in I Tim. 2 say that women should not be teaching and having authority over men in the church. God says something pretty simple: "I do not permit it." Now find me the church that says this without apology or excuse? Furthermore, the scriptures are crystal clear that if a man has sexual relations with another man, it is a sin. But where are the churches saying this? Rather than directing cultures and communities to follow God, in fear the church cowers at the frown of the culture. Perhaps it's because the church and the culture have become the same! Or perhaps we are witnessing the church falling to the powerful cultural movements like a sandcastle on the beach. When the church uses the same guiding principle as the culture, and these principles are wrong, then the church is no different from the culture around it.

There are still other factors involved in grape juice Christianity. In order to understand grape juice Christianity better we also need to recognize the idea of the democratization and pop acculturation especially of Evangelical Christianity. The historian, Nathan Hatch has examined and outlined the democratization of American Christianity in his excellent work, *The Democratization of American Christianity*.

> American Protestantism has been skewed away from central ecclesiastical institutions and high culture; it has been pushed and pulled into its present shaped by a democratic or populists orientation.[14]

The democratization of American Christianity meant that there was never to be a king over the people of God. But wait, is the church really a democracy? In fact, the church is a monarchy. This is exactly why Jesus claims to be king upon his resurrection and ascension. He is seated at the right hand of God the father almighty, and he is the king to whom every knee shall bow. Yet, Americans as the saying goes don't bow to anyone. We are all equal. In fact, instead of bowing the knee to a king, Patrick Henry inspired Americans that they should "bow with utmost deference to the majesty of the people."[15] According to Hatch, the American Revolution brought these kinds of beliefs into the Protestant churches which had created a cultural ferment over the meaning of freedom. "Turmoil," Hatch argued, "swirled around the crucial issues of authority, organization and leadership."[16]

This tendency to be moralistic, individualistic, and democratic meant that American Evangelical Christianity was deeply flawed in major areas of thinking, all of which would create an approach to worship utterly perverted in its orientation. When combined with what Hatch referred to as a position of anti-authority in religious matters meant that American Evangelical Christianity was fundamentally flawed in its ecclesiology as well. The church is not a democracy because Jesus is the king. He has not established the church on democratic or popular principles but rather he has commanded that the church ruled by elders who have divine though ministerial authority over the members of the church—the church follows the instructions of her king. If the rule of elders over laymen in the church

---

14. Hatch, *Democratization of American Christianity*, 5.
15. Hatch, *Democratization of American Christianity*, 6.
16. Hatch, *Democratization of American Christianity*, 6.

sounds undemocratic, it's because it's not democratic. It's the rule of King Jesus through leaders that he appoints in the church.

If we stop for a moment and consider how radical democratic impulses are when situated in the context of worship, then we should be seriously worried about worship as something that is inherently God-centered, but in the context of American history has become essentially man-centered. If America's democratic individualism is correct, then the individual's will, interests or "vote" is the center of everything in the world. This replaces God-centered Christianity with a man-centered religion of some sort, which is especially pernicious in worship since everything in worship is to be offered to God because he is God and because he is the center of everything. It stands in direct contrast to scriptural worship as we have outlined in this little study.

To make matters even worse, the American obsession with moralism and democracy is simultaneously situated in an American obsession with entertainment. In his book, *Life: The Movie: How Entertainment Conquered Reality*, Neal Gabler outlines how American culture has been overtaken by entertainment. He argues that our culture's "bottomless appetite for novelty, gossip, and melodrama" has turned everything including religion into one vast public entertainment.[17] Not too many years ago my family used to enjoy a game called Trivial Pursuit. It was incredibly popular. This may be an apt summary of today's grape juice worship practices: trivial pursuit. Worship has been transformed from a God-centered, reverent activity into the pursuit of the trivial, the inane and the vapid, and most unfortunately, it's all in the name of Jesus. The following quote decries the fall of high culture to entertainment—I would beg the reader to replace the word, arts with worship (modifying the grammar) in order to feel the devastating effects of entertainment culture on the church's worship.

> Perhaps the most difficult adjustments to the imperatives of entertainment were those undergone by the arts which had, by definition, been arrayed against entertainment and had denied its sensationalist aesthetic. These had tried to hold the line even as everything else seemed to be succumbing around them, but not even art could finally resist the siren call of show business. The arts were forced either to surrender or to be

17. Gabler, *Life: The Movie*, 20.

marginalized to the point where they would cease to matter to any but a handful of devotees.[18]

If we combine the conquest of entertainment with the dreadful effects of subjective, moralistic, democratic, individualism in America, then historic Christian worship is effectively under complete cultural siege. Leigh Eric Schmidt notes,

> From Roger Williams to Ralph Waldo Emerson, the America Protestant mythos seemed designed to produce churches of one member. With the right of private judgment exalted if not fetishized, the spiritual hankerings of the lone individual overtook the collective authority of the church time and again. As Schaff saw it, an atomistic sectarianism had found its most fertile ground in the United states . . . In America he discovered "a variegated sampler of all conceivable religious chimeras and dreams; "here was a land in which "the arbitrary fancies and baseless opinions of an individual" repeatedly superseded the church as a historical body and living communion.[19]

When this devastating reality is also then combined with evangelicalism's moralistic approach to human behavior as evidenced in their long-standing obsession with the temperance movement then Christian worship is effectively gutted of its essential meaning and purpose. All of these dreadful influences are supposed to be counteracted in God-centered worship. Instead, grape juice worship has succumbed to them almost completely.

Christians have turned the scriptural ethical system on its head with scriptures being placed under the authority of an alien worldview rather than rejecting the foreign views based simply on the fact that such views are in conflict with God's word. It's painfully simple, which is why this chapter is saturated with a strong sarcastic tone. It's time we either started following our principles or started another Reformation not against the Roman Catholics, but against the moralistic, individualistic, and entertainment-driven Protestants who have replaced God's word with man's words and man's teachings in worship. We need a Reformation against grape juice Christianity.

We may also note that teachers who are defending individualistic moralism fit closely into the same mold as the Pharisees and Sadducees

---

18. Gabler, *Life: The Movie*, 20.
19. Schaff, *Development of the Church*, 5.

in Jesus' day and Jesus leveled his harshest words against them. James has already warned that teachers will be judged more strictly for what they teach—and there are millions of Protestant teachers who are feeding their sheep a rotten, anti-biblical slurry that they are calling ethics.

The West, and America in particular, is crying for leadership from the church at its most basic level—but the church has failed. The church has failed to provide leadership in her teachings but most especially in her worship practices. The West, and America, is floundering. To say that America and the west is experiencing cultural decline is an understatement that sounds like the beginning of a bad joke.

> The United States, locked in the kind of twilight disconnect that grips dying empires, is a country entranced by illusions. It spends its emotional and intellectual energy on the trivial and the absurd. It is captivated by the hollow stagecraft of celebrity culture as the walls crumble.[20]

People in America are like the ancient Romans who had only known a steady, stable western dominated world and now the empire has fallen. Their emotions and interests had been captivated by the public games and when the government inspired entertainment finally died, they were lost and directionless. So, Americans like ancient Romans are longing to find someone and somewhere in the world with a sense of steadiness amidst the insanity that feels so overwhelming. This is what made St. Augustine's great work, *The City of God*, so compelling and so appealing after Rome was defeated for the first time in A.D 410.

If massive numbers of churches, who claim to believe the Bible are afraid to follow it in areas of such obvious simplicity as using wine in communion, then why would the world listen to the church? But imagine what might happen if these same millions of believers started doing what God said to do without any apology! They say that courage is contagious. How much more if the church was courageous in her worship? I challenge Christians everywhere to consider returning to the ancient and powerful simplicity of Christian worship that has wine and the blood of Jesus as central to worship. How wonderful this would be if it happened every single week in worship!

This chapter contains a most pointed a question, that is not merely about wine, it's the question of why, why won't Evangelical and Reformed Protestants simply do what God says to do in worship? Throughout the

---

20. Hedges, "American Psychosis," para. 2.

first one thousand eight hundred years the church practiced communion using wine, not grape juice. Let this sink in! For virtually the first two thousand years of Christian history almost everyone, almost everywhere used wine in communion! They did so because they were following the simple teachings of Jesus, not alcoholics anonymous or any other moralistic psychology that says scripturally bizarre things like this: once an alcoholic always an alcoholic?? This is like saying, once of thief, always a thief or once a liar always a liar—seriously undermining the gospel.

We need to step back and examine how radically unbiblical and alien these ideas are when compared to the scriptures that encourage us to know that when we are in Christ, we are new creatures—old things are passed away—and behold all things, new! The scriptures encourage us in the power of God's grace to break the chains of slavery to sin. One of the greatest Old Testament stories of salvation is set in the context of liberation from the land of slavery!! Salvation through the blood of Jesus sets us free and we are free indeed. Wine is the symbol of this freedom. Wine is God's chosen symbol for our liberation from sin, which is why Jesus said, "all of you drink it."

Here's even more good news. God knows that though free from sin in Christ, we will also struggle with sin in this sinful world. In order to help us along the way and to help us in the hard struggle with sin, he has given us sacraments that aid us. Yes, even the Lord's Supper, which provides through the power of the Holy Spirit aid, comfort, and affirmation in grace. In worship we should hear the gospel preached in a sermon and then by God's mercy we should be able to reach out to him as he stoops down to our level and feeds us with literal things like bread and wine. Yes, in the Lord's Supper God reaches down from heaven and touches us with reaffirming grace saying as it were: you are mine and I am yours, and I love you. Using wine in communion God says, I will help you struggle with drunkenness if you will trust in in me, symbolized in my blood. I will nourish you in your battle with these seemingly overwhelming struggles because I love you and have given myself for you on the cross—and because I have overcome. In the wine of communion God reminds us that he will be with us as he takes us into the future where one day we will eat and drink as the great enemies of Satan and sin shall be defeated forever.

The little book is a challenge to grape juice Christians with the strident test with which worship confronts us. The test is simple: are we willing to do what God says to do? Let the light of the Scriptures' teachings on wine help you to reject the false teachings of grape juice Christianity.

For some of you this may be a very hard move to make. However, listen to the words of J. Gresham Machen,

> Light may seem at times to be an impertinent intruder, but it is always beneficial in the end. The type of religion which rejoices in the pious sound of traditional phrases, regardless of their meanings, or shrinks from "controversial" matters, will never stand amid the shocks of life. In the sphere of religion, as in other spheres, the things about which men are agreed are apt to be the things that are least worth holding; the really important things are the things about which men will fight.[21]

Courage is contagious and so is faithfulness. There is something so exciting and thrilling when you find someone who tells the truth and "tells it like it is," especially after prolonged periods of nauseating silence or worst yet double speak; the phenomenon of clarity and courage awakens other people's heart to the same excitement—courage is contagious. This is true of cultures as well. Imagine, what might happen if the church actually took the simple words of Jesus seriously and started practicing a humble but potent Christianity in worship? I tell you that when even a single church does this, people are amazed, and attracted to it. I have seen it firsthand. When a church starts doing things that are in the scriptures, but which due to fear or other weak motives many churches have failed to do or refused to practice, then people begin to take notice—and they like it. May God bless his church in rejecting grape juice Christianity and turning fully to the blood of Jesus Christ as our only hope in life and in death!

If by faith and with genuine humility to the words of Christ, the church returns to frequent communion using the elements that God wants it to use, then this author believes that multiple other blessings may come to the church; and it's also my hope that these blessings will flood into the church like a raging river after the spring rains—like revival. The idea is quite simple—God blesses the humble, but he resists the proud, which is most emphatically true in worship. The logic flows from the simple idea that many of life's difficulties tend to fall into place when one simply puts first things first. And worship is first among all things. Perhaps the most basic guiding principle in worship is to say what God says and then do what he says to do. Then as the scriptures say, he will make your paths straight!

---

21. Machen, *Christianity and Liberalism*, 4.

Conclusion

I HOPE THIS LITTLE work on embodied worship has spurred you to reconsider the place and purpose of worship in your life, especially if you are a minister or elder in your church. I also hope that it will create a renewed interest in worship as the central matter of life. It is, if I may be so bold as to say, a call to another Reformation not in general but in worship primarily.

I have tried to outline in essential though admittedly skeletal form some guiding principles for worship, with particular interest in the role of the body and liturgy. The first and most basic principle of worship is what has traditionally been called the regulative principle—we only do what God wants in worship. God is the center of worship—not man. Everything is therefore structured in worship according to what God wants. When we meet with him in worship we celebrate his glory, his might, and his love. Worship offers the humble in Christ an opportunity to renew their covenant of love and to be filled with grace and adoration of God. We don't structure worship around theoretical seekers or someone who we want to get saved. We structure worship around the actual person to whom worship is given: God. God is at the center of worship.

From the regulative principle we then move to the second guiding principle found in I Cor. 14:40: all things should be done decently and in order. This principle requires us to think carefully about the elements of worship as they fit into the overall telos or purpose of worship. This one is a bit more ticklish than the regulative principle and it calls for wisdom and careful study of how best to glorify God in bringing to him the worship that he wants and in the most excellent and beautiful manner possible.

All of the previously mentioned principles of worship include a focus on the fundamental givenness of embodied worship. We are embodied beings who live physically in a physical world and worship is not disconnected from our embodied existence. I am amazed at the times in my life whether happy or sad when human touch made a powerful difference. When someone says encouraging words it's helpful, but when they take hold of your hands as they look you in the eye, it adds an embodied dimension that has a mysterious and powerful effect. It's deeply human. When, for instance, I've been touched, hugged and/or held in times of troubles, it adds an embodied feature that has a powerful effect. How could it be any different? When you are near someone who is overcome with grief at the death of their loved one, your instinct is to reach out and to touch them. We do this because we are embodied beings. The same is true of worship.

This little book is situated in the context of worship as a supernatural work of God. None of our activity or liturgy in worship means anything without the presence of God's Holy Spirit. As noted in the introduction, in worship by faith and in the Holy Spirit God opens the heavens for us to meet with him before his throne. Worship is like ascending the mountain of God to meet with him as he comes down to touch the mountain and dwells with us. The angels join us in this kind of worship as well.

This study of worship comes at a time that many are calling an inflection point in history? Over the past few years, I have been hearing that western civilization and America in particular is at an inflection point? The phrase inflection point has been taken from mathematics and indicates a point at which a line curvature changes from being concave (curving downward) to being convex (curving upward) or vice versa. Culturally an inflection point is a similar kind of deviation or change in direction and our culture is changing rapidly.

Only three seconds ago it was culturally acceptable that homosexuality was a deviant behavior. Only three seconds ago everyone casually accepted that the only two genders were male and female. Only three seconds ago it was considered racists to judge another person based solely on their skin color. Now, we are facing a world in which the political and intellectual elites are demanding that everyone positively affirm something they, only three seconds, ago all agreed was the opposite. In one of most brazen, Orwellian twists of language, critical race theory now unapologetically demands that white people accept ill-defined, moral guilt for their whiteness. Up is down and down is up and we are required to say this with appropriate affirmation and humility—say it! We need worship at the center of our lives especially in such crazy times so that we are redirected away from the lies we are being coerced into accepting. We need to hear the truth; we need to hear from God.

Worship helps us to remain steady and properly oriented in the midst of the raging stupidity of our times and of any times. If we are facing an inflection point in history (and we are) then there may have never been a better time in history for the church to take worship seriously.

As a word to pastors and elders, it's time to think of worship as a full, embodied experience that will empower God's people to face the present pressure with a faithfulness that worship provides us. This will require us to take worship more seriously. We will need to approach the whole worship experience with diligence, preparation, and prayer. Since worship is much more than a sermon, we need to think about every aspect of worship with regard to engaging the embodied reality of God's people. God's people need God and worship is the most powerful means by which God through Christ comes to his people and meets with them in an official, wonderful, mysterious, and grace-filled experience—we need this more than ever.

We need to call God's people to Christ in worship! As ministers we should call them to stand in his presence, call them to raise their hands in praise and prayer to him, call them to raise their voices to him in song, call them to kneel before him as they confess their sins, call them to eat and drink together in his presence. All of this involves powerful, robust theological instruction at every level and it's the church's responsibility to do so. Pastors and elders are in charge of organizing this meeting with God—and it's the most important meeting in the world. Every week we need to clean our house so to speak for this meeting. Imagine if the president were coming to meet with you! You would prepare everything carefully. You would sweep your house and clean for the occasion why would worship be different?

Another critical point in this study is that worship must be guided by faith and not fear. I think that many serious Christians are sincerely attempting to avoid what they perceive to be extremes in worship. On the one hand they want to avoid what they see as thoughtless rituals practiced by highly liturgical traditions such as the Roman Catholic

Church. On the other hand, they are afraid of the equally thoughtless extremes of emotionally charged charismatic worship and Pentecostal extremes. Such concerns can be healthy and good, and many people fancy themselves to be in the middle between these extremes. However, if you use the fear of extremes as a guide for worship, you are using the wrong standard. The word of God is our standard.

One good brother told me of a time when his church revised some songs they were using for their children. They came to a song that said I lift up my hands to you. In an attempt to "help" the children think correctly the church leaders changed the words of the song to say, "I lift up my heart." This is a classic example of fear replacing faith. Why would a Bible believing Christian feel the need to change the very words of the Scriptures in order to avoid what they feared was an extreme? Whenever we encounter words in the Scriptures and we feel the need to change them in order to "fit" the Bible into our theology, then we need to rethink our theology. It is not the Bible that needs to be adjusted; it's our theology that needs to be altered.

If the Bible says that it is an acceptable posture to raise your hands, then we must agree with the Bible. Of course, this does not eliminate the need to take seriously the abuses of some traditions, but at the most basic level we need to be willing to say that raising hands as stated in the Scriptures is an acceptable activity. We must still be vigilant to study the "hows," the "when," and the "where" of raising hands, but we should never dismiss altogether what the Bible plainly states.

Worship is the most central issue in all of life and it's time to take this seriously. The churches with Bible this and Bible that plastered all over their walls and sprinkled throughout their pamphlets are the same churches virtually obsessed with being relevant to the world, against which the Bible warns. The best example is the Lord's Supper. The simple idea of coming to Christ in the Holy Supper on a regular basis is lost to them in their obsession with relevance. What could be more relevant than eating and drinking? Aside from breathing it may be the most basic, human activity that takes us back to the creation scene when God tested Adam and Eve.

What could be more relevant to human love and dependence on God than coming to him in the Lord's Supper in worship? What could be more basic? And yet, where do you find an Evangelical church that serves this supper weekly and when they do serve it, it's like a child playing with a tea set because it's grape juice instead of wine.

So much for the Bible, the whole Bible and nothing but the Bible. You can see why these Evangelical slogans are maddening to those who actually take the scriptures seriously. America has recently been shaken through a pandemic that has caused reconsiderations on a massive number it items. One most centrally is the issue of worship.

At the beginning of the COVID-19 pandemic apocalyptic predictions of world-destroying proportions were used to shut down almost the whole world. Schools were closed, businesses shuttered, restaurants padlocked, gyms, hair salons and almost every imaginable business were bolted shut. The government's declared state of emergency did, however, recognize certain activities as "essential." But worship was not usually on the list.

When the dust settled, and monumental miscalculations were observed, many Americans assumed that life could open up and go back to "normal." But many Christian leaders had failed their flocks when satisfied with online or virtual worship. Worship seemed to be something that was not "essential" in times of extreme need. This is a problem. "Essential" services included liquor stores and marijuana shops, but churches were told to remain closed.

Now if according to many evangelicals, the church and her worship were personally satisfying but clearly optional then what was the fuss. But for those with heartfelt convictions that both the church and her worship are essential to life there was a serious problem.

It's amazing that even simple acts of obedience seem brave in a theologically weak culture filled with man-fearing religious leaders. We need a renewal of God-centered worship. In one of the earliest accounts of Christian practices from an outsider, Pliny the Younger, governor of Bythinia, wrote to the emperor to ask advice on what to do with a growing religion in the Roman world, Christianity. In the course of asking for advice and outlining his policies, the governor revealed that these Christians had a powerful simplicity in the way the honored Jesus as deity and their simple worship and basic but powerful ethical commitments. The same is true of another document from early church history, the Didache. Here you don't find the early Christians mapping out a program for taking over Roman culture—they worshipped! Again, their simplicity and commitments had a potency and attractiveness like nothing else around it.

The divine power of preaching, the mysterious grace in the sacraments, the soul-moving praise in worship, the vows, confession of sins, the assurance of forgiveness and much more are mere highlights of the precious and unique work of God that occurs nowhere else like this except where two or three are gathered—in worship. I call all Christians everywhere to reignite a passion for worship as the central feature of our lives. My prayer is that this little work on worship may have some good effect towards this end.

Bibliography

Adams, Jay E. *Preaching with Purpose: The Urgent Task of Homiletics*. Grand Rapids, MI: Zondervan, 1982.
Asprou, Helen. "'Music for People Living with Dementia is a Necessity, Says New National Campaign." *Classic FM* (blog), 2020. https://www.classicfm.com/discover-music/music-for-people-living-with-dementia-isnt-nicety/.
Ash, Christopher. *The Priority of Preaching*. Scotland: Christian Focus, 2009.
Barth, Karl. *Church Dogmatics*. Vol. 4.3.2, *The Doctrine of Reconciliation*. Edited by G. W. Bromiley and T. F. Torrance. Translated by G.W. Bromiley. London: T. & T. Clark International, 2004.
Bass, C. B. "Body." In *The International Standard Bible Encyclopedia, Revised*, edited by G. W. Bromiley, 1:528–31. Grand Rapids, MI: Eerdmans, 1979.
———. "Order." In *The International Standard Bible Encyclopedia, Revised*, edited by G. W. Bromiley, 3:613. Grand Rapids, MI: Eerdmans, 1979.
B. C. W. "Public Worship." In *Mercersburg Review*, 2:296–306. Mercersburg, PA: Alumni Association of Marshall College, 1850.
Beale, G. K. *We Become What We Worship: A Biblical Theology of Idolatry*. Downers Grove, IL: IVP Academic, 2008.
Block, Daniel I. *For the Glory of God: Recovering a Biblical Theology of Worship*. Ada, MI: Baker Academic, 2014.
Bond, Douglas. "How NOT to Sing at Christmas (or Any Other Time of the Year)." *Douglas Bond Books* (blog), December 25, 2019.
Burnet, George B. *The Holy Communion in the Reformed Church of Scotland: 1560–1960*. Edinburgh: Oliver and Boyd, 1960.
Calamy, Edmund, et al. *The Puritans on the Lord's Supper*. Grand Rapids, MI: Soli Deo Gloria, 1997.
Caldecott, Stratford. *Beauty for Truth's Sake: On the Re-enchantment of Education*. Grand Rapids, MI: Brazos, 2009.
Calvin, John. *Form of Ecclesiastical Prayers and Songs*, quoted in Jonathan Gibson & Mark

BIBLIOGRAPHY

Earngey, *Reformation Worship: Liturgies from the Past for the Present* (New Growth Press, 2018), p. 308.

———. *Institutes of the Christian Religion*. Edited by John T. McNeill. Translated by Ford Lewis Battles. Louisville: Westminster John Knox, 1960.

———. *The Necessity of Reforming the Church*. 1843. Reprint, Dallas, TX: Protestant Heritage Press, 1995.

Carson, D. A., ed. *Worship by the Book*. Grand Rapids, MI: Zondervan, 2002.

Chan, Simon. *Liturgical Theology: The Church as Worshiping Community*. Downers Grove, IL: IVP Academic, 2006.

Chapell, Bryan. *Christ-Centered Worship: Letting the Gospel Shape Our Practice*. Ada, MI: Baker Academic, 2009.

Cheaney, Janie B. "Everybody Sing! The Temporary Loss of Congregational Singing Highlights its Unique Value." *WORLD* (blog), March 28, 2020. https://wng.org/articles/everybody-sing-1620616659.

Clark, R., and D. McLaurin, III. *Lexham Theological Wordbook*. Edited by D. Mangum Duty et al. Bellingham, WA: Lexham, 2014.

Dabney, Robert L. *Evangelical Eloquence: A Course of Lectures on Preaching*. 1870. Reprint. Edinburgh: Banner of Truth Trust, 1999.

Davies, Horton. *The Worship of the English Puritans*. Grand Rapids, MI: Soli Deo Gloria Publications, 1997.

Eby, David. *Power Preaching for Church Growth: The Role of Preaching in Growing Churches*. Scotland: Mentor, 2009.

Eire, Carlos M. N. *War against Idols: The Reformation of Worship from Erasmus to Calvin*. Cambridge: Cambridge University Press, 1986.

Erskine, John. *Thoughts upon the Duty of a More Frequent Celebration of the Lord's Supper*. Edinburgh: Paterson, 1781.

Fortune, A. W. "Decently." In *The International Standard Bible Encyclopedia*, edited by G. W. Bromiley, 1:908. Rev. ed. Grand Rapids, MI: Eerdmans, 1979.

Green, Michael. "Editor's Preface." In *Between Two Worlds: The Art of Preaching in the Twentieth Century*, by John R. W Stott, i–x. Grand Rapids, MI: Eerdmans, 1982.

Gibson, Jonathan, and Mark Earngey. *Reformation Worship: Liturgies from the Past for the Present*. Greensboro, NC: New Growth Press, 2018.

Gordon, T. David. *Why Johnny Can't Sing Hymns: How Pop Culture Rewrote the Hymnal*. Phillipsburg, NJ: P&R Publishing, 2010.

Hart, D. G. *Recovering Mother Kirk: The Case for Liturgy in the Reformed Tradition*. Grand Rapids, MI: Baker Academic, 2003.

Hedges, Chris. "American Psychosis." *David Westerfield* (blog), June 22, 2010. https://davidwesterfield.net/2010/06/american-psychosis-article-by-chris-hedges/.

Henry, Matthew. *A Way to Pray: A Biblical Method for Enriching Your Prayer Life and Language by Shaping Your Words with Scripture*. Edited and revised by O. Palmer Robertson. Edinburgh: The Banner of Truth Trust, 2010.

Hoeksema, Herman. *In the Sanctuary: Expository Sermons on the Lord's Prayer*. Grand Rapids: MI, Reformed Free Publishing Association, 1981.

Hunter, James Davidson. *To Change the World: The Irony, Tragedy, & Possibility of Christianity in the Late Modern World*. Oxford: Oxford University Press, 2010.

Isbell, Sherman. "'Hear Ye Him:' Worship in the New Testament." In *Worship in the Presence of God: A Collection of Essays on the Nature, Elements, and Historic Views and Practices of Worship*, edited by Frank J. Smith, 61-73. Taylors, SC: Greenville Seminary Press, 1992.

Hatch, Nathan O. *The Democratization of American Christianity*. New Haven, CT: Yale University Press, 1991.
Jackson, L. Charles. *Riots, Revolutions, and the Scottish Covenanters: The Work of Alexander Henderson*. Grand Rapids, MI: Reformation Heritage Books, 2015.
Johnson, Terry L. *When Grace Comes Alive: Living Through the Lord's Prayer*. Scotland: Christian Focus Publications, 2003.
Jones, Mark. *Faith, Hope and Love: The Christ-Centered Way to Grow in Grace*. Wheaton, IL: Crossway, 2017.
Kineer, Jack. "Worship Is More Than a List." *The Orthodox Presbyterian Church* (blog), April 2002. https://opc.org/nh.html?article_id=172.
Frame, John M. *Worship in Spirit and Truth: A Refreshing Study of the Principles and Practice of Biblical Worship*. Phillipsburg, NJ: P&R Publishing, 1996.
Gabler, Neal. *Life: The Movie—How Entertainment Conquered Reality*. New York: Vintage, 2000.
Gusfield, Joseph R. *Symbolic Crusade: Status Politics and the American Temperance Movement*. Champaign, IL: University of Illinois Press, 1986.
Law, William. *A Serious Call to a Devout and Holy Life*. South Carolina: CreateSpace Independent Publishing, 2013.
Leithart, Peter. "At the Table." *First Things* (blog), June 30, 2017. https://www.firstthings.com/web-exclusives/2017/06/at-the-table.
———. *Blessed Are the Hungry: Meditations on the Lord's Supper*. Moscow, ID: Canon, 2000.
———. *From Silence to Song: The Davidic Liturgical Revolution*. Moscow, ID: Canon, 2003.
Letham, Robert. *The Lord's Supper: Eternal Word in Broken Bread*. Phillipsburg, NJ: P&R Publishing, 2001.
Littlejohn, Bradford. *The Mercerburg Theology and the Quest for Reformed Catholicity*. Eugene, OR: Pickwick, 2009.
"Liturgical Gestures." *Encylopedia.com* (blog), 2019. https://www.encyclopedia.com/religion/encyclopedias-almanacs-transcripts-and-maps/liturgical-gestures.
Lloyd-Jones, D. Martyn. *Preaching and Preachers*. Grand Rapids, MI: Zondervan, 1971.
———. *Studies in the Sermon on the Mount*. 2 vols. Grand Rapids, MI: Eerdmans, 1977.
Lukacs, Paul. *Inventing Wine: A New History of One of the World's Most Ancient Pleasures*. New York: Norton, 2012.
Luther, Martin. "Preface to Georg Rhau's Symphonoiaeiucundae." Translated by C. M. Jacobs. In *Luther's Works*, edited by J. Pelikan and H. T. Lehmann, 53:323. Minneapolis, MN: Fortress, 1965.
MacArthur, John. *Jesus' Pattern of Prayer*. Chicago: Moody, 1981.
———. *Worship: The Ultimate Priority*. Chicago: Moody, 2012.
Machen, J. Gresham. *Christianity and Liberalism*. London: Macmillan, 1923.
Mathison, Keith. *Given for You: Reclaiming Calvin's Doctrine of the Lord's Supper*. Phillipsburg, NJ: P&R Publishing, 2002.
Myers, Kenneth A. *All God's Children and Blue Suede Shoes: Christians & Popular Culture*. Wheaton, IL: Crossway, 1989.
Needham, Nick. *2000 Years of Christ's Power*. Vol. 1, *The Age of the Early Church Fathers*. Scotland: Christian Focus Publications, 2016.
Nevin, John Williamson. *The Anxious Bench*. (digitized) Office of Publication of the German Reformed Church, 1844.

———. *The Mystical Presence: A Vindication of the Reformed or Calvinistic Doctrine of the Holy Eucharist*. Philadelphia: Lippincott, 1846.

Newbigin, Lesslie. *Lesslie Newbigin: Missionary Theologian: A Reader*. Edited by Paul Weston. Grand Rapids, MI: Eerdmans, 2006.

Nicholls, W. *Jacob's Ladder: The Meaning of Worship*. Ecumenical Studies in Worship 4. London: Lutterworth, 1958.

Noll, Mark A. *The Scandal of the Evangelical Mind*. Grand Rapids, MI: Eerdmans, 1994.

O'Donnell, Douglas Sean. *God's Lyrics: Rediscovering Worship through Old Testament Song*. Phillipsburg, NJ: P&R Publishing, 2010.

O'Donovan, Oliver. *The Desire of the Nations: Rediscovering the Roots of Political Theology*. Cambridge: Cambridge University Press, 1996.

Old, Hughes Oliphant. *Worship: Reformed according to Scripture*. Louisville, KY: WJK Press, 2002.

Opperwall, N. J. "Order." In *The International Standard Bible Encyclopedia*, edited by G. W. Bromiley, 3:613. Rev. ed. Grand Rapids, MI: Eerdmans, 1979.

Owen, John. *A Brief Instruction on the Worship of God and Discipline of the Churches of the New Testament*. 1667. Reprint. Edited by William Goold. Edinburgh: Banner of Truth Trust, 1853.

Pettegree, Andrew. *Reformation and the Culture of Persuasion*. Cambridge: Cambridge University Press, 2005.

Piper, John. *Let the Nations Be Glad: The Supremacy of God in Missions*. Ada, MI: Baker Academic, 2010.

"Reading at Risk: A Survey of Literary Reading in America: Research Division Report No. 46." *Arts* (blog), June 2004. https://www.arts.gov/sites/default/files/ReadingAtRisk.pdf.

Rice, Howard L., and James C. Huffstutler. *Reformed Worship*. Louisville, KY: Geneva, 2001.

Robeck, C.M., Jr "Decently." In *The International Standard Bible Encyclopedia*, edited by G. W. Bromiley, 4:873. Rev. ed. Grand Rapids, MI: Eerdmans, 1979.

Ross, Allen P. *Recalling the Hope of Glory: Biblical Worship from the Garden to the New Creation*. Grand Rapids, MI: Kregel Academic & Professional, 2006.

Schaff, Philip. *The Development of the Church: "The Principle of Protestantism" and Other Historical Writings of Philip Schaff*. Edited by David R. Bains and Theodore Louis Trost. The Mercersburg Theology Study Series 3. Translated by John Williamson Nevin. Eugene, OR: Wipf & Stock, 2018.

Schmemann, Alexander. *For the Life of the World*. Yonkers, NY: St. Vladimir's, 2004.

Smith, James K. A. *Imagining the Kingdom: How Worship Works*. Ada, MI: Baker Academic, 2013.

———. *You Are What You Love: The Spiritual Power of Habit*. Grand Rapids, MI: Brazos, 2016.

Smith, Rob. "Music, Singing, and Emotions: Exploring the Connections." *Themelios* 37 (2012) 465–79.

Spring, Gardiner. *The Power of the Pulpit: Thoughts Addressed to Christian Ministers and Those Who Hear Them*. Edinburgh: The Banner of Truth Trust, 1986.

Stapert, Calvin R. *A New Song for an Old World: Musical Thought in the Early Church*. Grand Rapids, MI: Eerdmans, 2007.

Stewart, James. *Heralds of God*. Grand Rapids, MI: Baker, 1972.

Sulpicius Severus. "Sulpitius Severus on the Life of St. Martin." Translated by Alexander Roberts. In *A Select Library of Nicene and Post-Nicene Fathers of the Christian Church: Sulpitius Severus, Vincent of Lérins, John Cassian*, edited by P. Schaff and H. Wace. New York: Christian Literature, 1894.

Sweeney, Conor. *Abiding the Long Defeat: How to Evangelize Like a Hobbit in a Disenchanted Age*. Brooklyn, NY: Angelico Press, 2018.

The Orthodox Presbyterian Church. *The Directory for Worship in The Book of Church Order of the Orthodox Presbyterian Church*. 143. USA: Committee on Christian Education of the Orthodox Presbyterian Church. 2020.

The Westminster Confession of Faith. Edinburgh ed. Philadelphia: Young, 1851.

Todd, Margo, ed. *Reformation to Revolution: Politics and Religion in Early Modern England*. London: Routledge, 1995.

Todd, Margo. *The Culture of Protestantism in Early Modern Scotland*. New Haven, CT: Yale University Press, 2002.

Trueman, Carl. "Tragic Worship." *First Things* (blog), June 2013. https://www.firstthings.com/article/2013/06/tragic-worship.

Twitchell, James B. *For Shame: The Loss of Common Decency in American Culture*. New York: St. Martin's Press, 1997.

Ursinus, Zacharius. *Commentary on the Heidelberg Catechism*. Translated by G. W. Willard. 4th ed. Cincinnati, OH: Elm Street, 1888.

Vos, Geerhardus. *The Pauline Eschatology*. 1930. Reprint. Phillipsburg, NJ: P& R Publishing, 1991.

Walker, Andrew G., and Robin A. Parry. *Deep Church Rising: Rediscovering the Roots of Christian Orthodoxy*. London: SPCK, 2014.

Wirzba, Norman. *Food and Faith: A Theology of Eating*. Cambridge: Cambridge University Press, 2011.

Woodruff Tait, Jennifer L. *The Poisoned Chalice: Eucharistic Grape Juice and Common-Sense Realism in Victorian Methodism*. Tuscaloosa, AL: University of Alabama Press, 2011.

www.ingramcontent.com/pod-product-compliance
Lightning Source LLC
Chambersburg PA
CBHW060609230426
43670CB00011B/2046